303 Homemade Jelly Recipes

(303 Homemade Jelly Recipes - Volume 1)

Mimi Lockett

Content

303 AWESOME JELLY RECIPES 8

1. Cherry Chocolate Preserve 8
2. Simple Mango Marmalade 8
3. Truffle Tremor, Hot Soppressata And Pepper Jelly Crostini 8
4. 2 Ingredient Duck Sauce........................... 9
5. 3 Ingredient Strawberry Preserve 9
6. Aamer Morobba (Indian Mango Preserve) 10
7. Almond Butter & Jelly Chia Pudding 10
8. Almond Butter And Orange Thumbprints With Cranberry Preserves 10
9. Almond Ricotta Cake With Rasperry Jam And White Chocolate 12
10. Anise Cardamon Spiced Plum Jam 12
11. Anna Brone's Cardamom Carrot Marmalade 13
12. Anniversary Mortadella Melts With Fennel Onion Jam 13
13. Apple Rosemary Jam 14
14. Apricot Jam Crostata (Crostata Di Marmellata) 14
15. Apricot Jam Tart 15
16. Autum Spice Pear Jam 16
17. BLOOD ORANGE MARMALADE 16
18. Back To School Raspberry Granola Bars From Karen DeMasco 17
19. Bacon Jam 17
20. Bakewell Tart With Rhubarb Hibiscus Jam 18
21. Balsamic Chicken Sandwich With Peach Jam And Brandied Onions 19
22. Banana Jam 20
23. Beef Tenderloin With Shallot Marmalade 20
24. Better Turkey Burger With Feta And Onion Jam 21
25. Betty's Jelly Meatballs 21
26. Big Momma's Blackberry Jam Cake........... 22
27. Black Grape Jam, Ethereal With Body And Style Like No Other... Jam That Is........... 23
28. Black Tea Jelly 23
29. Blackberry Mulled Wine Jam........... 24
30. Blackberry Cream & Jelly Verrines 24

31. Blackberry Jelly........................... 25
32. Blood Orange Marmalade Sunset In A Jar 26
33. Blood Orange Marmalade {with Salted Butter On Toasted Crostini} 26
34. Blueberry Date Jam........................... 27
35. Blueberry Pudding, Jam & Custard 28
36. Bocconotti (Southern Italian Jam Pastries) 28
37. Boysenberry Blueberry Jam 29
38. Brandy Old Fashioned Jam........................... 29
39. Bread With Butter And Jam 29
40. Brie And Jelly French Toast 30
41. Brie And Onion Jam Crostini........................... 30
42. Buckwheat Thumbprint Cookies With Cherry Preserves 30
43. Calamondin Orange And Limequat Marmalade 31
44. Candied Bacon And Tomato Jam Ice Cream........................... 31
45. Caramelized Apple Jam 32
46. Caramelized Banana PB + J With Spicy Pepper Jelly 33
47. Caramelized Onion And Gruyere Cheese Tartlets With Fig Preserves........... 34
48. Carrot, Onion And Dill Marmalade........... 34
49. Champagne Rhubarb Jelly Shots 35
50. Cheddar Cheese Biscuits With Bacon Jam 35
51. Cherry Amaretto Jam........................... 36
52. Cherry Jam Margarita........................... 37
53. Cherry Jam With Lemon Pepper Shortbread 37
54. Cherry Amaretto Jam........................... 38
55. Chicken Thighs With Love Apple Jam........ 38
56. Chipotle Bacon Jam 39
57. Chocolate Overnight Oats With Strawberry Chia Jam 39
58. Christmas Bombe With Berry Preserves And White Chocolate Mousse........... 40
59. Cindy Mushet's Italian Jam Shortbread Tart (Fregolotta) 42
60. Coconut & Lemon Cupcakes With Lemon Marmalade Filling 43
61. Coconut Fried Shrimp W/ Horseradish Marmalade Sauce 44
62. Coconut Jam Drops 45
63. Coffee Jelly........................... 45
64. Coffee Jelly, With Spiced And Spiked

Options 45

65. Concord Grape Jelly 46

66. Country Ham Biscuit With Fig Jam 46

67. Cranberry Ginger Jam Donuts 47

68. Crescent Jam And Cheese Cookies 48

69. Crostata Alla Marmellata (jam Tarte) 49

70. Crostata Di Marmelatta Di Fico Fig Jam Italian Pie 50

71. Crostini With Duck Breast And Red Onion Jam 51

72. Crostini With Duck Confit And Red Onion Jam 51

73. Crostini With Fig Preserves, Gorgonzola And Crispy Shallots 52

74. Crostini With Mascarpone, Prosciutto And Strawberry Jam 52

75. Crostini With Whipped Goat Cheese And Hot Pepper Jelly 53

76. Dark Chocolate Tart With Kumquat Marmalade 53

77. Dark Chocolate Smoked Sea Salt Ice Cream With Concord Grape Jelly Ripple 54

78. Date & Rosemary Jam 55

79. Deviled Eggs With Spicy Tomato Jam And Pistachio Dukkah 55

80. Drunken Pisco Fig Jam 56

81. Duck Bacon Jam With Coffee & Thyme .. 57

82. Eton Mess With Rhubarb Gin Jam And Lemon Basil Meringue 57

83. Fall Harvest Preserves 59

84. Farmers Market Skillet Bread With Tomato Butter And Blackberry Peach Quick Jam 59

85. Fennel Marmalade 61

86. Fig Jam With A Twist 61

87. Fig Jam With Cardamom 62

88. Fig Lemon Preserves 62

89. Five Citrus Marmalade 62

90. Fizzy Strawberry Jellies 63

91. Fragrant Kumquat Marmalade 63

92. French Baguette, With Parmigiano Reggiano Cheese, Italian Organic Fig Preserve And Balsamic Glaze 64

93. Fresh Fig And Strawberry Jam 64

94. Fried Egg Toasts With Mascarpone, Apricot Jam, And Chives 65

95. Fried Green Tomato And Egg Sliders With Tomato Jam 65

96. Gilly's Rotisserie Chicken & Hot Pepper Jelly Sandwich 66

97. Ginger Peach Jam 67

98. Goat Cheese Ice Cream With Honey And Fig Jam 67

99. Goat Cheese Tart With Mango Habanero Jam 68

100. Goat Cheese With Tangy Clementine Jam And Fresh Thyme 69

101. Goat Ricotta Crostini With Spicy Onion & Garlic Jam 69

102. Golden Plum Preserves Ice Cream 70

103. Golden Raisin Scones With Apricot, Plum And Rose Petal Jam 70

104. Gooey PBJ Brownies 71

105. Gooseberry Jam 72

106. Grandma's Best Raspberry Jam 72

107. Grapefruit Marmalade 72

108. Green Tomato Jam 73

109. Grilled Flank Steak Sandwich With Sweet Onion Marmalade And Pear Horseradish Mustard 73

110. Grilled Fontina With Lingonberry Preserves 74

111. Grown Up Birthday Cake 75

112. Habanero Corn Cob Jelly 75

113. Habanero Jelly 76

114. Ham, Cheddar And Marmalade Toasties .. 76

115. Heirloom Tomato Marmalade 77

116. Herbed Biscuit Bites With Ricotta Cream And Onion Jam 77

117. Herbed Goat Cheese And Jam Crostini 78

118. Hibiscus Pear Preserves 78

119. Homemade Cranberry Jelly, In A Can 78

120. Homemade Kaya (Coconut Jam) 79

121. Homemade Strawberry Jelly 80

122. Homemade Apricot Jam The French Way 80

123. Honey Sweetened White Peach Jam With Lemon 81

124. Hot Pepper Jelly Grilled Cheese 81

125. Hot And Sweet Pepper Funk Jam 82

126. Instant Pot Strawberry Jam 82

127. Jam Cake With Black Walnuts 82

128. Jam Tart (crostata) Dolci (dessert) 83

129. Jam Filled Cheese Turnovers 83

130. Jam Filled Scones 84

131. John DeBary's Preserves Sour 84
132. Katy's Cranberry And Jam Tart 85
133. Kumquat Marmalade With Champagne And Figs 85
134. Kumquat Smoothie Jam 86
135. Late Season Cherry Tomato And Vanilla Jam 86
136. Lemon Earl Grey Jam 87
137. Lemon Financiers With Blackberry Jam ...87
138. Lemon Marmalade 88
139. Lettuce Jam 89
140. Lightly Spiced Plum Jam 89
141. Love Letter Jam 90
142. Low Sugar Plum Jam 91
143. Lychee Jelly Hearts 91
144. MELON JAM WITH STAR ANISE 92
145. Marbled Jam Cake 92
146. Marmalade Bread Pudding 93
147. Marmalade Glazed Salmon On Pea Shoots & Spring Greens With White Wine And Lemon Cream Sauce 93
148. Melon Jam 94
149. Meyer Lemon Cured Preserves 95
150. Meyer Lemon Key Lime Marmalade 95
151. Meyer Lemon Vanilla Bean And Ginger Karma Marmalade 96
152. Mint, Rose And Rhubarb Jam 96
153. Mozzarella In Carrozza With Sun Dried Tomato And Roasted Red Pepper Jam 97
154. Mrs. Wheelbarrow's Focaccia With Apricot Jam, Caramelized Onion, And Fennel 98
155. Mrs. Wheelbarrow's Jam Tarts 99
156. Muh's Pepper Jelly 99
157. Multigrain Marmalade Muffins 100
158. Mushroom Confit Polenta Tart With Tomato Fig Jam 100
159. My Blancmange With Fig Marmalade 101
160. My Husbands Favorite Jam Tart 102
161. My Meyer Lemon Marmalade 102
162. My Mother's Strawberry Jam 103
163. My Aunt Jagica's Cookies With Jam 103
164. Nam Prik Pao (Chile Jam) 104
165. No Cook Raspberry Lime Freezer Jam ... 105
166. No Bake Orange Marmalade Cake 105
167. Nutty Thumbprint Cookies Filled With Figgy Pudding Jam 106
168. Oat Streusel Jam Bars 106
169. Oatmeal Jam Bars 107
170. Old Fashioned Apple Jelly Cake 107
171. Olia Hercules' Watermelon Rind Jam 108
172. Oma Jam 108
173. Onion Jam 109
174. Open Face Steak Sandwich With Red Onion Jam And Blue Cheese 109
175. Orange & Lemon Marmalade Cake 110
176. Orange Marmalade Glazed Chops 110
177. Orange Marmalade Tarts With Bittersweet Chocolate Ganache And Mascarpone Crème . 111
178. Orange And Apricot Jam Squares 112
179. Orange Pumpkin Torte With Cranberry Jelly And Ricotta Mascarpone Whipped Cream 112
180. Pasta Flora Jam Tart 113
181. Paula Wolfert's Herb Jam With Olives And Lemon 114
182. Peach Jam With Lavender And Honey .. 114
183. Peach Marmalade 115
184. Peanut Butter & Jelly Crunch Bread 115
185. Peanut Butter & Jelly Mug Cake 116
186. Peanut Butter & Jelly Overnight Oats 116
187. Peanut Butter & Jelly Sandwich 116
188. Peanut Butter And Jam Scones 117
189. Peanut Butter And Jelly Crispy Brown Rice Bars 117
190. Peanut Butter And Jelly Croissants 118
191. Peanut Butter And Jelly Picnic Cheesecake (Vegan) 118
192. Peanut Butter And Jelly Pie 120
193. Peanut Butter And Jelly Sandwich Cookies 121
194. Peanut Butter And Jelly On Whole Wheat Ice Cream 121
195. Peanut Butter And Raspberry Jam Galette 122
196. Peanut Butter And Jam Cookie Sandwiches 123
197. Pear Pineapple Ginger Jam 123
198. Pear And Black Pepper Preserves 124
199. Pelion Orange Marmalade (Greek Recipe) 124
200. Pepper Jelly Drumsticks 125
201. Pepper Punch Plum Jam 125
202. Pineapple Ginger Preserves 126
203. Pistachio Mascarpone And Blackberry Jam

Stuffed French Toast 126

204. Plum Jam With Rosemary And Ginger ... 127

205. Plum Jam With A Little Bite To It 127

206. Plum Pucker Jam And Elephant Ears 128

207. Plum And Star Anise Jam 128

208. Plum Jam With Tea Biscuit 129

209. Poached Eggs With Tomato Balsamic Jam And Aioli 129

210. Polpettone With Onion Shallot Jam Over Creamy Root Vegetable Purée 130

211. Port Wine Jelly 131

212. Proscuitto, Goat Cheese, And Fig Pear Balsamic Jam Rolls 132

213. Pumpkin Buckwheat – Spelt Pancakes With Pumpkin Plum Jam 132

214. QUICK AND EASY RASPBERRY JAM 133

215. Quick Blueberry Jam 133

216. Quince Jelly Tart With Cinnamon Cream Cheese 133

217. RUSTIC WHITE PEACH & CITRUS BLUEBERRY JAM TART WITH MAPLE CRUMBLE 134

218. Rapturous Morel Marmalade 135

219. Raspberry Chia Seed Jam 135

220. Raspberry Lemon Balm Jam 136

221. Red Pepper Jam! 136

222. Rhubarb Vanilla Jam 137

223. Ricotta And Cherry Jam Crostata (crostata Di Ricotta E Visciole) 137

224. Roasted Grape & Huckleberry Jam Galette 138

225. Roasted Grape Agave Jam 138

226. Roasted Jam 138

227. Roasted Pears With A Lemon, Quince (Jam) And Brandy Sauce 139

228. Roasted Strawberry Balsamic Jam 140

229. Roasted Tomato Jam 140

230. Roasted Vegetable, Goat Cheese, And Spinach Quesadilla With Spicy Tomato Jam 140

231. Rosemary Fennel Cookies With Marmalade 141

232. Ruby Red Raspberry Jam 142

233. Russet Potato And Jam Cake 143

234. STRAWBERRY CHIPOTLE JAM GLAZED SALMON TACOS 143

235. Sarah K's Greengage Jam 144

236. Savory Corn And Basil Muffins With Ricotta And Tomato Jam 144

237. Seven Minutes To Heavenly Raspberry Jam 145

238. Short Rib Jam 146

239. Shrimp Cooked In Smoked Sausage And Roasted Red Bell Pepper Jam Sauce 147

240. Shrimp And "grits" With Kahlua Bacon Jam 147

241. Sicilian Blood Orange Marmalade 148

242. Simple Concord Grape Jam 148

243. Sliders With Onion Jam And Fried Bananas Foster 149

244. Small Batch Strawberry Rhubarb Jam 150

245. Smoked Trout, Bacon And Tomato Sandwich With Crème Fraiche Pepper Jelly Topping 150

246. Smoky Shitake Cranberry Cauliflower Galette With Marmalade Mustard Mascarpone 151

247. Sour Cherry & Marzipan Jam Bars 152

248. Sour Cherry, Coriander & Candied Ginger Jam 152

249. Sour Cherry Black Pepper Jam 153

250. Spiced Cider Jellies 154

251. Spiced Plum And Port Jam 154

252. Spicy Sweet Potato Pommes Frites With Raspberry Preserves 155

253. Steak Sandwich With Peach "jam" And Brie 155

254. Strawberry Balsamic Jam Infused With Star Anise And Vanilla Bean 156

255. Strawberry Cardamom 'Smoothie' Jam ... 156

256. Strawberry Cardamom Jam 157

257. Strawberry Chia Jam 157

258. Strawberry Jam 158

259. Strawberry Jam Filled Doughnut Muffins 158

260. Strawberry Jam With Cardamom 159

261. Strawberry Lemon Jam 159

262. Strawberry Lemon Preserves 160

263. Strawberry Red Currant Jam 160

264. Strawberry Rhubarb Jam 161

265. Strawberry Vanilla Chia Seed Jam 161

266. Sufganiyot (Israeli Jelly Doughnuts) 162

267. Sufganiyot (Jelly Donut) Cake 162

268. Sungold Tomato Preserves 164

269. Sweet & Savory Tomato Jam 164

270. Sweet Cherry Pinot Grigio Jam 164

271. Sweet Onion And Rosemary Jam With Sage Butter Crostini..165

272. Sweet And Savory Burger With Fig Jam, Goat Cheese, And Arugula 166

273. Tangerine Passion Fruit Marmalade 167

274. Tennessee Jam Cake 167

275. Thai Tea Jam 168

276. The Ultimate Bacon Jam Recipe 168

277. Toasted Goat Cheese Crostini With Basil And Red Onion Jam 169

278. Tomato Balsamic Jam.................................169

279. Tomato Pomegranate Jam 170

280. Tomato Preserves.......................................170

281. Tomato Basil Jam Filled Mini Phyllo Shells 170

282. Turkey Bacon Sliders On Homemade Parmesan Gaugeres With Bacon Moscato Marmalade 171

283. Valencia Orange Marmalade 172

284. Vanilla Bean Semifreddo Swirled With Jam 173

285. Vanilla Scented Sour Apricot Preserves..174

286. Vanilla Chestnut Jam 174

287. Vanilla Tomato Jam 176

288. Veal Marrowbones With Oxtails Marmalade 176

289. Vegan Almond And Toasted Oat Jam Bars 177

290. Vegetables Wrapped In Beef With Soy Marmalade Ginger Sauce 177

291. Whole Wheat Jelly Doughnuts (Sufganiyot) 178

292. Wild Maine Blueberry Jam.........................178

293. Wine Jelly, White Chocolate And Caviar Verrine...179

294. Wintery Braised Red Cabbage, Plus Some Jelly 180

295. Wintery Sunday Morning Muffins With Blood Orange Marmalade 180

296. Yellow Plum And Apricot Jam 181

297. Buckwheat Crepes With Homemade Fruit Jam 181

298. Kumquat Preserve.......................................181

299. Marbled Muscadine Marmalade & Cream Cheese Brownies.................................182

300. Plum Jam 182

301. Polenta Pound Cake With Strawberry Jam Glazing..183

302. Roasted Carrots With Orange Marmalade 183

303. Tomato Jam, Mozzarella & Spinach Panini 184

INDEX 185

CONCLUSION 190

303 Awesome Jelly Recipes

***

---

1. Cherry Chocolate Preserve

Serving: Makes approximately 600 ml jam | Prep: | Cook: | Ready in:

Ingredients

- 2 pounds (1 Kg) sweet cherries, pitted
- 2 cups sugar
- 1/4 cup water
- 30 grams cocoa
- 2 tablespoons brandy

Direction

- Place the cherries in a saucepan with a thick base and add sugar. Bring to a boil, lower the heat medium to low and let boil without lid for about 2 hours. Stir occasionally to prevent sticking. Let aside to cool and the next day boil again for about 2 hours. All liquids must pulverize and jam will be very thick.
- Dissolve cocoa and brandy in 1/4 cup of water and pour into the jam, stir and boil for a while until most of liquids evaporates. It can be done in a day but the traditional way and the best flavor achieved by assigning cooking in 2 days. Store in sterilized jars.

---

2. Simple Mango Marmalade

Serving: Makes about 2 1/2 cups | Prep: | Cook: | Ready in:

Ingredients

- 1 navel orange, thinly sliced, peel and all , the slices then quartered
- 1/2 of a large lemon, thinly sliced, peel and all, the slices then quartered
- 3 cups water
- 3 cups diced red mangoes (small dice) - I used 3 mangoes
- 1 cup granulated sugar
- 1/8 teaspoon salt

Direction

- In a medium sauce pan combine the orange slices, lemon slices and water. Bring to a boil and then simmer for about 30 minutes.
- Add the diced mango, sugar and salt, bring back up to a simmer and then continue to simmer for about 20 more minutes.
- Using a potato masher or similar item, mash the mixture until it's thick and a little chunky. Cool, refrigerate and enjoy!

---

3. Truffle Tremor, Hot Soppressata And Pepper Jelly Crostini

Serving: Serves 6 to 8 | Prep: | Cook: | Ready in:

Ingredients

- 1 foot-long baguette sliced in to 1/4 inch pieces
- 1/4 pound thin-sliced hot or sweet Soppressata, rounds cut down the middle into half moons
- 1 Jar 1 Jar Red Pepper Jelly - we prefer Stonewall Kitchen brand
- 1/2 pound Cypress Grove Truffle Tremor Cheese (chilled for easy slicing)
- 1 handful Baby Arugula or other spicy flavored micro greens

- 3 tablespoons White or Black Truffle Oil (Optional)
- Sea Salt, to taste

Direction

- Slice your bread. Toast it, or if using optional Truffle Oil, brush the bread with Oil before toasting, finishing with a very light sprinkle of Sea Salt.
- Remove cheese from the fridge and cut off the back portion of the rind for easier slicing. Warm a flat edged knife in a cup of hot water and cut thin, triangular slices of cheese. Wipe your knife and rewarm in water between each slice. Note: If slicing proves difficult or cheese breaks apart, feel free to let it come to room temperature and spread it/press it onto the bread - it will be just as tasty!
- Place a triangle of cheese in the middle of your bread round. Place two half-moon pieces of soppressata onto the cheese folded in half, or in whatever formation looks nice, pressing the pointed edges into the cheese to affix.
- Pop in a few arugula leaves (to enhance the spicy flavor and for color).Dot with red pepper jelly to taste.

4. 2 Ingredient Duck Sauce

Serving: Makes 1/4 cup | Prep: 0hours5mins | Cook: 0hours0mins | Ready in:

Ingredients

- 3 tablespoons apricot jam
- 1 1/2 tablespoons red wine or white vinegar

Direction

- Add the jam and vinegar to a small bowl.
- Using a fork, stir until well-blended. May be stored in a covered container, in the fridge, for up to 2 weeks.

5. 3 Ingredient Strawberry Preserve

Serving: Serves 8 | Prep: | Cook: | Ready in:

Ingredients

- 4 cups Fresh cut, hulled strawberries
- 1 1/2 cups Fine cane sugar
- 1/2 cup Lemon Juice

Direction

- Wash and clean the strawberries thoroughly.
- In a large bowl mix the sugar and strawberries and let it sit for about 10 mins.
- Into a heavy bottom, stainless steel saucepan/ IP on sauté mode, transfer the strawberry mixture along with the lemon juice.
- Cook on low heat (sauté mode in IP) for about 20 mins until the berries release juices and sugar dissolves and the mixture starts to slow boil. Stir in between.
- Mix well with a spatula and mash the berries lightly leaving tiny chunks in the mixture.
- Once the mixture is thick and coats the back of a wooden spoon, turn off the heat (press cancel button on IP)
- Make sure you have prep the canning jars/glass jars for storing the preserve. Glass jars should be hot (wash with hot water) and sterilized and dry.
- Transfer the preserve into the jars and make sure it's airtight.
- Store in cool dry place or refrigerate and use. This strawberry preserve will stay fresh for about 1-2 months.
- This preserve pairs so well with creamy peanut butter and some banana slices to make awesome sandwiches.

6. Aamer Morobba (Indian Mango Preserve)

Serving: Serves 6-8 | Prep: | Cook: | Ready in:

Ingredients

- 8 mangoes (I prefer Ataulfo), cut into 1" long slices
- 1 tablespoon very finely minced ginger
- 4 Serrano peppers, seeded and finely minced
- 1 cup water
- 2 cups white sugar (use less if mangoes are very sweet)
- 2 cinnamon sticks
- 5 cardamom pods, slightly crushed
- 2 tablespoons lemon juice
- 1/2 teaspoon white vinegar
- 1 pinch kosher salt

Direction

- Heat the sugar and water together on medium heat. Add the ginger, Serrano peppers, lemon juice, cinnamon and cardamom. Stir frequently until the liquid has reached the consistency of a thick syrup. Now fish out the cinnamon sticks and the cardamom pods.
- Add the mangoes. Stir gently making sure that the mangoes do not disintegrate in the syrup. If the mangoes are a little unripe, you need to cook them a little longer, but if your mangoes are ripe, then it only needs to cook for a couple of minutes. They should be soft and cooked through, but definitely not falling apart. Keep an eye on them!
- Add a pinch of salt and the vinegar and mix everything gently. You can serve this on the side to a variety of Indian flat breads, or papads or eat it straight up as dessert!

7. Almond Butter & Jelly Chia Pudding

Serving: Serves 2 | Prep: | Cook: | Ready in:

Ingredients

- For the blueberry compote:
- 130 grams blueberries
- 1 piece Juice from ½ lemon
- For the chia pudding and Optional Toppings:
- 225 milliliters almond milk
- 1 teaspoon vanilla extract
- 2 tablespoons almond butter
- 1 tablespoon maple syrup or honey
- 2 tablespoons chia seeds
- 4 pieces blueberries
- 1 tablespoon honey

Direction

- Add the blueberries and lemon juice to a pan and heat over a medium/high heat for approximately 5 minutes (until you reach a thick compote consistency) then place the compote in a jar and refrigerate.
- Add all the pudding ingredients (except for the chia seeds) to a blender and blitz until smooth and fully combined, then add to a bowl and then add the chia seeds. Mix until well combined. Place in the fridge overnight to thicken.
- Once everything is ready - layer the chia mixture on top of the jam and serve with honey and fresh blueberries to top.

8. Almond Butter And Orange Thumbprints With Cranberry Preserves

Serving: Makes 40 cookies | Prep: | Cook: | Ready in:

Ingredients

- Cookie dough

- 1/2 cup unsalted butter, at room temperature
- 1/3 cup granulated sugar
- 1/3 cup firmly packed light brown sugar
- 2/3   cup almond butter (smooth)
- microplaned zest of one large orange (a generous 1/2 tablespoon)
- 1   teaspoon vanilla extract
- 1   large to extra-large egg, at room temperature
- 1 & 1/4   cups all-purpose flour
- 1/2   teaspoon baking soda
- 1/2   teaspoon baking powder
- 3/4   teaspoon kosher salt (Diamond brand)
- Shaping and Filling
- 1   cup smoked and salted almonds, or roasted and salted almonds
- 1   cup cranberry preserves (a jammy or jelly version)

Direction

- Place butter in large bowl or bowl of a stand mixer. Cream butter with hand or stand mixer briefly on medium (stand) to medium-high (hand) speed. Add all but about 2 tablespoons of the granulated sugar and all of the brown sugar. Beat until the mixture is aerated and has lightened in color, about 4 minutes, scraping the sides once in the process. Scrape the sides and bottom of the bowl, then add the peanut butter. Mix on medium until well combined, about 1 minute.
- Combine the orange zest and remaining granulated sugar on a cutting board. Mince through the mixture with a chef's knife several times in several directions. Using the flat edge of the blade scrape the mixture back and forth until a rough paste forms. Scrape the paste into the mixing bowl. Add the vanilla and egg to the bowl and mix on medium speed for 10 seconds, then scrape the bowl and mix an additional 10 to 20 seconds to combine. The mixture should be almost homogeneous.
- Combine the flour, baking soda, baking powder, and salt in a medium bowl and whisk for about 30 seconds to thoroughly combine. Add the flour mixture to the butter mixture.

Mix on low speed until the dough comes together, but still looks a bit rough, about 30 seconds. Scrape the sides and bottom of the bowl, and mix dough briefly on medium speed (8 to 10 seconds). Use a plastic bowl scraper or spatula to finish bringing the dough together.

- Transfer the dough (it will be soft) onto a long sheet of plastic wrap. Shape the dough into a 6 by 8 rectangle. The more evenly shaped the rectangle, the more evenly shaped the cookies will be, so take some time to square up the edges. Wrap the dough tightly, and refrigerate for at least 2 hours or up to 7 days.
- Heat oven to 350° F and line 2 half-sheet pans with parchment paper or silicon baking sheets.
- In a food processor pulse the almonds until a fairly fine meal forms, and no large pieces remain. If you have a jelled cranberry sauce whisk it with a fork to break it up into a more jam-like substance.
- Cut the dough into 5 even 8-inch long strips. Gently roll the strips back and forth to round out the edges. If they break apart a bit, just mash them back together. Sprinkle the almond meal over your work surface, and roll the strips in the meal to coat. Cut each strip into 8 even pieces, but leave the pieces in a log shape. Roll the log gently to round it again, then pull the pieces apart and place cut-side up on the prepared baking sheets in 5 rows of 4 per sheet.
- With the tip of your index finger make a generous indentation into each cookie. Fill the indentations with the cranberry preserves.
- Bake the cookies one pan at a time for 14 to 16 minutes, rotating the pan after 8 minutes. The cookies should be set around the edges with slight cracking on the tops. They will still be soft. Let the cookies cool completely on the pan.
- Store cookies in an airtight container at room temperature for up to 3 days, or in the fridge for up to 1 week.

9. Almond Ricotta Cake With Rasperry Jam And White Chocolate

Serving: Makes 1 cake | Prep: | Cook: |Ready in:

Ingredients

- 1 cup ground almonds
- 1/2 cup soft butter
- 1/2 cup sugar
- 4 eggs
- 1/2 cup whole wheat flour
- 1/2 teaspoon vanilla extract
- 1/2 cup Ricotta
- 1 pinch salt
- 1/2 cup white chocolate
- 4 tablespoons Raspberry jam or fruit coulis

Direction

- Grease Springform, cover with parchment paper and set in the refrigerator
- Wisk together butter and half of the sugar until creamy.
- Separate eggs yolks and egg whites, and add egg yolks to the butter-sugar mixture one by one.
- Stir in flour, almonds, vanilla extract and ricotta.
- Whisk egg whites with one pinch of salt, until almost stiff. Add the rest of the sugar and combine well until mixture in creamy and snowy. Finally, add the egg white to the ricotta mixture and pour in the Springform.
- Bake for 40-45 minutes in 350F. Let cool.
- For the topping, heat the raspberry jam with 50ml water and spread on top of the cake. Chill in the refrigerator for about an hour
- Using a vegetable peeler, shave the white chocolate and sprinkle in top of the jam.

10. Anise Cardamon Spiced Plum Jam

Serving: Makes (8) 4 oz jars | Prep: | Cook: |Ready in:

Ingredients

- 4 pounds Ripe, Mixed Plums - roughly chopped. (Around 8 cups chopped fruit)
- 2 cups Sugar
- 3 tablespoons Bottled Lemon Juice
- 1/4 teaspoon Cardamom Seeds – removed from pods, freshly ground or crushed in a mortar
- 1/4 teaspoon Ground Star Anise
- 1/4 teaspoon Ground Ginger

Direction

- Put the plums and sugar in a non-reactive pot and bring to a simmer over medium-low heat. Be sure to stir regularly so that the fruit doesn't stick and burn to the bottom of the pot. Cook for around 5 minutes, until the juice covers the fruit.
- Remove from the heat and pour into a strainer or mesh colander over a large bowl. Give the fruit a stir to drain as much of the juice as possible. Don't worry about being gentle – it's OK to smash up the fruit a bit.
- Set the fruit aside in the strainer (I suggest leaving it over the bowl to capture any late breaking juice). Return the juice to the pot and boil over high heat. Once it starts to boil, turn down the heat a touch and simmer, stirring often until the juice is thick & syrupy – about 10-15 minutes.
- Return the plums and any spare juice to the pan. Add the lemon juice and spices and bring to a simmer. Stir very frequently until the mixture is thick and ''jammy' – around 15 minutes. As it thickens, the jam will spew hot bubbles when you stir – so stand back. Take it from burned hand girl.
- Be sure you have some hot, buttered toast here – you'll want a taste, or two! Ladle hot jam into hot, sterilized jars – I like the 4 oz. jars,

ideal for sharing! Center a lid on top, screw on a jar ring until just finger tight. Process in a hot water bath for 5 minutes. When you remove them from the pot, check that they seal within 1 hour then resist moving them for 24 hours. Resist.

11. Anna Brone's Cardamom Carrot Marmalade

Serving: Makes 2 or 3 half-pint jars | Prep: | Cook: | Ready in:

Ingredients

- 2 cups water
- 1 tablespoon green cardamom pods
- 1 Meyer lemon, zest and juice
- 1 orange, zest and juice
- 2 cups carrots, grated (~3 large carrots)
- 2 cups sugar
- 1 teaspoon ground cardamom

Direction

- In a saucepan or Dutch oven, combine the water, cardamom pods, and lemon and orange zest and juice. Bring to a boil and simmer for ~15 minutes. Remove from heat and remove cardamom pods with a slotted spoon, discard.
- Add the other three ingredients and simmer for 30-45 minutes, stirring constantly, until the liquid has reduced to the point where only a little of the sugar syrup pools when you drag your spoon across the bottom. Remove from heat.
- If canning, fill sterile, glass half-pint jars with the marmalade and secure with lids and bands. Process in a water bath for 10 minutes. Otherwise, refrigerate.

12. Anniversary Mortadella Melts With Fennel Onion Jam

Serving: Serves 2 | Prep: | Cook: | Ready in:

Ingredients

- 4 ounces Swiss cheese, freshly grated
- 2 tablespoons finely minced red onion
- 2 tablespoons full fat good quality mayonnaise
- 1/2 large or 1 small red onion, thinly sliced
- 1/2 large or 1 small bulb fennel, cored, outer tough layers removed and thinly sliced
- 1 sweet-tart apple, peeled and grated away from the core (I used a Gala)
- 2 tablespoons butter
- 1 tablespoon fresh thyme leaves
- 1 tablespoon apple cider vinegar
- 1 tablespoon brown sugar, packed
- salt and pepper, to taste
- 4 slices mortadella (2 per sandwich, or more if you prefer)
- 4 slices rye bread, well buttered on what will be the outside of the sandwich

Direction

- In a small bowl, mix the Swiss cheese, diced red onion and mayonnaise to make a Swiss cheese spread. This can be made and kept in the fridge for up to 5 days.
- In a medium sauce-pan with a lid, melt 2 tablespoons of butter over medium heat. To the melted butter, add the sliced red onion, fennel and thyme leaves. Cover and cook low and slow until soft and caramelized, about 15 minutes, stirring frequently.
- To the fennel and onion, add the grated apple, apple cider vinegar, and brown sugar and stir to combine. Cook another 3-5 minutes on medium-low heat to meld all of the flavors. Salt and pepper to taste. This jam can be made ahead and kept in the fridge for up to a week.
- For sandwich assembly and cooking: place half of the cheese spread on the un-buttered side of a slice of rye bread, top with 2 slices

Moraxella and finally half of the fennel-onion jam and cap with another slice of rye, buttered side out. Repeat for the second sandwich. Heat a lightly-buttered non-stick griddle or grill pan over medium-low heat and cook the sandwiches so that the bread is crisp on the outside and the cheese spread is melty. This is best done low and slow so that the insides are warm and the cheese melts without the bread burning. My husband is the sandwich griller in my house and he recommends 10 minutes per side on 4/10 heat on the stovetop.

13. Apple Rosemary Jam

Serving: Makes about 20 ounces of jam | Prep: | Cook: | Ready in:

Ingredients

- 5-6 red apples
- 1-2 lemons
- 2 1/2 cups sugar
- 1 teaspoon rosemary

Direction

- Fill a large bowl with cold/ice water and add the juice of 1/2-1 whole lemon (I found the juice of 1/2 a lemon was enough to keep the apples from browning, see below).
- Peel, core and quarter the apples and put them in the cold lemon water. Like the original recipe states, I found this kept the apples from browning before they were diced.
- Remove the apples from the lemon water one at a time and dice them. I diced mine very finely, which was more time consuming up front but eliminated the need for blending the jam further later on. Discard the lemon water.
- Add the apples to the bottom of a sauce pan with high sides (to prevent splattering), as well as the sugar, juice of the remaining lemon(s), and rosemary. (If you decided to use pectin, add it now.)

- Bring the apple mixture to a boil and stir often for 30-40 minutes until your desired consistency is reached. If necessary, the original recipe suggests using a hand blender about halfway through to break up any larger apple chunks - just be careful not to get burned!
- When the jam is ready, spoon into jars sterilized by your method of choice. I have found that just baking the jars at 225 degrees for about 20 minutes while the jam is cooking works just as well as a water bath method, especially since this is a smaller amount of jam that can be consumed more quickly. If you try baking the jars just be sure to put the jars in first before turning on the oven and let the jars warm up with the oven to prevent cracking.

14. Apricot Jam Crostata (Crostata Di Marmellata)

Serving: Makes 1 crostata (serves 8) | Prep: | Cook: | Ready in:

Ingredients

- For the apricot jam:
- 2 pounds (1 kilogram) apricots
- 2 1/4 cups (500 grams or 17 1/2 ounces) sugar, approximately
- For the crostata:
- 2 cups (250 grams) all-purpose flour
- 1/2 cup (110 grams) superfine white sugar
- 1 stick (125 grams) chilled butter, chopped into pieces
- 1 egg plus 1 yolk, beaten (save the white for brushing on top of the pastry for a shiny crust)
- zest of 1 lemon

Direction

- For the apricot jam:
- Halve the apricots and remove the pits. Place them into a medium-sized, heavy-bottomed saucepan and place over low heat. No need to

add water but just watch the apricots carefully and give them the occasional stir so they don't stick and brown on the bottom of the pan. As the pan heats, they will release their own juices and the fruit will begin to simmer. You can help them along by squashing them a little with a wooden spoon as you do your occasional stir. Simmer for approximately 30 minutes.

- At this point, the fruit will be completely soft and fallen apart. Pass it through a very fine sieve over a bowl to remove the skins. Weigh your smooth apricot purée, then place back in the pot over low heat and add the sugar — Artusi calculates that you'll need 800 grams of sugar for every kilo of apricot purée (so 4/5 of the weight of the apricots), which for this amount is usually about 500 grams (17 1/2 ounces).
- Heat until the sugar dissolves, stirring often. Continue simmering on low until you reach the consistency desired. If you let this go quite a while, you will get a harder set jam, but even just a short 10 minutes or so will give you a very soft, lovely jam, perfect for this crostata, which has additional cooking time in the oven.
- If not using right away, pour the bubbling hot jam into sterilized, dry jars and close the lids. Let them sit on the kitchen bench to cool until you hear that satisfying pop of the lids as they seal.
- For the crostata:
- Combine the flour and sugar in a large bowl or in the bowl of a food process. Cut the cold butter into the flour and sugar by pulsing the processor or, if using hands, rub the butter into the flour until you get a crumbly mixture and there are no more visible butter pieces. Mix in the beaten egg and the yolk along with the lemon zest until the pastry comes together into a smooth, elastic ball. Let it rest in the fridge for at least 30 minutes. Artusi says if you do this the day before, even better.
- After the dough has rested, preheat the oven to 350° F. Divide the dough into two pieces, one slightly larger than the other. Roll this larger one out to about 3-millimeter thickness

to cover your pie dish. Roll out the rest of the pastry and with a pastry cutter or sharp knife, cut long strips about 2 centimeters wide. Fill the pie with jam and crisscross your lattice strips over the top. If you like, use the leftover egg white to brush gently over the top of the pastry. Bake at 350° F (180° C) for about 25 minutes, or until the pastry is golden brown and the jam bubbling.

15. Apricot Jam Tart

Serving: Serves 12 | Prep: | Cook: | Ready in:

Ingredients

- Almond filling
- 4 ounces butter
- 1/2 cup sugar
- 1 egg
- 1 cup almond powder
- 1 teaspoon almond extract
- 1 teaspoon vanilla extract
- 1 teaspoon flour
- Apricot jam tart
- 1 3/4 cups all-purpose flour
- 1/3 cup sugar
- 1 tablespoon lemon zest
- 1/2 teaspoon baking powder
- 1/2 teaspoon salt
- 6 ounces unsalted butter, chilled, cut in small pieces
- 2 eggs, lightly beatn
- 3 tablespoons ground amaretti cookie
- 1 3/4 cups apricot jam
- 1 egg, for brushing

Direction

- 1. In a mixer cream the butter (room temperature) and add the rest of the ingredients.
- Blend flour, sugar, lemon peel, baking powder, and salt in processor until combined. Add butter; using on/off turns cut in until

mixture resembles coarse meal. Add 2 eggs; using on/off turns, process until moist clumps form. Gather dough into ball. Flatten into disk. Wrap in plastic and refrigerate overnight. Let soften slightly before rolling out. Preheat oven to 375. Butter 9-inch diameter tart pan with removable bottom. Set aside 1/3 of dough. Roll out remaining dough on lightly floured surface to 14-inch round. Transfer to prepared tart pan. Trim overhang to 1 inch. Fold in dough to make double-thick sides. Freeze rest 15 minutes. Spread the almond filling in cooled tart shell. Spread the jam over the almond filling, sprinkle amaretti crumbs over jam. Roll out reserved dough to 11x6 inch rectangle. Cut into eight 1/2-inch-wide strips. Arrange strips atop jam to form lattice. Brush lattice with beaten egg. Bake tart until crust is golden, about 45 minutes. Cool at least 6 hours to allow jam to set. Cut into wedges and serve.

16. Autum Spice Pear Jam

Serving: Makes 10 cups | Prep: | Cook: | Ready in:

Ingredients

- juice of 1 Lemon
- juice of 1 Lime
- 3 pounds Bartlett pears
- 2 pounds sugar
- 1/4 teaspoon ground ginger
- 1/2 teaspoon ground coriander
- 3 tablespoons pear liqueur
- 5 2 cup sterilized jars with tight-fitting lids

Direction

- Peel, quarter and core pears. Cut pears into 1/4 inch cubes.
- In a large bowl, combine the pears, lemon juice and lime juice. Mix well.
- Transfer 2 pounds of the pears to a large, deep pot. Set the remaining 1 pound of pears aside.

- Add the sugar, ginger, coriander and 1 1/2 tablespoons pear liqueur to the pot. Stir well, cover, and let stand for three hours.
- Bring the mixture to a boil, skimming the foam as necessary. Boil for 4 to 5 minutes.
- Add the remaining pears and liqueur to the mixture.
- Spoon jam into sterilized jars and secure lids.
- Boil the jars for 30 minutes.
- Allow to Cool

17. BLOOD ORANGE MARMALADE

Serving: Makes about 9 cups | Prep: | Cook: | Ready in:

Ingredients

- 7 to 9 blood oranges (2 lbs)
- 10 cups water
- 8 cups white sugar
- 2 tablespoons Cointreau or Grand Marnier
- sterilized canning jars and lids
- candy thermometer

Direction

- Cut each orange in half and then slice as thinly as possible with a very sharp knife.
- Put the sliced orange slices in a large heavy bottomed pot.
- Add the water and bring to a boil. Then lower the heat and simmer for 20 minutes.
- Turn off the heat, add the sugar and mix. Then leave overnight to develop flavor and color.
- The next day; bring the mixture to boil and simmer until the mixture reaches the jelling point of 220 degrees. Use a candy thermometer. This will take longer than you think, so the thermometer is an accurate way of knowing when the jell point is reached.
- Stir in the orange liquor (Cointreau or Grand Marnier).
- In the meantime, have canning jars and lids sterilized and ready.

- Carefully spoon the hot marmalade into each jar, wipe the rims of each jar and screw on the band or seal the jar.

18. Back To School Raspberry Granola Bars From Karen DeMasco

Serving: Makes 16 bars | Prep: 0hours10mins | Cook: 0hours40mins | Ready in:

Ingredients

- 1 cup (115g) pecan halves, coarsely chopped
- 1 1/2 cups (190g) all-purpose flour
- 1 1/4 cups (115g) old-fashioned rolled oats
- 1/3 cup (65g) sugar
- 1/3 cup (75g) packed dark brown sugar
- 1 teaspoon kosher salt
- 1/2 teaspoon baking soda
- 3/4 cup (170g) unsalted butter, melted
- 1 cup (320g) raspberry jam

Direction

- Heat the oven to 350°F (175°C), with a rack in the center. Butter an 8-inch (20cm) square baking pan. Line the bottom and sides with parchment paper, leaving a 1-inch (2.5cm) overhang on two opposite sides for easier lifting when the bars are done. Butter the parchment. Spread the pecans in a pie plate or on a rimmed baking sheet and toast in the oven until lightly browned and fragrant, about 5 minutes. Let cool.
- Whisk together the flour, oats, sugars, salt, baking soda, and cooled pecans in large bowl. Pour in the melted butter, and using a wooden spoon or rubber spatula, stir until well combined.
- Press two-thirds of the oat mixture (about 3 cups/470g) into an even, firmly packed layer on the bottom of the baking pan. Using an offset or rubber spatula, spread the raspberry jam evenly across the surface of the dough,

leaving a 1/4-inch (6mm) border uncovered at the edges (the jam will melt and spread closer to the edges). Evenly sprinkle the remaining oat mixture over the jam.

- Bake until the top is golden brown, about 40 minutes, rotating the pan halfway through baking. Let the granola bars cool completely in the pan on a rack, about 3 hours. (Or go ahead and sneak one while they're still warm — they'll be a little crumbly but so good.) Lift up the overhanging ends of the parchment paper and transfer the granola almost-bars to a cutting board. Cut into 2-inch (5cm) squares. Store in an airtight container at room temperature.

19. Bacon Jam

Serving: Makes 1/2 cup | Prep: | Cook: | Ready in:

Ingredients

- 1/2 pound applewood or cherrywood-smoked bacon, sliced crosswise into 1/2-inch wide pieces
- 1 medium-size shallot, diced
- 1 teaspoon seeded and chopped jalapeno pepper
- 1/4 cup packed light brown sugar
- 1/4 cup apple cider vinegar
- 2 tablespoons fresh orange juice
- 2 tablespoons bourbon
- 3 pieces peeled fresh ginger, each about the size and thickness of a quarter
- 1 bay leaf
- 1/2 teaspoon honey
- Freshly ground black pepper to taste

Direction

- Cook the bacon in a large skillet over medium heat until browned and crisp and the fat is rendered, 7 to 10 minutes, stirring often and adjusting the heat as necessary. Using a slotted spoon, transfer the bacon to a paper towel-lined plate to drain, reserving 1 to 2 tablespoons of the bacon fat in the skillet.

- Add the shallot and jalapeno to the skillet and cook over medium-low heat until the shallot is softened, about 2 minutes, stirring often and scraping up the brown bits from the bottom of the skillet. Return the bacon the skillet and add the brown sugar, cider vinegar, orange juice, bourbon, ginger, and bay leaf. Cover the skillet and let come to a boil, then reduce the heat and let simmer gently, uncovered, until most of the liquid has evaporated, 10 to 15 minutes, stirring occasionally.
- Remove and discard the bay leaf. Transfer the bacon mixture to a mini food processor and pulse until the bacon is finely diced but not pureed, 10 to 15 times, pausing several times to scrape down the side of the bowl.
- Place the Bacon Jam in a small bowl and stir in the honey and a couple of grindings of black pepper. Serve with assorted cheeses and crackers, or as a delicious condiment for a grilled burger, steak, or chicken.

20. Bakewell Tart With Rhubarb Hibiscus Jam

Serving: Makes one 9-inch tart, plus extra compote | Prep: | Cook: | Ready in:

Ingredients

- For the tart:
- For the almond cream
- 1 cup slivered almonds
- 1 1/2 tablespoons all-purpose flour
- 2/3 cup sugar
- 1   stick plus 1 tablespoon (9 tablespoons) unsalted butter, at room temperature
- 1   large egg plus 1 large egg white
- 1/2 teaspoon almond extract
- Zest of 1 lemon
- For the tart crust
- 150 grams all-purpose flour

- 30 grams almond meal or finely ground almonds
- 57 grams powdered sugar
- 1   stick plus 1 tablespoon (9 tablespoons) very cold or frozen unsalted butter, cut into small cubes
- 1   large egg, with its yolk gently broken up
- For the rhubarb-hibiscus jam (halve this recipe if you do not want a lot of extra jam):
- 2 pounds rhubarb
- 1 1/4 cups dark brown sugar
- 8   dried hibiscus flowers
- 6   dried hibiscus flowers, crushed, mixed with 1 tablespoon sugar (for optional garnish)

Direction

- Start by making the almond cream, as it has to chill for the longest amount of time. Finely ground the almonds and flour in a food processor. Add the sugar and process again. Then add the butter, extract, and lemon zest and blend until smooth. Mix in egg and egg white and process until no lumps remain. Transfer filling to a medium bowl, cover, and chill for at least 3 hours. (You can also make this 2 days in advance.)
- To make the tart crust, pulse the flours, sugar, and salt together in a food processor. Scatter the butter pieces over top and pulse until it's coarsely cut in—the size of oatmeal flakes and peas.
- Add the egg a little at a time, pulsing after each addition. When the egg is all in there, process in long 10-second pulses until the dough forms clumps and curds (this typically takes me 5 to 8 of these long pulses). The sound of the machine will change just before you get to this point, so listen carefully!
- Turn the dough out onto a piece of plastic wrap spread on a work surface. Very gently, bring all of the disparate pieces together. Blanket with plastic wrap and flatten into a disc. Chill the dough in the refrigerator for 2 hours (if you chill it for more time than this, you'll need to let it soften just a little at room temperature before rolling it out).

- Butter a 9-inch fluted tart pan with a removable bottom. On a floured sheet of parchment paper, roll the dough out to a 12-inch round, occasionally lifting it up and sprinkling some flour underneath. (You can also roll the dough out between 2 pieces of lightly-floured plastic wrap.)
- Use the paper as a guide to help you lift the dough into the tart pan. Peel off the paper, then gently lift and nudge the dough into the sides of the pan. Reserve any extra dough (for repairing cracks, for extra insurance!) in the refrigerator. Cover with plastic wrap and freeze for at least 30 minutes (and preferably longer).
- While your crust freezes, make the rhubarb jam. Trim the ends off the rhubarb stalks and then cut any large ones in half lengthwise, Cut the lengths into 3/4-inch chunks. You should have about 6 cups of rhubarb; set 2 cups aside.
- Add the remaining 4 cups of rhubarb to a medium sauce pan with the brown sugar and hibiscus flowers. Stir so that everything is combined, then turn the heat to medium low. Cover the pot and cook for 15 minutes, stirring from time to time just to make sure the sugar isn't burning.
- Remove the cover, increase the heat to medium, and cook for around 15 minutes, stirring constantly, until the rhubarb has completely broken down and the consistency is thick.
- Add the remaining rhubarb to the pot and stir to combine.
- Pour the compote into a large baking dish or a sheet tray to cool. Once cool, remove the hibiscus flowers.
- While the jam cools, par-bake your tart crust. Preheat the oven to 375° F and position a rack in the center. Butter a piece of nonstick aluminum foil and place it butter side down tightly against the dough. Place on a baking sheet and bake on center rack for 20 to 25 minutes.
- Carefully remove the foil. If the crust is puffy, gently press it down with the back of a spoon.

Bake for 5 additional minutes, then transfer to a rack and cool to room temperature.
- When your tart is partially baked, the rhubarb jam is cool, and the almond cream has chilled for 3 hours, you're ready to assemble and do the final bake!
- Preheat the oven to 350° F with a rack in the center. Spread the compote in a rather thin layer over the base of the shell. Save any extra throughout the week in the fridge. Then dollop the almond filling over top and spread it carefully with an offset spatula. If using, sprinkle the hibiscus sugar over top. Bake tart until golden and tester inserted into center of filling comes out clean, about 45 minutes. Cool tart in pan on rack. The whole tart can also be made half a day in advance. Let stand at room temperature.

21. Balsamic Chicken Sandwich With Peach Jam And Brandied Onions

Serving: Serves 4 | Prep: | Cook: | Ready in:

Ingredients

- For the chicken and brandied onions:
- 1 pound boneless free-range chicken breast, cut into strips
- 1 cup balsamic vinaigrette
- Sea salt, to taste
- Freshly cracked pepper, to taste
- Olive oil
- 1 red onion, thinly sliced
- 1 tablespoon brandy
- 1 loaf of bread from the bakery (I used French bread), sliced
- Peach jam (see below)
- Your favorite mayonnaise (or a vegan substitute)
- 1 head of lettuce (Boston, green, or red leaf would work)
- For the peach jam:

- 1 peach, peeled and chopped
- 2 tablespoons organic sugar
- 1 teaspoon brandy
- 1 pinch sea salt

Direction

- For the chicken and brandied onions:
- Marinate the chicken for at least one hour and up to 12. When you're ready to cook, preheat a grill or a grill pan over medium-high heat. Drizzle the grill with a little olive oil and cook chicken strips for 4 minutes per side. Remove and set aside.
- Meanwhile, in a small pan, heat a glug of olive oil over medium heat and add the onion slices. Season with salt and pepper and cook for 6 to 7 minutes, stirring often.
- Add the brandy and continue to cook until the alcohol is absorbed, about 2 to 3 minutes. Remove from the heat and set aside.
- Lay out the slices of bread. Spread the jam on one side and the mayonnaise on the other. On top of the jam, add the chicken, onion, then the lettuce. Voilà!
- For the peach jam:
- Add the ingredients to a pan set over high heat. Bring to a boil, then reduce heat to medium and continue to cook for about 7 minutes. Using a potato masher, smash the peaches until the big lumps are gone.
- Turn off heat and transfer to a jar to cool. The jam will keep for up to 3 weeks in the refrigerator (if you don't eat it all first!).

22. Banana Jam

Serving: Makes 3 cups | Prep: 0hours0mins | Cook: 0hours0mins |Ready in:

Ingredients

- 6 large bananas (22 to 24 ounces, post-peeling), broken in half
- 1 1/4 cups granulated sugar

- 2 tablespoons brown sugar
- Juice of 2 limes
- 2 tablespoons water
- 1/2 teaspoon kosher salt
- 1 tablespoon dark rum
- 1 teaspoon vanilla extract

Direction

- Combine the bananas and sugars in a medium pot. Mash with a fork until the fruit is chunky and the sugar syrupy. Set over medium-low heat and bring to a simmer. Add the lime juice, water, and salt. Continue to cook at a steady simmer—stirring occasionally—for about 10 minutes, until slightly thickened. Remove from the heat and stir in the rum and vanilla.
- Spoon the hot jam into jars. I just seal with a lid and keep in the fridge—but sterilize if you'd like.

23. Beef Tenderloin With Shallot Marmalade

Serving: Serves 6 to 8 | Prep: | Cook: |Ready in:

Ingredients

- 2 tablespoons unsalted butter
- 4 tablespoons olive oil
- 1 pound shallots, halved
- 2 fresh rosemary sprigs
- Kosher salt
- Freshly ground black pepper
- 1 tablespoon sherry vinegar
- Pinch of sugar
- 1 (4 pound) beef tenderloin

Direction

- Heat the butter and 2 tablespoons of olive oil in a large skillet over low heat. Add the shallots and rosemary sprigs, season with salt and pepper, and cook for about 1 hour, until the shallots are tender and caramelized. Remove and discard the rosemary and stir in the vinegar and sugar. Transfer the shallots to the bowl of a food processor and blend until slightly chunky.

- Meanwhile, preheat the oven to 400°F. Drizzle the remaining 2 tablespoons of olive oil over the beef and season with salt and pepper. Place on a large rimmed baking sheet. Roast for 35 to 40 minutes, until a meat thermometer inserted into the thickest part of the meat registers 125°F. Remove from the oven and transfer the meat to a cutting board. Tent with aluminum foil and let rest for 20 minutes.
- Slice the meat into ½-inch thick slices and arrange on a serving platter. Spoon the marmalade over the top and serve.

24. Better Turkey Burger With Feta And Onion Jam

Serving: Serves 4 | Prep: | Cook: |Ready in:

Ingredients

- 1 large yellow (or vidalia) onion
- 1 tablespoon olive oil
- 1 teaspoon paprika
- 1/2 teaspoon soy sauce
- 1 splash red wine
- 1 pound lean ground turkey
- 1 teaspoon cumin
- 1 teaspoon garlic powder
- 1 teaspoon each salt and pepper
- 4 brioche buns
- 8 ounces feta cheese, cut into slices
- 1 arugula
- 1 large tomato, sliced thick

Direction

- Place a large skillet over medium-low heat. Slice the onion into very thin slices and set aside.

- Heat olive oil in skillet and add paprika, cooking for 10 seconds until smoky and sweet smelling. Add onions and soy sauce then quickly stir to coat.
- Slowly sweat onions until translucent, about 10 minutes. Remove half of the onions and add to a large mixing bowl to cool.
- With the heat still on the remaining onions, stir in the splash of red wine and cook for another 10 minutes until very soft and jam-like. Set aside for finished burger.
- Preheat grill to medium-high heat. Return to your mixing bowl with cooled onions and add ground turkey, cumin, garlic powder, salt and pepper. Get your hands in there and mix (because it's fun!) then shape into 4 even sized patties.
- Grill turkey patties for about 4 minutes per side or until nice grill marks have appeared and the burger is medium-firm to the touch and cooked through.
- Toast brioche buns and slather one side with a bit of onion jam. Build burgers with a slice of feta, a bit of arugula, a tomato slice, and top with jam slathered bun. Enjoy!

25. Betty's Jelly Meatballs

Serving: Serves 3-4 dozen | Prep: | Cook: |Ready in:

Ingredients

- Meatballs:
- 1 pound lean ground beef-I used ground turkey to make it a little more lean, a mix of both would also work.
- 1 egg beaten
- 1/2 cup fine bread crumbs
- 3 tablespoons chopped fresh parsley
- 1/2 cup finely chopped onion
- 1 teaspoon salt and pepper to taste
- 1 tablespoon Worcestershire sauce
- 1/2 teaspoon freshly ground black pepper
- Sauce:

- 1   12 ounce bottle of Heinz Chile Sauce
- 1   10 ounce jar of Grape Jelly
- 1 teaspoon fresh lemon juice
- 2 tablespoons brown sugar
- 1 tablespoon soy sauce

Direction

- Mix meat mixture and make small meatballs 1/2 inch- 1 inch in circumference. My Aunt adds them raw to the hot bubbling sauce but sometimes I bake them ahead of time in the oven, on a parchment or aluminum foil lined pan at 375 degrees F for about 20-25 minutes or until light brown. I then add them to the sauce and let them simmer for about 15 minutes on very low.
- For the sauce, just mix up all the ingredients and bring to a boil in a medium/large sized pot, you also need room for the meatballs. If you are adding the meatballs raw, gently place them in the sauce and let them simmer for about 30 minutes until cooked through and infused with the sauce. Serve hot with toothpicks as an appetizer or over rice as a main course with some veggies on the side.
- Tip: My Aunt mentioned you can freeze the sauce once it has cooled. Cook the meatballs before you freeze them. When ready to use, thaw the sauce and bring to a simmer in a pot and then add the thawed meatballs and let simmer for about 20 minutes. Serve hot.

26. Big Momma's Blackberry Jam Cake

Serving: Serves 16 | Prep: | Cook: | Ready in:

Ingredients

- Blackberry Jam Cake
- 1 cup golden raisins
- 1 cup black walnuts
- 3 cups cake flour
- 1 teaspoon ground cinnamon
- 1 teaspoon ground allspice
- 1 teaspoon freshly grated nutmeg
- 1/2 teaspoon ground cloves
- 1 teaspoon baking soda
- 8 ounces unsalted butter, softened
- 1 1/2 cups dark brown sugar, packed
- 1/2 teaspoon salt
- 3 large eggs
- 1 cup blackberry jam, homemade and seedless if possible
- 1 cup buttermilk
- coconut caramel glaze, recipe follows
- Coconut Caramel Glaze
- 1/2 cup dark brown sugar, packed
- 2 ounces unsalted butter
- 1/4 cup half and half
- 1/4 cup sweetened shredded coconut
- 2 tablespoons unbleached all purpose flour
- 1/2 teaspoon vanilla extract

Direction

- Blackberry Jam Cake
- Preheat the oven to 350. Grease and flour a large bundt pan. Place the raisins in a small saucepan and cover with water. Bring to a boil, turn off the heat and allow the raisins to cool completely; drain well. Place the walnuts on a small baking pan and toast in the oven until lightly browned and fragrant, about 5 minutes. Let them cool and chop them evenly.
- Sift the flour, cinnamon, allspice, nutmeg, cloves and baking soda into a bowl and set aside. With an electric mixer, cream the butter with the brown sugar and the salt on medium-low speed until light and fluffy. Add the eggs, one at a time, scraping the bowl as you go. Add the jam and mix it in completely. Add the reserved dry ingredients alternately with the buttermilk, scraping the bowl completely once or twice. Fold in the raisins and walnuts. Pour the batter into the prepared pan.
- Bake until a pick inserted into the cake comes out clean, about an hour. Let the cake cool in the pan for 20 minutes then turn it out onto a rack to cool completely. Place the cooled cake

- onto a serving dish or cake stand and drizzle with the coconut caramel glaze.
- Coconut caramel glaze
- Place the brown sugar, butter, half and half, coconut and flour into a large shallow, heavy saucepan. Set over medium low heat and cook while stirring until the mixture is completely blended and begins to boil.
- Continue to boil gently while whisking until the mixture begins to thicken, about 7-10 minutes. Remove from the heat and stir in the vanilla. Scrape the glaze into a heat proof dish and press plastic wrap to the surface to prevent a skin from forming. Chill in the fridge until it is cool and thickened but will still dollop off of a spoon.
- Using a large spoon, drizzle the glaze, bit by bit, over the top of the bundt cake. Guide the glaze with the spoon so that the entire cake has drizzles of glaze running down the sides.

27. Black Grape Jam, Ethereal With Body And Style Like No Other... Jam That Is.

Serving: Makes 4 half pint jars | Prep: | Cook: | Ready in:

Ingredients

- 2 pounds Black Seedless Table Grapes
- 1 cup pineapple or orange juice
- 2-3 cups unrefined sugar
- 1/8 teaspoon sea salt

Direction

- Remove 2 pounds of grapes from the stems. Give them a wicked good rinse to remove any build up or stray stems.
- Place into a blender, (with your pineapple or orange juice) and blend until smooth-as-can-be.
- Place grape mixture into a large pot with 2 to 3 cups of sugar, juice and a pinch of sea salt.
- Bring to a boil over medium-high heat.

- Simmer and Stir, stir, stir for 10-15-20 minutes. This step may seem tedious but it is necessary to prevent scorching.
- You want to cook your jam until it has set. Your jam will go from a frothy, foamy wet mixture to a thick syrup, to a heavy syrup that will coat your spoon. At this stage you are ready to test your jam to see if it will gel. Place a small amount on a frozen spoon or plate, or simply place some in a shot glass and refrigerate it for a few minutes. If it seems to have solidified you are golden. If it is still quite wet you need five more minutes. I find 15-20 works just right for me.
- Place hot jam into sterile jars. Wipe rims entirely clean, secure lids and rings into place and place into a stock pot, cover with water and bring it up to a boil. Process in boiling water for 8 to 10 minutes. Carefully remove from the water bath and leave the jars un-bothered for 24 hours. Store as long as needed, the flavor is best if used within 6 months to a year.
- Note: The more sugar you use, the easier it will be to gel. I found that 3 cups is about right for a "normal" tasting preserve. Typical recipes call for 4 cups of sugar to 4 cups of smashed (high pectin) fruit. I have found that Smaller jars work best for keeping jams. They always seem to set better in small jars. Do not try to double the recipe, it is a labor of love and if you try to double up your jam will not gel.

28. Black Tea Jelly

Serving: Serves enough for a small dinner party | Prep: | Cook: | Ready in:

Ingredients

- 2 cups of your favorite black tea (I use Taylor's of Harrogate Scottish Breakfast), strongly brewed and cooled to room temperature
- 2 packets (1/2 an ounce) powdered gelatin

- 1/4 cup sugar

Direction

- Brush a 4-cup mold or bowl lightly with vegetable oil.
- Sprinkle the gelatin evenly over the tea and let it soften for about 5 minutes. Meanwhile, put a kettle on to boil. When the water boils, measure out 1½ cups and stir in the sugar until it dissolves. Add the tea and gelatin and stir until the gelatin dissolves, about a minute.
- Carefully pour the liquid into the mold and refrigerate for several hours, until set. To unmold the tea jelly, set it in a bowl of very hot water for about 30 seconds, place a serving plate over the top, hold your breath, and flip. If you don't hear a squelching noise, followed by a plop, jiggle the mold a little. Once it's safely on the plate, decorate the edges of the gelatin mold with berries or whatever else you'd like, parade it into the dining room and serve with heavy cream or vanilla ice cream on the side.

29. Blackberry Mulled Wine Jam

Serving: Serves 12 halfp pint jars plus extra for the fridge | Prep: | Cook: | Ready in:

Ingredients

- 2 cups merlot (something rather fruity)
- 4 cinnamon sticks
- 15 whole cloves
- 3 whole star anise
- 10 cups fresh washed blackberries
- 3 tablespoons minced candied ginger
- 1 cup orange juice
- 2 boxes NO SUGAR NEEDED fruit pectin (1.75 oz each)
- 2 cups sugar
- 2 tablespoons unsalted butter

Direction

- If you are canning - sterilize your jars and get your canning station ready. Put a couple of spoons in the freezer.
- Pour the wine into a large pot and bring it to a simmer with the cinnamon, cloves and star anise. I put the cloves in a tea egg which makes it easier when you fish them back out. Allow this mixture to simmer on very low heat for 10 minutes.
- Remove the spices, then add the blackberries, orange juice, and ginger. Bring the mixture to a rolling boil. Meanwhile whisk the sugar and pectin together - this will keep the pectin from lumping up. When the berries are boiling, stir in the sugar, pectin and butter. The butter will keep the mixture from foaming up too much and butter makes things better in general. Once the jam has reached a rolling boil again you can turn down the heat and keep it at a low boil for about 5 minutes, stirring often. Now look at a spoonful - do you want all whole berries or some mashed? I like some mashed so I run through the jam (gently) with a potato masher. Do the jam test - pour a little down the back of a frozen spoon. Run your finger through it. It should make a path that stays open. If not, boil a few more minutes and test again. Your jam is done!
- If you are canning - carefully ladle jam into the jars, clean the rims, place the lids on top and secure with the rings. Boil in the jam pot for 10 minutes then remove and leave them alone until they have cooled completely and the seals have set. Please research before canning - safety first!!!

30. Blackberry Cream & Jelly Verrines

Serving: Makes 6 '125ml capacity' verrines | Prep: | Cook: | Ready in:

Ingredients

- 1 1/2 cups caster sugar

- 150g (frozen) blackberries
- 3 gelatine leaves (or 1 1/2 teaspoons gelatine powder)
- 1/3 cup mascarpone cheese, whisked a bit to loosen and break structure
- 1/2 cup single cream
- 1 teaspoon vanilla extract
- 2 tablespoons raw, flaked almonds
- 2 tablespoons light brown sugar
- zest of 1-2 limes and wedges to garnish

Direction

- Blackberry syrup: Place 1/2 cup of sugar and 1 cup water in a pan on medium heat, stirring till the sugar is dissolved. Add the blackberries and gently stir. Allow to cook till the blackberries are soft and can be squashed. Remove from heat and let cool. Blitz in a food processor or with a hand-held immersion blender. Now this next step is crucial - because the jelly will lose some of its sweetness when it cools down, taste the syrup now and add more sugar if necessary, stirring to make sure it dissolves well. Strain 160ml of the liquid mixture for the jelly. (Refrigerate the rest of liquid and strained out blackberry mass/puree for use later in the verrines)
- Blackberry jelly: if using gelatine leaves, soak them first in water for 4-5 minutes till the soften and swell, then add to 160ml warm blackcurrant syrup (if blackcurrant syrup is cold, gently reheat it till warm but not boiling), stirring till it dissolves. If using powder, sprinkle onto a few tablespoons of warm water and leave to stand for a few minutes, then combine with warm blackcurrant syrup and mix till dissolved. Note that I used gelatine leaves so my instructions for the powder are a guide. When the liquid is ready, gently pour equal portions into your 6 tumblers. Cover and leave to set for a couple of hours (or overnight).
- Cooled, whipped cream: By the time you're making the cream, the jelly should be set and ready to be topped. Cool your mixing bowl and whisking attachment in the freezer for a half hour before whipping the cream. When the utensils are cool, combine the cream, 1/2 cup of sugar and vanilla extract in the bowl and whip till light and soft. To this creamed mixture, add your mascarpone and gently fold in. You can use the cream as is or add a tablespoon of the set-aside blackberry puree (leftover from step 1) or do both.
- Set out the glasses with the set jelly and ladle into each glass a teaspoonful of the blackberry puree (leftover from step 1). Top/fill up with the whipped cream. Do this for all the verrines.
- When you're done, place in the fridge for at least an hour or overnight, covered to 'set'.
- Sugared Almonds: Pre-heat your top grill to the highest. In a baking tray, place the flaked almonds and gently sprinkle the light brown sugar on top of the almonds. Place the tray 6 inches down from the heat source and let brown for 3-4 minutes. Remove from oven, pour onto a bowl or unto a plate and let cool for a few minutes.
- When ready to serve verrines, (give your guests long handle spoons) sprinkle with sugared almonds and some lime zest. Serve with a lime wedge and have your guests squeeze some lime juice over the top - the fragrance is wow. If you have key limes which I've heard so much about but never used, go ahead and avail yourself!
- Enjoy

31. Blackberry Jelly

Serving: Makes 2 jars | Prep: | Cook: | Ready in:

Ingredients

- 2 1/2 pounds wild blackberries
- 2 pounds preserving sugar (not all may be needed)

Direction

- You will also need a jelly bag or a large muslin cloth and a colander.
- Wash the brambles and put them in a heavy stock pot or jam pan with a little water – the residue from the washing will be enough. Bring them to the boil and simmer for about 20-25 minutes, until completely soft.
- If you have a jelly bag, use it according to the instructions. Otherwise place a colander over a tall pot (you can use the same pot you cooked the brambles in, rinsed, while the brambles have been decanted to a bowl).
- Pour the brambles into the bag or muslin cloth and leave to drip overnight.
- The next day squeeze the bag with fruit pulp to maximize the yield and decant the juice to a measuring jug. For every 1l (4 cups) of the juice use 750g (3 1/2 cups) jam sugar.
- Pour the juice and the sugar into the pot again and bring to a gentle simmer. Let it cook for about 30-40 minutes until the temperature reaches 105C/200F – or a blob dropped onto an ice cold plate sets to jam/jelly consistency.
- While the jelly cooks, wash two jam sized jars, kilner or lidded, in hot water. Place them in an oven heated up to 120C240F and immediately switched off.
- When the jelly is ready leave it to slightly cool down, about 10 minutes, and then carefully fill the jars. Close them tightly and leave for at least a few days to mature before eating.

32. Blood Orange Marmalade Sunset In A Jar

Serving: Makes 3-4 medium sized jam jars | Prep: | Cook: | Ready in:

Ingredients

- 2 1/2 pounds organic blood oranges, rinsed
- 1 1/4 pounds sugar
- 2 lemons

Direction

- Sterilize the jam jars in boiling water for 5 minutes.
- Fill a large pan with water and bring to the boil.
- Cook the oranges for about 25 minutes or until soft (mine needed 25 minutes but they were small with thin skin). Take them out and keep some of the water.
- Quarter the cooked oranges (don't peel them, you use the whole orange!), take out their seeds and put them aside (you will need them).
- Cut the lemons in half and keep their seeds as well. In a small pan, heat up some of the blood orange cooking water (it should come up to 3/4"), add the lemon seeds and orange seeds and let them cook for 5 minutes.
- Shred the quartered oranges in a food processor for a few seconds.
- Put them in a large pan, add the sugar, the juice of the 2 lemons and the water used to boil the seeds. Bring to the boil gently (the sugar has to dissolve first) and boil for 18-20 minutes.
- Dip the rim of your sterilized jars in spirit and wash out the lids of the jars with the alcohol as well. Fill your jars with the marmalade and close well immediately.

33. Blood Orange Marmalade {with Salted Butter On Toasted Crostini}

Serving: Makes citrus sunshine in a jar | Prep: | Cook: | Ready in:

Ingredients

- Blood Oranges {Moro, Tarocco or Sanguinello}
- Granulated Sugar
- Water
- {optional: a dash of Campari}

Direction

- Wash the oranges in warm water, rubbing the skins to take off any wax coverings {especially if you cannot find organic or sustainably grown oranges}.
- Trim the tops and bottoms from the blood oranges, reserving the peel caps. Cut the orange peel lengthwise into thirds or quarters and carefully peel the fruit, removing as much pith as possible.
- Here is what makes citrus marmalade different from other fruit jam: for an added layer of flavor {& a dash of bitterness}, you want to add in the citrus peel, which needs to soften - and here's how: place the orange peel in a large saucepan, cover with cold water and slowly bring to a boil. Boil over medium-low heat for about 10 minutes. Drain. Return the saucepan to the stove, cover with fresh cold water and boil for another 10 minutes. Drain again {& repeat a third time, if peel is not soft to the touch}.
- Let the peel cool for a few minutes. Take a small spoon and carefully scrape away all white pith from inside each peel segment, then stack a few peel segments and with a sharp knife cut into very fine julienne strips.
- While the peel is boiling, separate the orange segments from the membrane. Save juices and squeeze the membranes to remove any additional juice, collecting juice and segments in a large saucepan. Discard the membranes.
- Add the julienned peel and enough water to cover segments & peel. Slowly bring the saucepan to a boil, stirring occasionally. Reduce the heat and boil gently, stirring frequently, until the peel is very soft - about 30-40 minutes. Test the peel by pressing between two fingers.
- Pour in the water, a cup at a time {make sure to keep count!}, until the fruit is just covered. Bring back to boiling. Now gradually stir in the sugar {same amount of cups as water previously added} and heat up to a strong boil. Stir! For the perfect marmalade fruit/sugar ratio, I add the same amount of sugar as water {not too sweet, not too bitter}.

And if the batch turns out too sweet, adding some Campari will bring back the bitterness.
- While boiling and stirring, keep an eye on the consistency: the marmalade will begin to gel after about 10-12 minutes. Let it cool for a few minutes, then pour into sterilized glasses & seal. Voila, bright year-round citrus sunshine in a glass :)

34. Blueberry Date Jam

Serving: Makes 1 heaping cup | Prep: | Cook: | Ready in:

Ingredients

- 12   pitted dates
- 6 cups frozen Maine blueberries (about 24 oz of blueberries)

Direction

- Place blueberries (do not thaw ahead of time) and dates in a medium saucepan. Cover.
- Turn heat to medium and cook, covered, for about 10-14 minutes. Start peaking at it at 10 minutes. If the berries already look quite wrinkled and reduced, it's go time.
- Uncover and continue to cook, stirring constantly, for 3-5 additional minutes. Use a wooden spoon. You'll know that it's done when you pull the spoon across the bottom of the pan and the mix does not return to that spot (aka, you will still be able to see the path the spoon made on the bottom of the pan)
- If you have an immersion blender, you can puree the mix right away. If you don't have an immersion blender, wait for the mix to cool before pureeing to a smooth, even consistency.

35. Blueberry Pudding, Jam & Custard

Serving: Serves 6 | Prep: | Cook: |Ready in:

Ingredients

- For the pudding:
- 50 grams plain wholemeal flour
- 1 piece egg
- 75 milliliters unsweetened almond milk
- 25 pieces blueberries
- For the custard:
- 600 milliliters coconut milk
- 3 tablespoons honey or maple syrup
- 1 piece vanilla pod
- 9 pieces egg yolks

Direction

- Preheat the oven to 200C/390F.
- Add coconut oil to the bottom of each muffin tin, then heat for 5 mins in the oven.
- Add the coconut milk, honey/maple syrup and vanilla for the custard to a saucepan and heat gently over a medium heat until warm, but not boiling.
- Add the beaten egg yolks to the custard pan and stir continuously until everything is combined, then turn down to a low heat for another 15 minutes until thickened, whisking occasionally.
- Once everything is ready - add the toppings of your choice and enjoy!

36. Bocconotti (Southern Italian Jam Pastries)

Serving: Makes about 8 | Prep: | Cook: |Ready in:

Ingredients

- 2 cups (250 grams) all purpose flour
- 1/2 cup (110 grams) sugar
- 1 stick (½ cup or 125 grams) of cold butter, diced
- 1 large (not jumbo) whole egg plus 1 yolk, beaten (save the white for brushing on top of the pastry for a shiny crust)
- zest of one lemon, finely grated
- 4 cups (560 grams or 20 ounces) quince jam (or sour cherry jam or pastry cream)
- powdered sugar for dusting (optional)

Direction

- Combine the flour and sugar in a large bowl or in the bowl of a food processor. Cut the cold butter into the flour and sugar by pulsing the processor or, if using hands, rub the butter into the flour until you get a crumbly mixture and there are no more visible butter pieces. Mix in the beaten egg and the yolk along with the lemon zest until the pastry comes together into a smooth, elastic ball. Let it rest in the fridge for at least 30 minutes.
- Roll the dough on a lightly floured surface until about 3mm (1/10 inch) thick. Cut 8 discs about 3 3/4-4 inches in diameter (9.5-10cm) -- I use a bowl I have about this size across the widest part, flip it over onto the rolled out dough and trace around it. Fill a muffin tray or ramekins with the pastry discs, pressing them down gently to be smooth and even. Prick the base with the tines of a fork.
- Fill the pastries (I used roughly 1/4 cup or a couple tablespoons) with jam.
- Gather together the leftover dough and roll it back out to 3mm thickness. Cut out discs to cover exactly the top of the pastries (mine were about 3 1/4 or 8cm in diameter).
- Beat the leftover egg white and brush some over the edges of the pastries before putting the discs on top. Press down the edges very gently to seal and, if desired, you can brush the egg white on the top of the pastries too, this will give them a bit of shine, if you are going to serve them without a dusting of powdered sugar.

- Bake in an oven pre-heated to 180C/350F for 20 minutes or until the tops are golden brown and crisp.

37. Boysenberry Blueberry Jam

Serving: Makes 1 jar | Prep: | Cook: |Ready in:

Ingredients

- 2 packages organic frozen boysenberries
- 1 1/2 C water
- 1/2 large package blueberries
- 1 C organic brown sugar
- 1/2 meyer lemon juice and zest
- 1/2 sachet liquid natural pectin
- 1 clean mason jar and screw on lid

Direction

- Boil the lid of the jar and keep in the water till ready to seal. Put the washed and clean jar in a 275 F oven for 10 minutes to sterilize. Keep in oven till ready to fill.
- Put the frozen fruit and water in a heavy saucepan over medium high heat for a few minutes. Add sugar lemon zest and juice, stir and bring to a boil.
- Lower temperature to medium heat and let rapidly simmer for about 20 minutes.
- Add the fresh blueberries, boil 5 more minutes.
- Add pectin, boil and then simmer until jam reduces to your desired consistency, mine was quite syrupy. Turn off heat.
- Using clean tongs, remove a jar from the oven and place it on a wooden cutting board. Pour the jam carefully into the jar without dirtying the outer edge (you may want to use a funnel for this). Using the tongs, remove the lid from the boiling water and place on top of the jar of jam. Seal. Store at room temperature for 24 hours before opening and/or refrigerating.

38. Brandy Old Fashioned Jam

Serving: Makes 4 cups | Prep: | Cook: |Ready in:

Ingredients

- 8 cups pitted cherries (frozen cherries are your best bet around the holidays. I recommend using a mix of half sweet and half tart cherries)
- 2/3 cup freshly squeezed orange juice
- 2 tablespoons grated orange zest
- 1 1/2 cups sugar
- 1/2 cup brown sugar
- 1/4 cup brandy
- 2 teaspoons Angostura bitters

Direction

- Place cherries, orange juice, and orange zest in a large pot over medium high heat. Cook until cherries are soft and releasing juice, about 10-15 minutes.
- Transfer jam to a blender, or use an immersion blender to blend most of the cherries into a smoother consistency. If desired, you can leave a few whole cherries in there for added texture. Return blended cherries to medium high heat.
- Add the sugars and stir to mix thoroughly. Bring to a boil and continue cooking over medium high heat, stirring often, until mixture thickens, about 25-30 minutes.
- Remove from heat and stir in the brandy and bitters. Ladle jam into jars and seal tightly. Jam will keep in refrigerator for 2-3 weeks.

39. Bread With Butter And Jam

Serving: Makes your choice | Prep: | Cook: |Ready in:

Ingredients

- Slices of soft, white sandwich bread

- Finest (cold) salted butter
- Top notch strawberry jam

Direction

- Take a few slices of bread and butter each one. Spread the strawberry jam over the butter, on each slice.
- Sit back and eat individually, not sandwiched (doubles the pleasure)
- Sing in your head

40. Brie And Jelly French Toast

Serving: Serves 1 | Prep: | Cook: | Ready in:

Ingredients

- 2 pieces thick bread slices
- 1 tablespoon red currant jelly
- 1 tablespoon butter
- 4 pieces brie cheese slices

Direction

- Melt butter in a skillet over medium-high heat.
- Spread the jelly on one slice of toast and top with cheese slices.
- Spread the jelly on one slice of toast and top with cheese slices.
- In a shallow dish whisk together the egg, milk, salt, and sugar with a fork until combined.
- Dip both sides of bread in egg mixture.
- Fry slices until golden brown, then flip to cook the other side.
- Sprinkle with powdered sugar.
- Sprinkle some more.
- Top with syrup. Enjoy!

41. Brie And Onion Jam Crostini

Serving: Serves 12 crostini | Prep: | Cook: | Ready in:

Ingredients

- 1 Large red onion, thinly sliced
- 2 teaspoons Olive oil
- 1/2 teaspoon Salt
- 1/4 teaspoon Mustard powder
- 2 teaspoons Brown sugar
- 3 tablespoons Balsamic vinegar
- 2 sprigs Fresh thyme chopped
- few grinds of black pepper
- 1 Baguette
- 1 Wheel or log of Brie
- 2 tablespoons Chopped walnuts

Direction

- In a large frying pan, warm the oil and then add onion slices. Sprinkle with a nice pinch of salt and gently cook over medium low heat until deeply brown. This will take about 20 minutes. Be patient this needs to be done low and slow.
- Add the mustard powder, brown sugar, pepper, thyme and vinegar. Cook, stirring often until vinegar evaporates, about 5 minutes. Set aside until ready to assemble crostini.
- Cut the baguette into 3/4 inch slices brush with olive oil. Toast at 350 degrees until golden. Slice the Brie into twelve pieces.
- On each crostini spread onion jam, place a piece of Brie and sprinkle walnuts on top. Bake in the oven a few minutes until cheese is slightly melted but not runny. Serve immediately.

42. Buckwheat Thumbprint Cookies With Cherry Preserves

Serving: Makes 36 to 40 cookies | Prep: | Cook: | Ready in:

Ingredients

- 1 1/3 cups (130 grams) walnuts or pecans

- 1/2 cup plus 1 tablespoons (70 grams) buckwheat flour
- 2/3 cup (65 grams) oat flour
- 1/4 cup plus 2 tablespoons (55 grams) white rice flour, preferably superfine, OR ½ cups plus 2 tablespoons (55 grams) Thai* rice flour
- 1/2 cup (100 grams) sugar
- 1/4 teaspoon salt
- 1/8 teaspoon baking soda
- 1/4 cup (60 grams) cream cheese, cold, cut in chunks
- 12 tablespoons (170 grams) unsalted butter, slightly softened, cut into chunks
- 1 tablespoon water
- 1 teaspoon vanilla
- Powdered sugar for dusting
- About 1/4 cup (80 grams) cherry preserves

Direction

- Combine the nuts, buckwheat flour, oat flour, rice flour, sugar, salt, and baking soda in a food processor fitted with the steel blade and process until the nuts are finely ground -- or leave up to half of them a little coarser for texture if you like. Add the cream cheese, butter, water, and vanilla. Process just until a smooth soft dough forms. Scrape the bowl and blend in any stray flour at the bottom of the bowl with your fingers.
- Scrape the dough into a bowl and cover it with plastic wrap. Refrigerate for at least two hours, but preferably 24.
- Preheat the oven to 325° F. Position racks in the upper and lower thirds of the oven.
- Shape slightly more than level tablespoons of dough into 1 1/4-inch balls. Place 2 inches apart on cookie sheets lined with parchment paper. Bake 15 to 20 minutes, until the cookies are well browned on the bottom (you'll will have to tip one up gently and have a peek underneath) -- if in doubt bake a minute or so longer. Rotate the pans from top to bottom and front to back halfway through the baking time to ensure even baking.
- When the cookies are done, set the tray on racks. For thumbprint cookies, immediately press the handle of a wooden spoon about halfway into the center of each hot cookie.
- Let the cookies cool completely before storing or filling. Unfilled cookies may be kept in an airtight container for at least 2 weeks. Shortly before serving, use a fine-mesh strainer (or tea strainer) to dust the cookies with powdered sugar and, for thumbprints, fill depressions with preserves.
- *Thai rice flour is even finer than superfine flour and weighs less per cup, so you need a greater volume to get 55 grams.

43. Calamondin Orange And Limequat Marmalade

Serving: Makes 2 cups | Prep: | Cook: | Ready in:

Ingredients

- 25 calamondin oranges
- 5 Limequats
- 2 cups cane sugar
- 2 cups water

Direction

- Slice calamondin oranges and limequats in half and remove seeds, thinly slice and set aside. Do not peel fruit.
- Add sugar and water to sauce pan and then add fruit and allow to simmer till rind of fruit is translucent and a thermometer reads 220 degrees.
- Transfer to a glass jar and refrigerate till set.

44. Candied Bacon And Tomato Jam Ice Cream

Serving: Makes about 1 quart | Prep: | Cook: | Ready in:

Ingredients

- Tomato Jam and Candied Bacon
- 3 cups finely diced peeled, seeded very ripe tomatoes (about 4 decent size tomatoes)
- 1/3 cup granulated sugar
- 1/2 teaspoon pure vanilla extract
- 4 slices bacon
- 1/2 cup light brown sugar
- Making the ice cream
- 2 cups heavy cream
- 1 cup whole milk
- 3/4 cup granulated sugar
- 1/8 teaspoon salt
- 2 teaspoons pure vanilla extract
- The tomato jam
- The chopped bacon slices.

Direction

- Tomato Jam and Candied Bacon
- The day before you want to eat your ice cream ,in a medium sauce pan cook the diced tomatoes and granulated sugar over medium heat until the tomatoes become soft and "jammy". This may take between 20 and 30 minutes. Stir often while cooking and press the tomatoes with a wooden spoon to break them up.
- Once cooked, take the pan off the heat and stir in the vanilla extract. Cool and place in a covered container and refrigerate.
- Place the brown sugar and bacon slices in a plastic bag and shake to coat the slices thoroughly. Prep a rimmed baking sheet by covering with parchment paper and setting a wire rack over. Lay the bacon slices on the wire rack and bake in a preheated 375F oven for 20 to 30 minutes or until well browned. Cool and chop the slices in very small pieces and refrigerate.
- Making the ice cream
- Again, the day before you want ice cream, heat the cream, milk, sugar and salt in a medium sauce pan, whisking all the while, until the mixture is lukewarm and the sugar has dissolved. Cool and refrigerate in a covered container overnight.

- The next day, stir the 2 teaspoons of vanilla extract into the cream/milk mixture and then process in an ice cream maker per your maker's instructions until you get a soft serve consistency.
- Stir the bacon bits into the tomato jam and then pour about half of the ice cream into an appropriate size container. Place 2 dollops of the tomato-bacon jam on top and then stir slightly into the ice cream. Place the rest of the ice cream over, add 2 more dollops and stir again. (Save a couple of spoons of jam for your morning toast).
- Cover and freeze the ice cream for a few hours to harden before serving.

45. Caramelized Apple Jam

Serving: Makes 6 to 8 half pint jars of jam | Prep: 1hours0mins | Cook: 0hours30mins |Ready in:

Ingredients

- 12 nice sized apples - a firm variety such as Granny Smith, Honeycrisp, or Cripps, peeled, cored, and chopped into I" pieces - about 7 cups
- 6 to 7 tablespoons fresh lemon juice, or more as you like
- 3 cups sugar
- 2 cups fresh apple cider
- 1/4 cup apple cider vinegar
- 2 tablespoons honey
- seed from 1 vanilla bean
- 2 tablespoons Calvados (OPTIONAL)
- 1 tablespoon water
- 6 half pint jam jars, with lids and screw tops, properly sterilized

Direction

- NOTE: I make sure that I have assembled all my ingredients before I begin cooking the jam. Working with caramel requires full concentration, and it is best to have all ingredients ready. Place the lemon juice in a large bowl. Peel, core and chop 3 apples at a time and thoroughly mix them into the lemon juice until all the apples are prepared and covered with lemon juice. Cover with plastic wrap and set aside.

- In a very large jam pot or enamel Dutch oven, place 2 and 1/2 cups sugar and 1/2 cup of the cider over a medium high flame. Stir constantly to dissolve the sugar, and continue cooking to boiling. Reduce the heat and continue to stir, producing a light caramel colored syrup. This will take anywhere from 10 to 15 minutes. I usually need 10 minutes.

- Immediately add the apples, the rest of the cider, the apple cider vinegar, and the honey to the jam pot. Bring the mixture to a rolling boil, and skim the film that rises to the top with a spoon, then reduce the heat, add the seed from the vanilla bean, (if you want to add Calvados, do so now), and cook, stirring often, for about 30 minutes. Keep the mixture simmering. The apples will retain their shape throughout the cooking process, but become soft.

- After the apples have cooked for 25 minutes, put the remaining 1/2 cup of sugar and a tablespoon of water in a 2 or 3 quart saucepan over medium high heat. Stirring constantly, make a much darker caramel syrup - quite brown in color, being careful to not burn yourself as you prepare the caramel syrup. It may take less time for this batch of syrup to become darker. Pour this syrup immediately into the apple mixture, and stir the mixture well. Don't worry if the caramel seizes a bit - keep stirring and the caramel with soften and meld with the apple mixture. Allow to cook for another 15 minutes, stirring constantly.

- Depending on the apples you use, some of the chopped apples make break down towards the end of the cooking process. If that is NOT the case, take a potato masher, and smash about 50% of the apples in the mixture - retaining some pieces for chunkiness, but allowing half of the mixture to take on a jam-like texture. At

this point, almost all liquid should be evaporated.

- Fill jam jars, making sure that you pack the jam well, and process in a hot water bath according to your preferred instructions. I process for 15 minutes. Take out of the hot water bath, wait for the "ping" sound that indicates that the jams are sealed, and allow jams to sit for a day. Any jam that does not have a secure seal should be placed in the refrigerator.

---

46. Caramelized Banana PB + J With Spicy Pepper Jelly

Serving: Serves 1 | Prep: | Cook: | Ready in:

Ingredients

- Caramelized Banana
- 1   banana
- 1 teaspoon coconut oil
- 1 1/2 teaspoons maple syrup
- Assembly
- 2   slices hearty bread (gluten free if needed)
- 1-2 tablespoons peanut butter
- 1-2 tablespoons spicy pepper jelly
- 1/2 teaspoon coconut oil
- 1 teaspoon maple syrup

Direction

- First, make the caramelized bananas by stirring 1 tsp coconut oil and 1 1/2 tsp maple syrup together in a saucepan over medium high heat.
- Slice the bananas into small discs and transfer to pan. Cook each side 4-7 minutes, until golden brown.
- While bananas are cooking, spread about 1-2 tbsp peanut butter on one slice of bread, and 1-2 tbsp jelly on the other slice (you've made pb + j's before - use the amount of each spread you like best).

- When bananas are caramelized, evenly distribute on top of peanut butter.
- Add about 1/2 tsp coconut oil and 1 tsp maple syrup to the same pan used earlier and swirl to combine. Place both slices of bread, dry sides down, in the pan and cook until brown and crispy, about 5 minutes.
- Press the slices together to form a sandwich, and enjoy.

47. Caramelized Onion And Gruyere Cheese Tartlets With Fig Preserves

Serving: Makes 2 dozen tartlets | Prep: | Cook: | Ready in:

Ingredients

- 1   Package frozen puff pastry sheets, thawed
- 2-3   Caramelized onions
- 3/4 cup Grated gruyere cheese
- 1 tablespoon chopped fresh thyme
- 1/4 cup Good quality fig preserves
- Freshly ground black pepper

Direction

- Preheat oven to 400 degrees. On a lightly floured surface, roll out thawed puff pastry. Using a 2-inch fluted cutter, cut out 24 rounds from the pastry and distribute between two sheet pans covered with parchment paper. Lightly prick the tops of the pastry with a fork. Place another piece of parchment over the tops of the pastry rounds and set an additional sheet pan onto the pastry to ensure rounds do not rise in the oven. Bake for 20 minutes, remove parchment paper and top sheet pan and continue to bake for another 10 minutes or until very lightly browned.
- Spread the grated gruyere cheese evenly over each round. Next, add a single layer of caramelized onions to each pastry. Sprinkle with a bit of fresh thyme and a dash of freshly

ground pepper to taste. Bake the tartlets for another 10 minutes, or until pastry is golden brown and the cheese has melted. Let cool then top each round with a small dollop of fig preserves.

48. Carrot, Onion And Dill Marmalade

Serving: Serves 4 eight-ounce jars | Prep: | Cook: | Ready in:

Ingredients

- 2 pounds carrots, peeled and grated
- 1/2 cup packed combined fresh thyme, dill and zest of 1 lemon
- 4 cups sugar
- 1 pound Vadalia onion, Walla Walla or Texas Sweet 1015, coursely chopped
- 2 tablespoons of bottled lemon juice
- Juice of 2 oranges
- 2 tablespoons minced crystallized ginger

Direction

- In a large nonaluminum saucepan, combine carrots with just enough water to barely cover, and bring to a boil.
- Reduce to low and simmer for 20 minutes. Drain and return carrots to saucepan.
- Tie herbs in a cheesecloth and add to carrots. Add sugar, onions, citrus juices and crystallized ginger.
- Bring mixture to a boil over medium heat. Continue to boil slowly, stirring occasionally, until marmalade is thick and clear, about 40 minutes. Remove and discard cheesecloth.
- Ladle marmalade into hot, sterilized jars, wipe rims, seal and process for 10 minutes in a boiling water bath. If you do not have a canning set-up, use your double pasta pot, four bottles should fit nicely.
- Process for 10 minutes. Remove jars and set to cool. Check the lids to make certain they are

tightly sealed. Store upright in a cool, dark place. If you do not want to can this you can store it in the refrigerator.

- Refrigerate after opening.
- Note: For those afraid that there isn't enough acid to waterbath can this recipe safely, the ph in this marmalade is 3.5 and anything under 4.6 is considered acidic enough for safe canning.

49. Champagne Rhubarb Jelly Shots

Serving: Makes 30 squares | Prep: | Cook: | Ready in:

Ingredients

- Rhubarb Syrup
- 1 pound rhubarb, cut into 1/4-inch pieces
- 1 cup lemon juice
- 1 cup water
- 2 cups sugar
- Rhubarb Jelly
- 2 cups rhubarb syrup, divided
- 8 packets powdered gelatin, like Knox
- 1 cup lemon juice
- 1/2 cup gin
- 1/4 cup sugar
- 3 cups champagne

Direction

- Rhubarb Syrup
- Combine all ingredients in a medium saucepan on medium-low heat and simmer for about an hour, or until liquid turns a bright ruby red and rhubarb has softened.
- Cool to room temperature, and strain through a mesh strainer.
- Rhubarb Jelly
- Wipe a 9 x 13-inch rectangular baking pan with about a teaspoon of vegetable oil. Heat 1 1/2 cups of the rhubarb syrup in a small saucepan, until it is hot but not boiling, and whisk in 2 packets of gelatin. Whisk for 2 to 3 minutes, and allow to cool slightly. Pour

through a mesh strainer (to get out any lumps of gelatin) into the prepared baking pan, and refrigerate for about an hour, until solidified.

- Now heat 1 cup of lemon juice with remaining 1/2 cup of rhubarb syrup and 1/4 cup of sugar in a small saucepan, stirring until sugar is dissolved and mixture is hot but not boiling. Remove from heat and whisk in remaining 6 packets of gelatin, stirring for 2 to 3 minutes. Pour through a mesh strainer into a large mixing bowl. Whisk in gin, followed by champagne, and pour into baking pan, over the rhubarb layer. Refrigerate for 4 to 5 hours or overnight.
- Once the jelly has solidified, run a thin spatula around the edges to loosen it from the pan. Set a large cutting board over the top of the pan, and carefully invert, so that the jelly flips onto the cutting board in one big rectangle. Using a straight, sharp knife, cut jelly into 1-inch squares and refrigerate until ready to serve.

50. Cheddar Cheese Biscuits With Bacon Jam

Serving: Serves 12-16 | Prep: | Cook: | Ready in:

Ingredients

- Cheddar cheese biscuits
- 3 cups all-purpose flour
- 1 1/2 tablespoons baking powder
- 1 teaspoon salt
- 1/3 cup sugar
- 1 1/2 stick butter, divided
- 1 1/2 cups grated sharp cheddar, or cheese(s) of your choice
- 1 1/2 cups milk
- Bacon jam
- 1 pound good smoked bacon
- 1 medium onion, diced
- 3-4 cloves garlic, minced
- 1/4 cup brown sugar
- 1/2 cup strong black coffee

- 1/4 cup maple syrup
- 2 tablespoons apple cider vinegar
- 2 tablespoons balsamic vinegar
- 1/2 teaspoon allspice

Direction

- Cheddar cheese biscuits
- Preheat oven to 375. Sift all dry ingredients together. Cut one stick butter into tablespoon-sized pats, and cut into dry ingredients with a fork or pastry blender until it looks like coarse crumbs.
- Toss with grated cheese (I often use a combo of whatever kinds of firm cheeses I have in my fridge).
- Add milk, and stir just enough for dry ingredients to all come together. If dough is too dry and crumbly add a little more milk.
- Turn out onto a floured board and knead only two or three times -- enough to incorporate everything. Form into a ball and pat or roll out to about 1 inch thick.
- Use a small biscuit cutter -- I find a small tomato paste can, both ends cut out, makes a great cutter for cocktail sized biscuits -- to cut out biscuits. Place on ungreased baking sheet. At this point, if you're making in advance, you can freeze the biscuits on the baking sheet, then remove to a plastic bag. Allow to thaw before baking.
- Melt remaining half-stick of butter and brush tops of biscuits. Bake until golden brown, and cool on a rack.
- Bacon jam
- Cut bacon into 1-inch pieces and toss into heavy Dutch oven. Cook over medium high heat, stirring periodically, until starting to crisp.
- Dice onion and mince garlic, and add to bacon. If you're concerned about the fat content (It IS bacon, after all), drain off some of the fat first, leaving 3 tablespoons or so. Lower heat to medium and cook until onion starts to brown, about 8 minutes or so.
- Add remaining ingredients. Reduce heat to a simmer, cover, and cook for an hour or two.

Stir occasionally, and add water if it gets too thick.
- When bacon is very tender, remove from heat and let cool for 30 minutes or so. Transfer to food processor -- you may need to do this in batches, depending on the size of your processor -- and pulse until mixture is the consistency you want.

51. Cherry Amaretto Jam

Serving: Serves 8 4oz jars plus another big jar for the fridge | Prep: | Cook: | Ready in:

Ingredients

- 8 cups cherries - pitted and stemmed (about 3 lbs - ish)
- 1/2 cup amaretto
- 1/2 cup water
- 1 1.75 oz package NO SUGAR NEEDED pectin
- 1 tablespoon fruit fresh
- 1 tablespoon vanilla
- 1 teaspoon almond extract

Direction

- This is so easy, put a spoon in the freezer - then just put everything but the pectin in a large saucepan and bring it to a boil, add the pectin just as it is starting to boil. Stir it down and simmer for 5 minutes or so. You can use a potato masher to break the cherries up some as they boil. Dribble a bit of the liquid down the back of the frozen spoon, if it looks jammy, you are ready!
- ** CANNING STEPS ** if you choose to can - wash the jars and put them in a single layer in a big pot and boil them for 10 minutes (I do this while I am working on the jam). Turn off the heat and remove them to drain / dry on a clean tea towel. Drop the flat top things into the hot (not boiling) water. As you fill each clean warm dry jar, wipe the rim, cover with a

disc, and screw a ring on - not too tight. When they are all jarred, back into the pot to boil for 10 more minutes then back onto the tea towel to cool. You will hear the pop pop pop as they seal. That's it!!!

52. Cherry Jam Margarita

Serving: Serves 1 | Prep: 0hours10mins | Cook: 0hours0mins | Ready in:

Ingredients

- 1 tablespoon Cherry Jam
- 1 ounce Lime Juice (about the juice from one 1 lime)
- 1/2 ounce Simple Syrup
- 1 1/2 ounces Silver Tequila
- Dash Angostura Bitters
- Lime wedge and/or a Cherry (optional garnish)

Direction

- In a rocks glass add ice and set aside. In a cocktail shaker, combine all ingredients, except for garnishes. Fill shaker with ice and put the cap on. Shake vigorously for about 30 seconds, or until shaker is extremely cold.
- Strain cocktail into your prepared rocks glass and garnish with lime wedge or a cherry if using. Serve immediately.

53. Cherry Jam With Lemon Pepper Shortbread

Serving: Serves 12 | Prep: 2hours0mins | Cook: 0hours20mins | Ready in:

Ingredients

- Cherry Jam:
- 1 1/3 cups cherries, pitted and quartered

- 1/4 cup 2 teaspoons granulated sugar
- 1/2 cup cherries, pitted and quartered, divided
- Lemon-Pepper Shortbread
- 4 ounces unsalted butter, softened
- 1/3 cup confectioner's sugar
- 3/4 teaspoon vanilla extract
- 3/4 teaspoon freshy ground black pepper
- 1/8 teaspoon table salt
- 1 lemon, zested
- 1 cup all-purpose flour
- 1 pinch Turbinado sugar, for sprinkling

Direction

- Cherry Jam:
- Place 1 1/3 cup cherries and granulated sugar in saucepan. Stir to evenly combine.
- Over high heat, stir cherries and sugar constantly, scraping the bottom of the pot to keep the sugar from burning. Stir until mixture is dark and thick, about 5 minutes.
- Add 1/4 cup cherries to mixture, stirring constantly. Bring mixture back to a boil, about 30 seconds.
- Add remaining 1/4 cup cherries, stirring constantly. Bring mixture to full boil, about 1 minutes.
- Immediately remove pot from stove and pour jam in clean bowl to cool. When jam has reached room temperature, cover and place in refrigerator.
- Lemon-Pepper Shortbread
- In stand mixer fitted with paddle attachment, cream butter and confectioner's sugar on medium speed until light and fluffy, about 3 minutes.
- Add vanilla, black pepper, salt and lemon zest. Paddle on medium speed until combined, about 30 seconds.
- Add flour to mixture. Paddle on low speed until just combined.
- Turn dough out onto counter and shape into rectangle with 1/4" thickness. Cover in plastic wrap; refrigerate at least 1 hour.
- Preheat oven to 325 °F. Prepare cookie sheet with Silpat or parchment paper.

- When dough is chilled, remove from refrigerator and unwrap. Using a 1.5" round cookie cutter, cut 12 rounds from the dough. Place on prepared cookie sheet and sprinkle with turbinado sugar.
- Bake at 325 °F until golden, about 20 minutes. Remove from oven and allow to cool on rack.
- To serve: spoon desired amount of jam over shortbread.

54. Cherry Amaretto Jam

Serving: Makes 4x250 ml (1 cup) | Prep: | Cook: | Ready in:

Ingredients

- 2,5 pounds sweet cherries (2 pounds if pitted)
- 300 milliliters cherry juice
- 1 packet vanilla
- 500 grams gelling sugar 2:1
- 1 pinch ground cardamom
- 4 tablespoons almond extract/amaretto

Direction

- Wash and stone the cherries.
- In a saucepan, puree a third of the cherries, then mix well with the remaining cherries, the cherry juice, vanilla and gelling sugar. Cover and let stand in a cool place for 3 hours.
- Cook the cherry mass under stirring let bubble for 4 minutes, then check is gelling point is reached.
- Stir in cardamom and almond extract/amaretto
- Fill jam into hot rinsed jars and seal immediately.
- Tip: Make cherry coconut by substituting the almond extract with coconut syrup or coconut liqueur.

55. Chicken Thighs With Love Apple Jam

Serving: Serves 8-10 | Prep: | Cook: | Ready in:

Ingredients

- 12-15 Large bone in Skin on Chicken thighs
- 5 Cloves garlic
- 4 cups sliced yellow onion
- 2 cinnamon sticks or 1.5 tablespoon of ground cinnamon
- 1/2 cup Chopped fresh ginger
- 3/4 cup honey
- 3-4 green cardamon pods
- 2 cups Pomegranate Juice
- 3 Large cans crushed San Marzano Tomatoes (not with basil)
- Salt & Pepper
- 2 cups Chicken Stock
- Fresh Mint
- Fresh Cilantro
- 1/2 cup Chopped toasted pistachios

Direction

- Heat olive oil over medium heat ...add Onions, Ginger, Cinnamon Stick, Crushed cardamom pods, 1 tablespoon of ground cumin, Urfa Pepper and season with salt & pepper.
- Lower heat and saute until onions soften and get a wee bit brown on the edges, about 15 minutes.
- Add tomatoes, pomegranate juice & honey, stir well and cook down stirring occasionally for at least 3 hours, maybe more, you want it to get dark and sticky, almost like barbeque sauce, it should reduce down at least by half-- You can do this a day ahead.
- Dry Chicken thighs well and season on both sides with Salt, Pepper & remaining Cumin.
- Working in batches brown the Chicken on both sides, make sure they have room or else they will steam and the skin will get rubbery...you want it nice & crisp, but the thighs should not cook through.

- Once all the chicken is finished layer them in a large Dutch oven or any other oven proof dish large enough to hold them in 1 or 2 layers.
- Pour over chicken and bake at 350 degrees for 1 hours.
- Right before serving cover with a flurry of chopped pistachios, mint & cilantro. Can be made 1 day ahead and reheated (even better actually)

56. Chipotle Bacon Jam

Serving: Makes about 3 cups | Prep: | Cook: | Ready in:

Ingredients

- 1 pound bacon
- 1   medium onion, chopped
- 4   cloves garlic, minced
- 1/4 cup cider vinegar
- 1/4 cup brown sugar
- 1/2 cup dried apricots, chopped
- 1/2 cup coffee
- 1 - 2 tablespoons chipotles in adobo sauce, chopped

Direction

- Cook bacon until crisp and remove from pan onto paper towels to cool. Drain excess bacon fat into a small dish and reserve.
- Add chopped onions and minced garlic to the bacon grease remaining in the pan and sauté until onions are translucent. In the meantime, whisk together cider vinegar and brown sugar and add to the onions.
- Once fully incorporated, add in the apricots and coffee and bring to a quick boil before reducing the heat.
- Roughly chop the cooled bacon and add back to the pan along with chipotles and adobo sauce stirring to combine. Reduce the heat and simmer until the liquid is mostly evaporated.

- Allow the mixture to cool and then pulse in a food processor (about 10 pulses) until combined but still a bit chunky.
- Allow to cool completely as mixture will continue to thicken. Serve with pimento cheese and crackers… or just a spoon!

57. Chocolate Overnight Oats With Strawberry Chia Jam

Serving: Serves 4 | Prep: | Cook: | Ready in:

Ingredients

- Chocolate Oatmeal
- 2 cups Almond Milk
- 1 cup Oatmeal
- 1/3 cup Chia Seeds
- 1/4 cup Cocoa Powder
- 1 teaspoon Cinnamon
- 1/4 teaspoon Salt
- 1/2 teaspoon Vanilla Extract
- 3 tablespoons Maple Syrup
- Strawberry Chia Jam
- 2 cups Frozen Strawberries
- 1/2 cup Cold Water
- 3 tablespoons Agave
- 1/2 cup Chia Seeds

Direction

- In a large mixing bowl combine all the ingredients for the chocolate oatmeal and whisk together until completely mixed. Cover with wrap or a lid and place in fridge overnight.
- Place the Frozen Strawberries, Cold Water, and Agave in a blender and blend until smooth. You made need to add water in order to achieve a smooth consistency. Do so by adding 1 tablespoon at a time. Place in a sealed airtight container and store in fridge overnight.
- In 4 separate jars or cups place a small layer of the Chocolate Overnight Oats and then top

with the Strawberry Chia Jam. Continue until both mixtures are used. Top with an additional toppings you desire.

58. Christmas Bombe With Berry Preserves And White Chocolate Mousse

Serving: Serves 10-12 | Prep: | Cook: |Ready in:

Ingredients

- For the Hot Milk Sponge Sheet
- 1 cup (100 grams) sifted (before measuring) unbleached cake flour (I use King Arthur)
- 1 teaspoon baking powder
- 3 large eggs, at room temperature
- 2 large egg yolks, at room temperature
- 1 teaspoon pure vanilla extract
- 3/4 cup (150 grams) sugar
- 1/4 cup (60 grams) whole milk
- 2 tablespoons (30 grams) unsalted butter, cut into small pieces
- Cranberry-Raspberry Spread and White Chocolate Mousse Filling
- 6 ounces cranberries, rinsed
- 1/3 cup sugar
- 1/3 cup raspberry preserves
- 9 ounces white chocolate (see note), finely chopped
- 1 1/2 cups whipping cream
- 3 tablespoons water
- 3 tablespoons kirsch (or water)
- 1/2 cup strained apricot preserves
- 3 tablespoons finely chopped pistachios

Direction

- For the Hot Milk Sponge Sheet
- Position a rack in the lower third of the oven and preheat the oven to 400° F. Line the bottom (not the sides) of a 12 by 16-inch half sheet pan (or 11 by 17-inch jelly roll pan) with parchment paper.

- Whisk the flour with the baking powder. Sift the mixture three times and return it to the strainer set over a bowl.
- Whip the eggs, yolks, sugar, and vanilla in the stand mixer at high speed for 2-4 minutes until the batter is light-colored, tripled in volume, and when the whisk is lifted the mixture falls in a thick fluffy rope that dissolves slowly on the surface of the remaining batter foam.
- While the eggs are beating, heat the milk and butter in a small saucepan until it the butter is melted and the mixture is extremely hot to the touch. (It must be very hot when you add it to the batter.)
- Remove the bowl from the mixer. With the strainer or sifter, sift one-third of the flour over the eggs. Fold with a large rubber spatula until the flour is almost blended into the batter. Repeat with half of the remaining flour. Repeat with the rest of the flour. Pour all of the hot milk mixture over the batter and fold gently but authoritatively, scraping batter up from the bottom of the bowl and rotating the bowl until the milk and butter are incorporated. Scrape the batter into the pan, and spread it evenly, taking care that the batter in the center is not deeper than the batter at the edges (or your sponge sheet will over cooked and/or dry at the edges).
- Bake 10 to 12 minutes until the cake is golden brown on top and springs back when gently pressed with fingers.
- Remove the cake from the oven and run a slim metal spatula around the edges to detach the cake from the pan. Cover the pan with a sheet of parchment paper longer than the pan at both ends. Hold the ends of the paper and the pan together and invert the whole business onto the counter (or on another baking sheet — but not on a rack) — so the top of the cake rests directly on the parchment. Leave the pan on top so that the cake steams a little as it cools. The top of the cake will stick to the parchment — this is correct. Let the cake cool completely while you make the cranberry raspberry spread.

- Cranberry-Raspberry Spread and White Chocolate Mousse Filling
- Make cranberry-raspberry spread: Put the cranberries in a small saucepan with 1/4 cup sugar. Cover and cook until about 2/3 of the berries are burst (4-5 minutes). Scrape the mixture into a medium coarse strainer with the raspberry or cherry preserves. Mash and press as much of the mixture through the strainer as possible, using a rubber spatula. This will take some effort—keep on mashing and rubbing into the strainer. Scrape the strained mixture from the underside of the strainer into the bowl. Continue to press the mixture, even with your fingers, until there's only 2-3 tablespoons of dry cranberry skins and raspberry seeds left behind to discard. You should have about 2/3 cup strained cranberry spread. Set aside.
- To assemble and freeze the cranberry-raspberry jelly roll (for lining for the bombe mold): Tear off a sheet of foil the size of the sponge sheet and set it on the counter next to the sponge. Lift the pan off of the sponge sheet and peel off the parchment liner. Using the parchment under the cake, flip the cake over onto the foil. Peel the parchment from the cake, taking all or most of the skin off of the cake as well. If any of the skin remains, remove it with a knife.
- Spread all of the cranberry-raspberry in a very thin even layer over the sponge sheet. Starting with one long edge, use the foil underneath the cake to help roll the cake as tightly as possible to form a 16 or 17-inch jelly roll. To tighten a jelly roll, imagine it as rolling a sleeping bag as tightly as possible so that you can squeeze it back into its impossibly small bag. Start with the sponge sheet on a piece of foil on the counter with one long side facing you. Start at the edge of the cake that's nearest you—and using the foil under the cakes as necessary, fold the least amount of cake possible over itself to start the roll, and keep the roll as round and tight as possible as you roll the cake away from you. When the roll is complete, squeeze and tighten it as follows:

Roll the entire jelly roll back towards the center the foil. Pull the far end of the foil towards you and over the jelly roll to cover it. Hold a ruler or straight edge on top of the foil against the bottom of the jelly roll. Use your other hand to anchor the foil under the cake against the counter so it won't slide while you press the edge of the ruler away from you, against the top foil (which should be free so it will slide forward) as you tighten the jellyroll inside the foil.

- Wrap the jelly roll tightly in the foil. Freeze for several hours or overnight for easiest handling. You can do this days or weeks in advance!
- To line the bombe with jelly-roll slices: Have a 6-cup half dome shaped bowl or bombe mold at hand (mine is 7 1/4 inches in diameter and 3 1/2 inches deep). There is no need to line it or grease it.
- Remove the frozen jelly roll from the freezer and unwrap it. Without thawing, trim ragged ends if necessary (and reserve the trimmings). Use a sharp serrated knife to cut slices 1/4 inch thick. Line the mold with slices as follows: place 1 slice in the center of the bottom of the mold. Next fit 7 (or more, as needed) slices around the center slice, pushing and fitting them together (assertively!) so that no space whatever is left between them (take this seriously or you will end up with mousse showing between the jelly-roll slices. Fit the next 9 or more slices around the mold, starting up the sides. Finish by fitting the next 10 or so slices to completely line the mold, always pushing and fitting to eliminate any space between slices. Push the last slices even with the rim of the mold if possible, or trim them so that they are flush. Reserve, wrap and freeze all trimmings and extra slices. Set the lined mold aside while you make the mousse.
- To make the mousse and fill the mold: Put the white chocolate, water and kirsch in a medium stainless steel bowl. Bring 1 inch of water to a simmer in a wide skillet. Turn the heat off under the skillet (or remove it from an electric burner) and wait 30 seconds, then set the bowl

of chocolate directly into the hot water. Stir constantly until the chocolate is melted and smooth. Remove the bowl from the water and let the chocolate mixture cool until it is 85F — slightly cool when you dab a little on your lip. If the chocolate is too cool or cold, the mousse will be grainy, if it is hot, it will melt the whipped cream you are going to fold into it.

- Just before the chocolate is cool enough, whip the cream only until it is thickened and barely being to hold a share — when you tilt the bowl the cream should flow to one side, fluffy but still pourable and not at all stiff. Scrape the cream into the bowl of chocolate (not vice versa!) and fold carefully but quickly just until the two are incorporated. The mousse should seem far too soft to set — but it will firm up as it cools. Immediately (before the mousse even thinks about starting to set) scrape it all into the lined bomb mold and spread it evenly.
- Remove the remaining jelly-roll slices and trimming from the freezer. Set aside just enough slices to completely cover the top of the mouse if placed tightly together — do this by laying slices on a piece of parchment and then pushing the edges together to form a round layer the same diameter at the bomb mold or bowl — but don't put them into the mold yet.
- Dice any remaining slices and trimming with a sharp knife. Scatter the dice evenly over the mousse. Now (finally), fit the slices assembled into a layer over the dice cake pieces to form the bottom layer of the dessert. Place a cardboard round or flat plate smaller than the diameter of the mold inside the mold and press firmly to level and compact the bombe. Wrap and refrigerate the bombe for at least 6 hours before unfolding and serving. The bombe may be completely to this point up to 36 hours in advance.
- To unfold and finish the bombe: Invert the mold and rap the edges sharply on the counter to release the dessert onto a cake circle or cookie sheet. Simmer trained apricot preserves in a small saucepan for 2-3 minutes to make a glaze. Use a pastry brush to paint the entire

dessert with a very thin coat of glaze. Touch the bottom edges of the bombe with minced pistachios. Transfer to a serving platter. Refrigerate until serving.

59. Cindy Mushet's Italian Jam Shortbread Tart (Fregolotta)

Serving: Serves 8 to10 | Prep: | Cook: | Ready in:

Ingredients

- 12 tablespoons (6 ounces) unsalted butter, softened
- 1/2 cup (3 1/2 ounces) sugar
- 1/4 teaspoon pure almond extract
- 1 1/2 cups (7 1/2 ounces) unbleached all-purpose flour
- 1/8 teaspoon salt
- 1/4 cup (2 ounces) not too sweet apricot jam (or other jam of your choice)
- 1/3 cup (1 ounce) sliced natural almonds

Direction

- Heat the oven to 350 °F. Position an oven rack in the center of oven.
- Place the butter, and sugar in the bowl of an electric mixer fitted with the paddle attachment (a handheld mixer is fine; just allow a little extra time to reach each stage in the recipe). Beat on medium speed until the mixture is very light in color, about 3 to 4 minutes. Use a rubber spatula to scrape down the sides of the bowl. Add the almond extract and blend well, another 30 seconds.
- In a separate bowl, whisk together the flour and salt. Add the dry ingredients to the butter mixture and combine on a low speed just until the dough is thoroughly combined, about 30 to 40 seconds. Measure out 1/2 cup of the dough and set it on a small plate, then place the plate in the freezer (this will chill the dough and make it easier to crumble).

- Press the remaining dough into a 9 or 9 1/2-inch tart pan in an even layer (the edges can be a little higher than the rest, just be careful that the center is not the thickest point). If the dough is too sticky, just chill it briefly.
- Use a small offset spatula or the back of a spoon to spread the jam in a thin, even layer over the surface of the dough, leaving a border of about 1-inch around the edges.
- Remove the reserved dough from the freezer and crumble it into small pieces over the layer of the jam, allowing some of the jam to peek through. Sprinkle the sliced almonds evenly over the top of the tart.
- Bake for 40 to 50 minutes, or until the topping is a beautiful golden brown. Remove from the oven and place on a rack to cool completely. If your tart pan has a removable bottom, to unmold, center the tart pan on top of a large can so that it balances midair as the rim of the tart pan falls to the counter. Leave the bottom of the pan under the tart for support, or run a large spatula between the crust and the pan, using the spatula to guide the tart onto a plate. Alternately, cut wedges straight from the pan. Serve with tart whipped cream.
- Store the tart covered in plastic wrap, at room temperature for 3 to 4 days. The tart can be assembled ahead and frozen for up to 1 month. Assemble the tart, then wrap tightly twice in plastic wrap and freeze on a flat surface -- it may require a few minutes extra of baking time.

---

60. Coconut & Lemon Cupcakes With Lemon Marmalade Filling

Serving: Makes 12 | Prep: | Cook: | Ready in:

Ingredients

- Cupcakes
- 2 eggs
- 1 1/2 cups AP flour
- 1 1/4 cups sugar
- 1/2 (1 stick) cups unsalted butter (room temp)
- 1/3 (+ 1 tbsp) cups lemon juice
- 2 tablespoons milk (2%)
- 3 tablespoons grated lemon zest
- 1/3 cup greek yogurt (also 2%)
- 1 tablespoon poppy seeds
- 1/2 teaspoon vanilla extract
- 1/2 teaspoon salt
- 1/4 teaspoon baking soda
- 1/4 teaspoon baking powder
- toasted coconut cookie thins (for garnish, Trader Joe's has some)
- toasted sweet coconut flakes (also for garnish)
- Frosting & Marmalade
- 6 lemons
- 1 1/2 cups sugar
- 1 1/2 teaspoons coconut extract
- 1/2 teaspoon vanilla extract
- 8 ounces cream cheese (room temp)
- 16 tablespoons unsalted butter (room temp)
- 2 cups powdered sugar

Direction

- First, the marmalade. Juice the lemons and take out the seeds, and make sure you save the juice.
- I started to cut the peels into thin strips, and then got fed up and threw them into my food processor because I'm lazy. If you have one, I suggest you do it my way. If not, slice the lemon peels nice and thin.
- Either way you slice it (see, see what I did there? This is why I'm a writer, folks. Comedy gold.), throw the peels into a large pot and cover them with cold water. Bring it to a boil and boil for a minute, then drain them and rinse under more cold water. Do it a couple more times, but don't rinse on the last pass.
- Throw the peels back into the pot along with the lemon juice and sugar, bring it up to a simmer on medium, and let it cook for around 30 minutes, giving it the occasional stir. To test if it's ready, put a ceramic plate in the freezer, put a little bit of the marmalade on it, and stick it back in for a couple minutes. If you can push

the stuff on the plate with your finger and it wrinkles up, you're ready to go. If not, give it some more love on the stove.

- While that's happening, you can get to work on the cupcakes.
- Start by preheating the oven to 350.
- Get a bowl and whisk together the dry stuff: flour, salt, baking soda, and baking powder.
- Get another bowl and do the same thing with the yogurt, milk, vanilla, and lemon juice.
- Put the butter and sugar in your stand mixer and cream them together on medium for 2-3 minutes, until they're light and fluffy.
- Mix in the eggs one at a time, then the lemon zest.
- Next, mix in the dry stuff and the wet stuff, alternating until it's all in there.
- Stir in the poppy seeds, put the batter in a cupcake tin, then throw it into the oven for about 30 minutes. Let them cool for 5, then let them cool some more on a cooling rack while you make the frosting.
- This part's easy: cream together the butter and cream cheese in your stand mixer until they're…well, creamy. Then add the other frosting ingredients and mix. Even a monkey could do it.
- Once the cupcakes are at room temperature, scoop out a tablespoon from the tops of each and fill them with that sweet, tangy marmalade.
- Frost the cupcakes, top with the toasted coconut, and stick a cookie in the top of each. Unfortunately, due to the limitations of pastry-physics the cookies get all soggy and gross if you keep them in the cupcakes for long, so you gotta put them in the day you eat them.

61. Coconut Fried Shrimp W/ Horseradish Marmalade Sauce

Serving: Serves 3-4 | Prep: | Cook: | Ready in:

Ingredients

- Coconut Shrimp
- 1 cup all-purpose flour, split in 1/2 cup portions
- 1/2 teaspoon salt
- 1/2 teaspoon baking powder
- 1/4 - 1/2 teaspoons cayenne pepper,
- cracked black pepper, about 3 cranks of the pepper mill
- 2/3 cup water
- 7 ounces package shredded, sweetened coconut
- 3/4 cup panko, japanese-style bread crumbs
- 1 pound large or jumbo shrimp, peeled and deveined
- Oil for frying
- Horseradish-Marmalade Sauce
- 1/2 cup orange marmalade
- 2 tablespoons prepared horseradish
- 1 tablespoon plus 1 teaspoon rice vinegar
- 1/2 teaspoon crushed red pepper

Direction

- In a medium-sized bowl, whisk together 1/2 cup flour, salt, baking powder, cayenne and black pepper. Add water, whisk until smooth. Let stand 15 minutes.
- Meanwhile, in a shallow bowl, toss together coconut and panko.
- Pat dry shrimp. Add 1/2 cup flour to gallon storage bag. Toss shrimp in flour, then one by one, dredge shrimp in flour/water mixture and coat in panko/coconut mixture, may have to press to adhere to shrimp.
- Heat oil to 360 degrees, can use deep fryer or frying pan (I use cast iron) with 1" to 2" of oil. Place shrimp in fridge while oil is heating up. (This will give the coconut a chance to adhere to the shrimp)
- Fry, in batches, for 1-2 minutes, until golden brown.
- For Sauce: Whisk together marmalade, horseradish, rice vinegar, and crushed red pepper. Microwave for 20 seconds (to soften marmalade), and whisk until well blended. Add more horseradish, if necessary, to taste.

Do yourself a favor and double the sauce, you will be glad you did.

62. Coconut Jam Drops

Serving: Makes 20 | Prep: | Cook: | Ready in:

Ingredients

- 1 cup desiccated coconut, fine or coarse
- 1/4 cup almond meal
- 125g unsalted butter, softened
- 1/2 cup caster sugar
- 1 egg
- 1 teaspoon vanilla extract
- Sprinkling of cinnamon powder, to taste
- 1 cup plain flour, sifted
- 1 teaspoon baking powder
- 2 tablespoons (raspberry) jam

Direction

- Toast desiccated coconut in a pan on the cooktop, till golden. Set aside to cool. Toast almond meal in a pan, till dry and a bit bronzed.
- Beat butter and sugar with an electric mixer until pale and creamy, add egg and vanilla extract, cinnamon powder and pinch of salt and beat until light and fluffy, turn speed to low and add sifted flour, almond meal, baking powder and 1/2 cup coconut, beat until just combined into a soft dough.
- Drop teaspoonfuls of biscuit mixture into remaining coconut and roll to coat. Arrange balls on a baking paper lined tray allowing 5cm for spreading between each biscuit. Using the back of a wooden spoon, make a dent in the top of each ball and fill dents with a little jam taking care not to overfill.
- Bake biscuits at 170°C for 15 minutes until pale golden. Remove and cool on tray for 5 minutes before removing to a wire rack to cool completely.

63. Coffee Jelly

Serving: Serves 4 | Prep: | Cook: | Ready in:

Ingredients

- 1 envelope unflavored gelatin
- 1/2 cup cold water
- 1 cup very hot brewed coffee
- 1/3 cup white sugar plus 1 teaspoon, divided use
- 1/2 cup whipping cream
- 1/4 teaspoon almond extract
- toasted sliced almonds
- lemon zest curls

Direction

- Empty the gelatin granules into a glass loaf pan. Add the cold water and stir to soften gelatin.
- Add the hot coffee to gelatin and stir well to dissolve.
- Add sugar and stir.
- Refrigerate until jelly has set, about 3 hours.
- Chill 4 martini glasses in freezer.
- Cut the jelly into small cubes and return to fridge while you whip the cream.
- In a deep-sided bowl, add the cream, sugar and almond extract. Whip until soft peaks form.
- Gently stir the jelly cubes into the cream.
- Spoon into chilled glasses, garnish with almonds and lemon zest. Serve immediately.

64. Coffee Jelly, With Spiced And Spiked Options

Serving: Serves 4 | Prep: | Cook: | Ready in:

Ingredients

- 1/2 ounce unflavored gelatin

- 1 ounce cold filtered water
- 15 ounces hot fair trade coffee, brewed to your taste (Jamaica Blue used here)
- 2 tablespoons to 1/4 cup of sugar (turbinado or light Muscovado suggested), to taste
- peel of Meyer lemon (about an inch piece), optional
- one nickel size coin of fresh ginger, optional
- shot of Domaine de Canton or whiskey, optional
- dollops of whipped heavy cream, optional, spiked/spiced/sweetened or plain

Direction

- Sprinkle the gelatin onto the cold water and let sit for 3-5 minutes. The way I prefer to brew my coffee is to heat filtered water to 190 degrees. In a filter cone place the freshly ground coffee beans. Pour in a tease of the hot water (about 1/4 the amount) to wake up the ground beans; let that small amount of water filter through. Then pour in the remaining water to complete the brew. Whisk in the hot coffee to dissolve completely the softened gelatine. Sweeten to taste. Add a small peel of Meyer lemon, the ginger, and a shot of Domaine de Canton or whiskey, if desired. Cool, then remove the peel and ginger coin. Pour into a flat pan or mold or individual molds and chill for 3 hours or more.
- After chilling cut the coffee gelatin into cubes from the pan or unmold the aspic (place in hot water briefly to loosen). Garnish with whipped cream (spiked, spiced, sweetened if you like, or just plain) and a small Meyer lemon peel. In Asia coffee gelatin cubes are often served in a pool of condensed milk.

65. Concord Grape Jelly

Serving: Makes approximately 3 pints | Prep: | Cook: | Ready in:

Ingredients

- 2 quarts Concord grapes, stemmed
- 6 cups Sugar

Direction

- Briskly boil grapes on stovetop until whole grapes "pop" under the pressure of a spoon. Transfer to a canning sieve and press the pulp, reserve the juice that flows through.
- Squeeze the remaining pulp through cheesecloth to save every last drop of grape juice.
- Add all the juice to a saucepan with the sugar. Cook slowly until the sugar has dissolved.
- Rapidly boil the sweet juice until you reach the jellying point. Use the "plate test" to determine when the jelly is ready.
- Pour the boiling hot jelly into prepared canning jars. Leave ½-inch headspace if using Weck jars.
- Process in a boiling water canning bath for 10 minutes.

66. Country Ham Biscuit With Fig Jam

Serving: Makes 12 to 18 biscuit sandwiches | Prep: | Cook: | Ready in:

Ingredients

- For the jam:
- 1 pound dried figs
- 1/3 cup molasses
- 1/2 teaspoon kosher salt
- 3/4 teaspoon black pepper
- 1 1/2 teaspoons whole-grain mustard
- 1 1/2 teaspoons white sugar
- For the biscuits and assembly:
- 3 1/4 cups (1 pound) pastry flour
- 2 cups (10 ounces) bleached all-purpose flour
- 3 tablespoons baking powder
- 1 tablespoon kosher salt
- 1 tablespoon sugar
- 6 ounces cold butter, cut into small pieces

- 2 1/2 cups sour milk (add 2 1/2 tablespoons cider vinegar 2 3/8 cups milk)
- 12 tablespoons cold butter, cut into small pieces, plus 2 tablespoons (divided)
- 8 ounces country ham (prepared according to the producer's instructions); see headnote for substitutes
- Fig jam (recipe above)
- 1/2 cup sharp cheddar cheese, grated

Direction

- For the jam:
- Cut the stems off of the figs and discard. Combine figs and all other ingredients in a saucepan, and stir well. Add water just to cover.
- Bring pot to a simmer over medium heat, then lower heat and cook slowly, stirring regularly to prevent sticking. Add water as necessary to keep the jam from sticking or burning. Cook until figs have broken down somewhat (an hour or so). Purée gently with immersion blender or in a food processor, so that jam has a sticky but spreadable consistency.
- For the biscuits and assembly:
- Important note! Keep all ingredients for the biscuits cold throughout the process.
- Heat the oven to 500° F. In a large bowl, combine the flours, baking powder, salt, and sugar and blend well.
- Toss the 12 tablespoons of butter pieces into the flour and blend well with your fingers — you'll squeeze and pinch the butter into the flour until it's well-mixed and no piece of butter is larger than the fingernail on your smallest finger. The flour should resemble cornmeal. You want to do this step as quickly as possible so the butter does not begin to melt, but be thorough: getting the butter right is your best hedge against tough biscuits.
- Add milk to the flour and butter. Working quickly, mix the milk in with a rubber spatula, mixing only until the dough begins to hold together.
- Dump the dough onto floured work surface. Gather it together and pat briefly to flatten.

Fold the dough over on itself 3 or 4 times, then pat into a rough rectangle about 3/4- to 1-inch thick. Use a bench scraper to ensure dough isn't sticking to table.
- Use 2 1/2-inch biscuit cutter to cut biscuits from dough. Do not twist cutter as you cut the biscuits. If the biscuits stick to the cutter, dip it in a little flour before cutting. Place the biscuits onto a well-buttered baking sheet. They should be almost touching. Brush tops lightly with buttermilk.
- Bake for 15 to 20 minutes, until the biscuits are golden, well-risen and light; if they feel wet or heavy, bake them longer.
- Lower the oven to 450° F. Split 4 of the biscuits (save the rest for another use!) and place on a baking sheet. Put a piece of the remaining 2 tablespoons butter on each side of each biscuit.
- Next to the biscuits on the same baking sheet, divide the ham into 4 piles and cover with cheddar. Put the biscuits and ham into the oven and cook until the cheese and butter have melted.
- To assemble, put a pile of cheese and ham on the bottom half of each biscuit. Add 2 teaspoons of fig jam to the top half, close, and serve.

67. Cranberry Ginger Jam Donuts

Serving: Makes about 24 donuts | Prep: | Cook: |Ready in:

Ingredients

- Dough
- 4 1/2 teaspoons active dry yeast (2 packets)
- 1 cup warm water, 110° F
- 1/2 cup sugar
- 1/2 teaspoon baking powder
- 1/2 teaspoon freshly grated nutmeg
- 2 teaspoons salt
- 4 to 4 1/2 cups all purpose flour
- 1/4 cup soft butter or shortening
- 3 egg yolks

- 1 teaspoon vanilla extract
- Canola oil, for frying
- Confectioner's sugar to dust finished donuts
- Pastry bag and tip to fill the donuts
- Cranberry-Ginger Jam
- 12 ounces cranberries
- 2/3 cup water
- 3/4 cup sugar
- 1 tablespoon freshly grated ginger
- Juice and zest of one small orange
- Juice and zest of one lemon
- Seeds from one vanilla bean

Direction

- In the bowl of a stand mixer, whisk the yeast into the water along with 1 tablespoon sugar. Let sit until foamy, about 5 minutes.
- In a large bowl, whisk the remaining sugar, baking powder, nutmeg, salt, and 4 cups of flour together.
- Add the butter or shortening, egg yolks, and vanilla to the yeast mixture. Mix for about one minute to break up the butter or shortening.
- Slowly add in the dry ingredients, then switch to the dough hook and knead the dough for 2 minutes. The dough should be tacky and soft and may barely stick to the bottom of the bowl. If the dough seems very sticky, slowly add in more flour until just tacky. Once kneaded, transfer the dough to a lightly oiled bowl, cover, and let rise until doubled in size, about an hour.
- While the dough is rising prepare the cranberry jam by adding all of the ingredients to a medium saucepan. Bring to a simmer and cook over medium heat until the cranberries have softened and burst. Remove from heat and let the jam cool for 15 minutes, then use an immersion blender to blend until smooth. Fill a pastry bag fitted with a Bismarck tip or a large round tip.
- Transfer the risen dough to a lightly floured work surface and roll into a circle about 12 inch thick. Use a floured 2-inch round cutter to cut as many donuts as possible. Transfer the cut circles to a lightly floured baking sheet and

let rise, uncovered until almost doubled in size, 30 to 45 minutes.
- About 15 minutes before you are ready to fry the donuts, heat a large pot or Dutch oven with at least 2 inches of oil over medium heat until the oil reaches 350° F on a candy thermometer. Brush off any excess flour and fry the donuts for about 1 minute per side, being careful not to crowd the pan. When the donuts are deep golden brown on each side, remove them from the oil.
- Let the donuts cool slightly, then use the pastry bag to fill each donut with about 2 teaspoons of jam. Dust with confectioner's sugar and serve immediately. These donuts are best the day they are made.

---

68. Crescent Jam And Cheese Cookies

Serving: Makes about 30 cookies | Prep: | Cook: | Ready in:

Ingredients

- 1 cup unsalted butter, softened
- 7.5 ounces farmer cheese (cottage/ricotta-style cheese)
- 2 tablespoons sour cream
- 2 cups all-purpose flour, plus additional for rolling cookies out
- 1/4 teaspoon salt
- Raspberry Jam or preserves
- Milk, for brushing cookies
- Powdered sugar, for dusting

Direction

- Cream butter in a large bowl with an electric mixer until smooth. Force cheese through a sieve right onto creamed butter and stir it in. Add the sour cream and combine the mixture well.
- Whisk or sift together flour and salt in a separate bowl and gradually blend it into the

cheese mixture. Wrap the dough in plastic and chill it for at least 3 hours.

- Preheat oven to 200° C (400° F). Roll one-fourth of the dough out very thinly on a floured surface and chill the remaining dough until it is to be used.

- Cut the dough into 8 cm (3-inch) squares and put about 1/2 teaspoon jam or preserves in the center of each. Fold the dough in half on the diagonal, pressing firmly down to seal the two sides around the jam. Roll the triangle into crescents, starting at the wide end.

- Arrange crescents on a baking sheet (they won't expand terribly much, so just an inch or so between them is fine), brush them lightly with milk and bake them for 15 minutes, until they are golden.

- Transfer the cookies to a wire rack and dust them with powdered sugar. Continue making cookies in the same manner until all the dough is used.

---

69. Crostata Alla Marmellata (jam Tarte)

Serving: Makes two 20 cm tartes | Prep: | Cook: | Ready in:

Ingredients

- 500 grams pastry or cake flour, or Italian flour 00 (alternatively 460 g all-purpose flour + 40 g corn starch)
- 250 grams butter, chilled and cubed
- 140 grams icing sugar
- 3 egg yolks
- 1 whole egg
- zest of 1 large lemon (organic, not waxed, if possible)
- seed of 1 vanilla bean (or 2 tsp pure vanilla extract)
- 500 g your favorite jam or marmalade

Direction

- Sift the flour in a large mixing bowl. Add in the cubed butter and, using your fingertips, rub the butter into the flour until you get a crumbly mixture and there are no more visible pieces of butter.

- Mix in the icing sugar (sifted through a colander if it contains granules) and then lemon zest. Lightly beat the egg yolks and whole egg with a pinch of salt and the vanilla seeds or extract. Using a knife, mix the beaten eggs into the flour - butter mixture until the pastry comes together into a smooth, elastic ball. When preparing the pastry it is important that everything is cold (the ideal temperature is 13°C): keep your hands cool, or use the blades of two knives or a pastry scrapers for mixing the ingredients; alternatively ingredients can be mixed using a food processor.

- Once the dough comes into a ball, wrap it in plastic film and refrigerated for one day (if you can't wait so long, keep the dough in the fridge for at least 1 hour).

- Preheat the oven to 180°C.

- After resting, on a slightly floured counter - be careful since too much flour will alter the ideal ratio of flour to butter - rapidly work then roll out half of the pastry to 4 - 5 mm thickness and use it to line a buttered and floured 20 cm round tart pan (I recommend to make a thicker border for the tart by rolling the excess pastry into a thin rope, then placing it around the edges of the tart pan).

- Prick the base with a fork, line it with baking paper, fill it with baking beans (or rice) and blind-bake for 15 minutes. Then remove the baking paper and beans and let cool.

- In the meantime, roll out the excess pastry and cut into strips, about 1cm wide to create a lattice for the top of your tarts. Chill for about 10 minutes: it will be easier to handle when you go to transfer them onto the crostata.

- When the pastry base is cold, fill the tarts with your favorite jam (don't be shy, the jam layer should be thick) and place lattice strips over the top.

- Bake at 180°C for another 15 minutes or until golden on top. Once baked, the pastry should be golden, but still soft: it will crisp up slightly as it cools. Let cool in the pan before transferring to a serving plate.
- Notes (1) The remaining pastry, if not all is used straight away, can be frozen well wrapped in plastic, for up to 1 month. When you are ready to use the frozen pastry, transfer it to the refrigerator to defrost at least 6 hours in advance. (2) The blind baking is optional for the crostata alla marmellata but allows to cook the jam for a limited time, then avoiding it becomes dry and sticky; traditionally the pastry base is filled with jam when still unbaked, then decorated with strips and baked at 180°C for about 30 minutes until the pastry is golden on the edges.

70. Crostata Di Marmelatta Di Fico Fig Jam Italian Pie

Serving: Serves 6 | Prep: | Cook: | Ready in:

Ingredients

- Pie Crust
- 7.5 ounces flour, sifted
- 4 ounces butter, cold and cut up in small pieces
- 2 ounces icing sugar, sifted
- 1 egg
- 1 pinch salt
- 1/2 teaspoon lemon zest
- 1/2 tablespoon lemon juice
- Fig Jam with Grappa - see recipe I posted
- 3/4 cup fig jam

Direction

- Sift the flour with the icing sugar and salt. Add these ingredients in a food processor, add the cold butter in small cubes and the lemon zest. Pulse a few times to cut up the butter into the flour mixture. Add the egg and lemon juice. Pulse until the dough forms.
- Gather the dough on a marble top, divide the dough into a ball with 1/3 of dough and another with 2/3 of dough. Form each piece into a ball and flatten into a disk. Put each piece in plastic film and let rest for 1 hour in fridge.
- Preheat oven to 375°F.
- Start with the large piece of dough and roll it out between 2 parchment pieces of paper to 1/8 inch thick or less. Make sure it is all the same height all over.
- Remove the top parchment paper and turn over the pastry into an 8" pie pan (preferably with removable bottom). Press all around to adjust the dough into the pie pan. Remove the parchment paper and cut the excess dough, trimming with a knife so that it is flush with the top rim of the pie pan. Prick the dough with a fork all over the bottom.
- Cover again with the parchment paper and refrigerate while you roll out the second dough.
- Shape the smaller disk into a rectangle and roll it out between 2 parchment pieces of paper to 1/8 inch thick or less. Make sure it is all the same height all over.
- Remove the top parchment paper and cut strips the same width. Depending on how close you want to make the lattice you will need 8 or 10 strips.
- Remove the pie pan from the fridge, fill with the Fig/Grappa Jam and make the lattice on top. Moisten the ends of the dough with some water and press the ends down to adhere to the pie crust. If you want the lattice to be shiny, brush with lightly beaten egg yolk or milk.
- Bake tart until crust is golden, 35 to 45 minutes. Let cool on a rack.
- This is a rustic tart so we serve it as is but you can serve it with vanilla ice cream, crème anglaise or with a dollop of unsweetened whipped cream.

- You can make the Crostata the day before, keep it in the fridge overnight and bake it the next day.

71. Crostini With Duck Breast And Red Onion Jam

Serving: Makes about 30 crostini | Prep: | Cook: |Ready in:

Ingredients

- For the red onion jam
- 2 medium red onions, halved lengthwise and thinly sliced
- 2 tablespoons unsalted butter
- 1/4 cup sugar
- 1/4 teaspoon kosher salt
- Freshly ground black pepper
- 1/3 cup red wine
- 1 tablespoon sherry vinegar
- For the crostini and duck
- 2 large duck breasts, fat on
- 1 tablespoon vegetable oil
- Kosher salt
- 1 long, slender baguette
- Extra-virgin olive oil

Direction

- For the red onion jam
- In a large, covered pan over low heat, cook the onions, butter, sugar, salt and pepper to taste, stirring occasionally, until the onions are soft and slightly caramelized, about 30 minutes. Add the wine and vinegar and simmer uncovered, stirring occasionally, until thick, about 20 more minutes. Cool to room temperature before using. (Makes about 2 cups.)
- For the crostini and duck
- Using a very sharp knife, score the fat on each of the duck breasts and halve each breast lengthwise. Heat a large, heavy stainless steel or cast iron pan over medium-high heat,

adding the vegetable oil as soon as it is hot. Sprinkle each piece of duck generously with salt and gently place in the pan, fat side down. Sauté until the fat is golden brown, about 4 minutes, and then continue to cook, turning every minute or so to sear each side of the meat, until the duck is medium to medium rare, about 7 to 9 minutes total. Remove from the pan and let it rest until it is no longer hot.

- Heat the oven to 350 degrees. Cut the baguette on the diagonal into 1/4-inch slices and arrange them on a baking sheet. Brush the slices lightly with olive oil and bake until lightly browned, about 10-15 minutes. Do not overbake, or the crostini will be too hard.
- To assemble, slice each piece of duck into 1/4-inch slices. Arrange a slice on top of each of the crostini and top with a small dab of the onion jam. Serve immediately.

72. Crostini With Duck Confit And Red Onion Jam

Serving: Makes about 30 crostini | Prep: | Cook: |Ready in:

Ingredients

- For the red onion jam:
- 2 medium red onions, halved lengthwise and thinly sliced
- 2 tablespoons unsalted butter
- 1/4 cup sugar
- 1/4 teaspoon kosher salt
- Freshly ground black pepper
- 1/3 cup red wine
- 1 tablespoon sherry vinegar
- For the crostini and duck confit:
- Melissa Clark's Really Easy Duck Confit (get the recipe here: https://food52.com/recipes...)
- 1 long, slender baguette
- Extra-virgin olive oil

Direction

- For the red onion jam:
- In a large pan over low heat, combine the onions, butter, sugar, salt, and pepper. Cook, covered, stirring occasionally, until the onions are soft and slightly caramelized, about 30 minutes. Add the wine and vinegar and simmer uncovered, stirring occasionally, until thick, about 20 more minutes. Cool to room temperature before using. (Makes about 2 cups.)
- For the crostini and duck confit:
- Prepare duck confit and let it rest until it is no longer hot.
- Heat the oven to 350° F. Cut the baguette on the diagonal into 1/4-inch slices and arrange them on a baking sheet. Brush the slices lightly with olive oil and bake until lightly browned, about 8 minutes. Do not overbake, or the crostini will be too hard.
- While crostini are baking, shred the duck at room temperature with a fork.
- To assemble, arrange a tablespoon of the shredded duck confit on each crostini and top with a small dab of the onion jam. Serve immediately.

73. Crostini With Fig Preserves, Gorgonzola And Crispy Shallots

Serving: Serves a crowd | Prep: | Cook: | Ready in:

Ingredients

- 1   Loaf of French Bread, Cut into 1" Rounds and Each Slice Brushed with Olive Oil
- 8 ounces Crumbled Gorgonzola Cheese, Tossed with 1/2 teaspoon dried thyme
- 1   Jar Blackberry Farm Fig Preserves
- 5   Large Shallots, Thinly Sliced
- 2 tablespoons Rice Flour
- 1/2 tablespoon Good Olive Oil
- Salt

Direction

- Preheat oven to 400 degrees.
- In a small bowl toss the shallots in rice flour and olive oil. Spread shallots evenly on a baking sheet. Bake in oven for 15 minutes, stirring occasionally until the shallots are crisp. Lightly salt and let cool.
- Reduce oven to 350 degrees. Place bread rounds on a baking sheet and lightly toast. Remove and set aside.
- Set up an assembly line: bread rounds, fig preserves, gorgonzola and shallots. Spread the preserves on the toasted bread rounds, sprinkle with gorgonzola and then top with crispy shallots.

74. Crostini With Mascarpone, Prosciutto And Strawberry Jam

Serving: Serves many as an appetizer | Prep: 0hours0mins | Cook: 0hours0mins | Ready in:

Ingredients

- For the strawberry jam
- 3 cups diced strawberries
- 1/2 cup granulated sugar
- 1/4 teaspoon aleppo pepper
- 1/4 teaspoon sea salt
- For the crostini
- One or two baguettes, depending on how many bites you'd like
- Extra virgin olive oil
- 8 ounces mascarpone cheese*
- About 3 ounces thinly sliced proscuitto*
- The strawberry jam
- Aleppo pepper (optional)

Direction

- For the strawberry jam
- Place all ingredients in a small sauce pan and stir. Let the strawberries macerate in the sugar mixture for about 30 minutes.
- Simmer the mixture over medium heat for 10 to 15 minutes, mashing a bit as you go. The

mixture should be thick and "jammy". Transfer to a small bowl, cool to room temperature and then refrigerate for at least a few hours. (This can be made a day or two before serving)

- For the crostini
- Slice the baguette(s) on the diagonal about 1/2 inch thick. Brush one cut side with a little olive oil and bake in a preheated 350F oven for about 8 minutes until toasted a bit. Cool the slices.
- To assemble, spread a little mascarpone on the crostini and add a small spoon of the strawberry jam over. Drape a small piece of prosciutto over the top and sprinkle with a little Aleppo pepper if using. Now pour yourself a little "Bubbly"!
- *NOTE: Amounts are approximate and will depend on how many little bites you plan to make. Leftover ingredients can certainly be used to spread on toast or crackers.

75. Crostini With Whipped Goat Cheese And Hot Pepper Jelly

Serving: Serves a crowd | Prep: | Cook: | Ready in:

Ingredients

- Hot Pepper Jelly
- 3/4 pound red jalapenos
- 2 cups cider vinegar, divided
- 6 cups sugar
- large pinch salt
- 1 packet Certo liquid pectin
- Crostini
- 1 baguette, thinly sliced
- 2 cloves smashed garlic
- olive oil, as needed
- salt and pepper, to taste
- 1 cup goat cheese, or more as needed
- 2 tablespoons heavy cream

Direction

- Hot Pepper Jelly

- Halve the jalapenos. Seed the jalapenos based on how spicy you want the jelly. (Since red jalapenos are sweeter than green jalapenos, I seeded half of the jalapenos, but left the seeds with the other half. It made for an only slightly spicy jelly. Final spice can also be adjusted with red pepper flakes at the end of cooking.)
- Transfer the peppers to a food processor or blender, with half of the vinegar. Transfer the mixture to a large pot. Add the remaining vinegar and sugar. Bring to a boil over medium heat. Boil for 10 minutes.
- Stir in liquid pectin. Boil for 1 minute, until jelly begins to thicken. Remove from heat, and ladle into sterilized jars. If keeping in the fridge, close the jars and refrigerate. If planning to keep on the shelves, process, covered, in boiling water for 5-7 minutes, or until sealed.
- Crostini
- Rub each baguette slice with garlic. Drizzle with olive oil and season with salt and pepper. Bake in a preheated 350 degree oven until golden brown, about 4-5 minutes. Let cool completely.
- Using a handheld mixer (or in your Kitchenaid), whip the goat cheese with the heavy cream until light and fluffy. Season with salt and pepper.
- Spread a layer of whipped goat cheese on each piece of crostini, and top with a dollop of hot pepper jelly.

76. Dark Chocolate Tart With Kumquat Marmalade

Serving: Serves 8 | Prep: | Cook: | Ready in:

Ingredients

- All Butter Tart Shell
- 1 1/4 cups AP flour
- 1 1/4 sticks butter, diced and very cold fixed after food52 tested

- 1/2 teaspoon kosher salt
- 3 tablespoons ice water
- The Filling: Kumquat Marmalade and Dark Chocolate Ganache
- 100   grams kumquats (about 13)
- 40   grams sugar (2.5-3 tablespoons)
- 350   grams 70% chocolate
- 175   grams heavy cream (3/4 cup)
- 1 pinch salt

Direction

- All Butter Tart Shell
- Pulse the flour and salt in a food processor. Add the butter. Pulse until the butter and flour start to look like corn meal. Add the water pulsing in between each tablespoon until the whole thing just barely begins to come together. If you don't need all the water, don't use it. Pour out onto a spread piece of saran wrap and work the dough together to form a cohesive ball. Flatten the ball into a disk and let it rest in the fridge for a while. At least a half hour, but up to a few days is ok.
- Take the dough out of the fridge and let it rest at room temp for a half hour or so. When it starts to feel malleable, roll it out until it's about 1/4 of an inch thick. I like to use rice flour on the surface and rolling pin to help with this. It prevents sticking without really incorporating itself into the dough.
- Mold the dough into your tart pan and again let it rest for a little while in the fridge while you preheat your oven to 350. Line the shell with parchment and fill with rice or beans or those fancy pie marbles. Bake for about 45 minutes, but really just look for the shell to brown a bit and pull away from the sides of the mold. Let the shell cool completely (I throw it in the fridge) while you make the marmalade and the ganache.
- The Filling: Kumquat Marmalade and Dark Chocolate Ganache
- MARMALADE: Slice the kumquats in half lengthwise and take out the seeds. Slice them thinly and mix in a bowl with the sugar. I usually do this while my dough rests before I roll it out. The fruit and sugar need to sit together for about an hour or more so that the kumquats release all their juice.
- After the kumquats and sugar are nice and soupy, heat them in a small sauce pan until they have a really good boil going. Let them boil together for a few minutes until they start to gel. When you tilt the pan the whole mass will move together. It'll gel more as it cools.
- GANACHE: The most important part here is a high quality chocolate. Don't bother with anything that doesn't taste good to eat on its own. Check the ingredients. The fewer the better. Ideally all you want to see is cocoa mass, sugar and cocoa butter. Some good stuff has a little vanilla and even some lecithin in it. But try the chocolate before you use it. If it's waxy don't bother.
- Heat the cream to a boil. Pour over broken up chocolate. Let the whole thing sit for a couple minutes. Add the pinch of salt. Whisk until smooth.
- ASSEMBLY: Spread marmalade in a thin layer at the bottom of the tart shell. Pour ganache over everything evenly while still warm. Smooth with an offset. Let it cool completely before cutting into it so the ganache can set.
- I like to garnish it with either a wheel of kumquat or a little pile of pistachio grains. The pistachio adds some crunch and a little color!

77. Dark Chocolate Smoked Sea Salt Ice Cream With Concord Grape Jelly Ripple

Serving: Serves 3 | Prep: | Cook: | Ready in:

Ingredients

- 200 milliliters whole milk
- 200 milliliters heavy cream
- 130 grams sugar
- 3 teaspoons cornstarch
- 50 grams cream cheese

- 20 grams sifted cocoa powder
- 30 grams dark chocolate
- 1/3 teaspoon smoked sea salt

Direction

- For the chocolate sauce in a small saucepan over medium heat combine 80ml water, 45gr sugar, cocoa powder and smoked sea salt, cook 2min stirring until uniform. Add the chopped dark chocolate, cook until completely melted and glossy.
- Dissolve the cornstarch in 50ml whole milk, leave to rest.
- For the ice cream in another small saucepan over medium heat combine the heavy cream, the leftover milk, 85gr sugar, stir, bring to an almost boil, add the cornstarch milk and cook constantly stirring until thickened. Take off heat, add the cream cheese and the chocolate sauce, stir until smooth and combined. Cool to room temperature, then transfer into the fridge overnight.
- Freeze in your ice cream maker according to the manufacturer's instructions. Spoon into an airtight container alternating layers of ice cream and the Concord grape jelly (6-8tsp), store in the fridge for at least 5 hours until set.

78. Date & Rosemary Jam

Serving: Makes 1.5 cups(ish) | Prep: | Cook: | Ready in:

Ingredients

- 10-15 Dates, pitted and diced (about 1/2 cup smooshed)
- 1/4 cup Maple Syrup
- 1 Shallot, diced
- 1/2 teaspoon Ginger, use a fresh nub if you have it!
- 2-3 sprigs Rosemary, chopped
- 1 Lemon, zest and juice
- 1/2 teaspoon Cider Vinegar
- Pinch Cayenne (optional)

- 1/2 teaspoon Kosher Salt
- 1/2 cup Water

Direction

- Put all your ingredients into a small saucepan and bring to a boil. Take it down to a simmer, stirring occasionally, until it reduces and gets "jammy" and sticky and the dates have broken down. Your spoon will start to leave nice drag marks. Takes about 20 minutes. Taste and season if it needs a little more lemon/salt/syrup.
- Let cool. Spoon into a pretty dish and top with more rosemary.

79. Deviled Eggs With Spicy Tomato Jam And Pistachio Dukkah

Serving: Makes 6 servings | Prep: 0hours0mins | Cook: 0hours0mins | Ready in:

Ingredients

- For the tomato jam:
- 2 tablespoons olive oil
- 1 medium yellow onion, finely diced (about 1 1/2 cups)
- 1 pinch salt, plus more to taste
- 1 (28-ounce) can Muir Glen Canned Diced Tomatoes
- 1 cup sugar
- 1 tablespoon white vinegar
- For the deviled eggs and pistachio dukkah:
- 6 large eggs
- 3 tablespoons whole-milk Greek yogurt
- 2 teaspoons olive oil
- 1 teaspoon dijon mustard
- 1 pinch kosher salt
- 6 tablespoons roughly chopped raw pistachios
- 1 tablespoon sesame seeds
- 1 teaspoon fennel seeds

- 1 teaspoon coriander seeds
- 1 teaspoon cumin seeds
- 1 teaspoon caraway seeds
- 1/4 teaspoon kosher salt
- 1/4 cup tomato jam
- 1 teaspoon harissa, plus more to taste

Direction

- For the tomato jam:
- Set a large (roughly 12-inch) skillet over medium heat. Add the olive oil, then chopped onion. Season with a pinch of salt. Sauté, stirring occasionally, until soft—about 10 minutes.
- Add the tomatoes, sugar, and vinegar. Stir. Adjust the heat as needed to keep at a steady simmer and cook, stirring often, until the syrup is thick and dragging a spoon along the pan leaves a distinct trail—about 25 minutes. Transfer to a heat-proof container and refrigerate to cool completely.
- For the deviled eggs and pistachio dukkah:
- Add the eggs to a saucepan. Add water to cover by 1 inch. Bring to a boil. Remove from the heat, cover, and let hang out for 12 minutes. Drain and rinse under very cold water. Let cool completely, then peel. (I find the best way to do this is to gently roll the egg against the counter to crack the shell into a million little pieces, then peel under running water. But you do you.)
- Make the dukkah. Combine all ingredients in a skillet big enough for them to be in a single layer. Set over medium-low heat and toast until golden and fragrant, stirring as needed so they cook evenly. Transfer to the mortar and pestle (or food processor). Add the salt. Smash until the texture looks right to you— chunky or fine or somewhere between.
- Make the spicy tomato jam: Mix 1/4 cup of tomato jam with the harissa.
- Assemble the eggs. Halve each egg. Collect the yolks in a bowl. Add the yogurt, olive oil, mustard, and salt to the yolks. Stir with a fork until completely smooth. Season with mustard and salt to taste. Transfer to a plastic bag and

cut the corner to create a makeshift piping bag. Pipe this mixture evenly into the egg whites.

80. Drunken Pisco Fig Jam

Serving: Makes (6-7) 1/2 pint jars | Prep: | Cook: | Ready in:

Ingredients

- 4 pounds Fresh Figs - preferably a darker variety; stemmed and quartered
- 3/4 cup Peruvian Pisco
- 4 cups Sugar
- 3 tablespoons Lemon Juice

Direction

- Wash, stem and quarter the figs. There is no need to peel the figs. Mix the figs, sugar and the Pisco in a non-reactive pot and let everything macerate for 1 hour.
- Add lemon juice to pot and bring to a boil over high heat. Stir at a high boil until the sugar is dissolved. Lower heat and simmer (stirring occasionally) for 30-40 minutes until the blend is thick and "jammy." It will not gel.
- For chunky jam, mash the figs in the pot with a potato masher. For a smoother jam, pulse it in a blender until smooth and re-heat until bubbly & thick. Remove from heat.
- Taste, and if you'd like your jam a bit more boozy add more Pisco 1/4 cup at a time.
- Ladle jam into jars and store in the fridge for up to 3 weeks.
- Alternatively: Ladle mixture into 6 sanitized, hot 1/2-pint glass canning jars, leaving 1/4-inch space at top of jars. Remove any air bubbles. Wipe jar threads and rims with clean damp cloth. Cover with hot lids; apply screw bands. Process jars in pot of boiling water 10 minutes. Cool jars completely. Store in cool dark place up to 1 year. *This recipe has not been tested for acidity levels.

- Delicious served with creamy, salty cheese or with pork. It also makes a great tart filling.

81. Duck Bacon Jam With Coffee & Thyme

Serving: Makes 2 cups | Prep: | Cook: | Ready in:

Ingredients

- 1 pound Uncured Duck Bacon
- 1 Small, Sweet Onion, chopped fine
- 2/3 cup Brewed Coffee
- 2/3 cup Cane Sugar
- 1/4 cup Balsamic Vinegar
- 1/2 cup Water
- 1 teaspoon Fresh Thyme Leaves, chopped

Direction

- Heat a non-stick pan over medium low. I used my Lodge Cast Iron pan with deep sides - it will keep you from getting a bacon grease burn now and will keep the jam in its place later. Add the duck bacon a few strips at a time and cook them in batches until they are crispy. As they finish cooking, remove them to clean bowl and set aside. Be careful - they spit.
- Now, DO NOT drain the pan. Giving the bacon drippings a moment to cool down, add the onions to the pan, turn the heat up to medium low again and cook them until they are soft. Deglaze the pan with the coffee, using a wooden spoon-make sure to scrape up all the duck bacon goodness from the bottom of the pan.
- Bring the coffee to a simmer and add the sugar, balsamic vinegar and water, followed by the bacon bits, along with a good stir. Turn the heat up to high and bring to a swift boil. Reduce the heat to medium low and simmer for 35-45 minutes until everything is thick and jammy, stirring regularly so that it doesn't stick. Add the fresh thyme and cook for an additional 5 minutes.
- Finally, we play the waiting game. Turn off the heat and let the whole thing sit for 30 minutes in the pan to cool. When you check back in it will be lovely, sweet and slick.
- When it is cool, and IF you can stop from devouring it by the spoonful, it can be stored in the fridge for up to 3 weeks. You'll eat is all long before then, but you could in theory. It will be sticky and may have some of the drippings solidified at the top after a stint in the fridge. Just let it sit at room temperature for 30 minutes, give it a stir and you are good to go.
- How do you use duck bacon jam? Let me count the ways: Delicious on a drop biscuit with a fried, runny egg. Crazy good warm with that drop biscuit, some peaches and whipped cream for a twist on a peachy shortcake. Nice folded into an omelet with a salty hard cheese. Speaking of hard cheese... use that same cheese and top a crostini with both the jam and the cheese and broil. Near instant impressive appetizer. Skip the crostini, cut yourself a slice of bread, slather with jam and add cheese and arugula - open-faced sandwich. Done. Heaven mixed into ice cream. You've heard of bacon ice cream. Well, time to elevate it. Just eat spoonfuls of it. No judgment here. I *may* have done this while making it.

82. Eton Mess With Rhubarb Gin Jam And Lemon Basil Meringue

Serving: Serves 4 to 6 people | Prep: | Cook: | Ready in:

Ingredients

- 1/2 cup fresh basil leaves
- Zest of 1/2 a small lemon
- 1/2 cup sugar
- 1/4 heaping cup egg whites (about 2 large eggs)
- Juice of 1/2 a small lemon (1 tablespoon)
- 3 stalks rhubarb

- Juice of 1/2 a small lemon (1 tablespoon)
- 1/4 cup sugar
- 2 tablespoons gin
- Pinch of kosher salt
- 1 punnet full of strawberries (about 2 cups)
- 2 tablespoons light brown sugar
- 1 cup heavy cream

Direction

- Basil-Lemon Meringue: Heat the oven to 225 F.
- Wash the basil and dry it well, and then move the leaves to the bowl of a food processor. Zest the lemon (directly into the food processor, for ease). Add 2 tablespoons of the sugar. Set the bowl aside.
- Empty the eggs whites and the lemon juice into a metal mixing bowl. Set the mixing bowl over a simmering pot of water, and beat the whites using an electric mixer on medium-low speed; whisk for about 3 minutes, or until the egg whites begin to froth. Add 3 tablespoons of the sugar, and increase the speed to medium; whisk until the egg whites are a bit stiff, 4 to 5 minutes. Now add the remaining 3 tablespoons sugar, and whisk again, another 4 to 5 minutes. Turn off the heat under the water bath, and move the bowl to the countertop.
- Pulse the food processor for about 20 to 30 seconds, until the basil and the lemon zest have incorporated into the sugar. (Wait to do this, until just before you add this sugar to the egg whites -- you don't want the basil to brown.) Add the basil-lemon sugar to the egg white bowl, and beat on medium speed, another 2 to 3 minutes. The egg whites should be tinted lightly green, flecked with basil, and stiff enough to form peaks.
- Move the meringue into a piping bag -- I simply used a large, zip lock bag with a hole snipped into one corner. (You could also just use a spoon to scoop little clouds, if you're going for a more rustic look.) Pipe the meringue onto a parchment paper-lined baking sheet; my batch yielded 16 meringues, but you choose how large or small to make them.
- Move the baking sheet to the oven for 1 hour, and then turn off the heat. Without opening the oven door, let the meringues rest for at least 1 hour, but up to overnight.
- Gin and Rhubarb Quick Jam: Cut the ends off the rhubarb stalks, and also cut away any bruised bits. Now slice the rhubarb into pieces, about 1/2-inch long.
- Move the rhubarb to a medium saucepan, along with the lemon juice, the sugar, the gin, the pinch of salt, and 1/4 cup of water. Turn the heat to high, until the liquid starts to bubble, and then lower the heat to medium low. Stir occasionally. Cook the rhubarb for about 20 minutes, or until the rhubarb is jammy, but retains its shape a bit. Let the jam cool; it should fall apart a bit when you stir it.
- Prepare the strawberries: Slice the tops off the strawberries, and then slice the strawberries into halves or quarters, depending on the size of the strawberries, and your personal preference. Move the strawberry pieces into a medium bowl, and stir in the brown sugar, until the strawberries are evenly coated. Cover the bowl with plastic wrap, and let it sit for at least 30 minutes, or until strawberry syrup collects at the bottom of the bowl.
- Prepare the cream: Whip the heavy cream. I like to keep the cream on the runny side, the consistency of stirred yogurt, but it's up to you. The cream should be cold when you whip it. Move it to the fridge for a little while after you whip it, so that it's also cold when you serve it.
- Put everything Together: There are really no rules for how, or in what order, you put together the meringue, the jam, the strawberries and the cream. You can crack the top of each meringue (for example, to fit them into a jar), or not. I recommend drizzling some of the strawberry syrup over the top of each, to finish.

83. Fall Harvest Preserves

Serving: Makes 12oz | Prep: | Cook: | Ready in:

Ingredients

- 2 cups black seedless grapes
- 1 cup Braeburn apple with peel
- 1.5 cups figs
- 1/4 lemon juice
- 1 cup sugar

Direction

- Thoroughly was all fruit and allow to drain dry.
- Cut apples and figs into equal sized pieces.
- Add grapes, figs, and apples to pot on medium heat. Cook on medium for 45 minutes, stirring occasionally. Make sure apples are very soft before moving to next step.
- If the mixture is too chunky, put in blender for a couple of seconds. This will make it smoother but still have a thick consistency.
- Add sugar to fruit mixture and simmer for an addition 45 minutes.
- Pour jam into a 12oz sterilized jar. Or eat warm on toast!

84. Farmers Market Skillet Bread With Tomato Butter And Blackberry Peach Quick Jam

Serving: Serves 8-12 | Prep: | Cook: | Ready in:

Ingredients

- Farmers Market Skillet Bread
- 2 Small Zucchini
- 1 Ear of Sweet Corn
- 1-2 Hot Peppers
- 1 cup Heavy Cream
- 10 tablespoons Unsalted Butter
- 1/3 cup Honey
- 1 1/2 cups All-Purpose Flour
- 1 1/2 cups Yellow Cornmeal
- 2 teaspoons Baking Powder
- 3/4 teaspoon Baking Soda
- 1/2 teaspoon Salt
- 2 tablespoons Dark Brown Sugar, Lightly Packed
- 1 cup Plain Greek Yogurt (Whole or 2%), Room Temperature
- 1 Egg, Room Temperature, Slightly Beaten
- Salt and Pepper, as Needed
- Tomato Butter and Blackberry Peach Quick Jam
- 1 pint Cherry Tomatoes
- Olive Oil, as Needed
- 8 tablespoons Unsalted Butter, Softened
- 1/2 pint Blackberries
- 1 Peach
- 1/3 cup Dark Brown Sugar, Lightly Packed
- 1/3 cup Sugar (Preferably Cane Sugar)
- Salt and Pepper, as Needed

Direction

- Farmers Market Skillet Bread
- If you are making the Tomato Butter and Blackberry Peach Quick Jam, it's best to make them before the skillet bread. Please see the instructions for both after their ingredient list below the Skillet Bread recipe. To begin the Skillet Bread: first, line a colander with a double layer of paper towels and place in a clean sink. Wash the zucchini and trim the ends. Coarsely shred the zucchini into the colander. Place a medium bowl over the shredded zucchini. Place heavy cans or a large jar in the bowl to help drain the zucchini. Let drain for at least a half hour and up to two hours.
- While the zucchini drains, shuck and wash the sweet corn. With a sharp knife carefully remove the kernels and reserve them. Do not throw away the cob. Wash and stem the hot pepper(s) (if the peppers are very hot, you may want to use gloves). If the peppers are greater than two inches in length then cut them in half width-wise. To reduce the heat,

you may remove some of all of the pepper seeds if you wish, but this is not necessary (I removed half of the seeds).

- Next, place eight tablespoons of butter into a medium saucepan. Add the cream. Using the back side of a knife, "milk" the corncob into the cream mixture by carefully applying pressure with the knife in an up and down motion. Discard the cob. Add the hot peppers to the mixture. Heat on the stove's lowest setting, stirring frequently, until the butter is melted and incorporated into the cream (do not allow to boil). Remove from heat and let cool completely. After the mixture cools, remove peppers with a slotted spoon. Rinse the peppers gently, dice, and add the diced peppers to the reserved corn kernels.

- Preheat oven to 375 degrees. Remove the bowl and cans from the zucchini. Carefully ring out the zucchini with the paper towels. Place the zucchini in an oven safe 13" x 9" roasting pan (Pyrex or similar). Add the remaining two tablespoons of butter and the 1/3 cup honey to the zucchini. Season the mixture with salt and pepper to taste. Give mixture a brief stir and place in the pre-heated oven. Cook for 30 minutes, stirring the mixture every 10 minutes. At the 30 minute mark, add the reserved corn kernels and the diced hot peppers. Roast 15 minutes more, stirring every few minutes, until the honey butter has reduced completely and the vegetables are slightly caramelized. Remove from the oven and allow to cool until no longer hot. Do not turn off the oven.

- Begin the dough: In a large bowl whisk together the flour and the cornmeal. Add the baking soda, baking powder and salt and whisk again. Add the brown sugar and once more. Using clean fingers, break up any clumps of brown sugar.

- Next, add the yogurt to the cooled cream mixture, whisking to incorporate. Add beaten egg and whisk to incorporate again. Add the wet cream/yogurt mixture to the dry flour/cornmeal mixture all at once, stirring gently with a wooden spoon until just combined. Add most of the cooled zucchini

mixture (reserve a scant 1/4 cup) and mix briefly and gently. The dough will be quite thick. Butter a 10 inch cast iron skillet. Spoon dough into skillet and smooth to the edges. Scatter remaining zucchini mixture over top. Bake in still heated (375 degrees) oven for 23-27 minutes, or until the edges are nicely browned and a toothpick inserted in the center comes out clean. Remove from oven carefully and allow to cool for at least 20 minutes before cutting. Serve with Tomato Butter and Blackberry Peach Quick Jam if desired. Store the bread and its fixings in the refrigerator.

- Tomato Butter and Blackberry Peach Quick Jam

- For the Tomato Butter: Preheat oven to 375 degrees. Rinse cherry tomatoes. If any tomatoes are larger than 1" in diameter, cut them in half. Place cherry tomatoes in an 8" x 8" baking dish. Drizzle with olive oil and season with salt and pepper. Give the tomatoes a gentle stir to combine. Place in preheated oven and roast for 20-25 minutes, or until softened, but not browned. Remove from oven and allow to cool completely.

- After the tomato mixture has cooled, carefully drain off as much residual liquid as possible. Place the tomatoes in a food processor. Add the softened butter and 1/2 teaspoon salt (or to taste) and process until combined. The mixture will not look very appetizing at this point - but do not fear. Scrape the mixture into a small bowl, cover and place in the fridge for two hours. After two hours, return the mixture to a clean food processor. Process until thoroughly combined (this should take two to three minutes). The mixture should now look like a lovely, soft, orange butter. Place the mixture in a clean bowl, cover and refrigerate for several hours before using. Makes approximately 1 1/2 cups.

- For the Blackberry Peach Quick Jam: Rinse fruit. Pit and coarsely chop peach (it is not necessary to peel the peach). Add blackberries, peach, and both sugars to a medium saucepan. Heat the mixture to a gentle boil over medium heat, stirring frequently to prevent burning.

Once mixture boils, reduce heat to low. Continue cooking 10-15 minutes, until the fruit is broken down and mixture reduces and thickens. Remove from heat and allow to cool.

- Place a thin mesh sieve over a medium bowl. Carefully pour the cooled blackberry/peach mixture into the sieve. With a spoon, press as much of the jam through the sieve as possible (it helps to scrape the spoon over the bottom of the sieve from time to time). Discard remaining seeds and peach skin in the sieve. Pour the jam into a glass jar (or small bowl), cover and refrigerate for several hours before using. Mixture will thicken as it cools, but the jam will be relatively thin (between a sauce and a jam in thickness). Makes approximately 1 scant cup.

85. Fennel Marmalade

Serving: Makes 1 pint(ish) | Prep: | Cook: |Ready in:

Ingredients

- olive oil
- salt
- 1 small bulb fennel, cored and thinly sliced
- 1 small onion, thinly sliced
- 1/2 cup brown sugar
- 1/2 cup orange juice
- grated zest of one lime

Direction

- Heat oil in a large sauté pan over medium heat. Add onion, fennel, and salt. Cover and cook until onion and fennel start to wilt, about 10 minutes. Stir in 1/4 cup of the brown sugar. Pour in the orange juice and reduce heat to the lowest setting. Simmer for about 45 minutes, stirring occasionally. If the mixture starts to seem dry while the fennel is still on the crunchy side, add a few more dribbles of orange juice. Do not let the mixture burn.

- After 45 minutes, add the rest of the brown sugar and raise the temperature. The mixture should bubble and caramelize. When most of the moisture seems to have evaporated, take the marmalade off the heat. Stir in the lime zest.
- Place marmalade in a jar or a covered bowl in the fridge until ready to use. Makes about one pint.

86. Fig Jam With A Twist

Serving: Makes 500ml jar | Prep: | Cook: |Ready in:

Ingredients

- 3 ripe figs
- 1 handful small yellow tomatoes
- 1 handful kumquats
- 1 cup dark muscovado shugar
- 1 pinch freshly ground black pepper
- 2/3 cup water
- 1 handful walnuts

Direction

- Halve the kumquats lengthwise and quarter the figs and tomatoes.
- Put in a deep 20" pot with the sugar, salt pepper, marsala and water.
- Bring to boil, reduce the heat to medium and cook until most of the liquid has evaporated, stirring occasionally, taking care not to mash up the fruit too much
- Just before you remove from the heat, add the broken walnut kernels and stir to coat
- Put in a sterilized jar straight away and close shut.
- Let it cool before transferring to the fridge
- It matures and the flavour deepens with time, if you have the patience to wait! It will keep for up to a month

87. Fig Jam With Cardamom

Serving: Serves lots of slices of toast | Prep: | Cook: | Ready in:

Ingredients

- 1 pound of fresh, ripe figs
- 1/4 cup + 1 TB red wine
- 1/2 cup water
- 2 TB + 1 tsp fresh lemon juice
- 1 strip of zest from the lemon
- 1 1/2 tsp vanilla extract
- 2 TB + 1 tsp organic turbinado sugar
- 1 tsp ground cardamom
- 1 stick of cinnamon
- A couple of rasps of nutmeg
- 1 pinch ground cloves

Direction

- Slice the lids off of the figs.
- Add them along with the rest of the ingredients to an awaiting pot, reserving 1/2 tsp of vanilla and 1 tsp of lemon juice.
- Bring to a boil, then turn down to a simmer. Let this cook for 45 minutes over a very low flame, or until it's thick and jammy, stirring frequently to keep it from scorching. Sprinkle some water into the pot if it looks like it's about to scorch, or if it's cooking too quickly and the figs have not broken down yet.
- When the jam has adequately thickened, add the last 1/2 teaspoon of vanilla and 1 tsp of lemon juice, remove from the heat and allow to cool a bit before transferring to small Mason jars fitted with lids. Store in the refrigerator.

88. Fig Lemon Preserves

Serving: Makes 8 half pints | Prep: | Cook: | Ready in:

Ingredients

- 4 pounds Fresh figs, washed, trimmed, halved and sliced
- 3 pounds Sugar
- 1 Cinnamon stick
- 3 Lemons quartered, thinly sliced
- 2 cups Pecan halves cut in half, or pieces

Direction

- Combine all ingredients except pecans in a large, heavy saucepan.
- Bring to a boil, stirring so nothing sticks to the bottom of pan.
- Once boiling, reduce heat and simmer for about an hour.
- Stir in pecans and spoon into hot, sterilized jars. Keeps in fridge for several weeks. This recipe can be processed in a water bath for 8 minutes.

89. Five Citrus Marmalade

Serving: Makes 9 half pint jars | Prep: | Cook: | Ready in:

Ingredients

- 2 pomelos
- 1 grapefruit
- 1 handful of kumquats
- 2 navel oranges
- 2 lemons
- 8 cups sugar
- 8 cups filtered water

Direction

- Day 1: Prepare the fruit and combine it with the water. To prepare the pomelos: Run either a sharp knife or a sharp vegetable peeler around the outside of the pomelos, removing the colored part of the rind and leaving behind the pith. Stack the pieces of rind in a pile and slice them into the thinnest strips you can manage. If the finished strips are on the long side, cut them in half or thirds (you want them to fit nicely into a spoon for the finished marmalade, not to be pomelo noodles). Set the finished pomelo rind aside in a mixing bowl. Now, cut off the layer of white pith to reveal the colored fruit. Use your knife to remove individual segments from the fruit, leaving behind the bitter membranes. Roughly chop the fruit segments into bite size pieces. Set the prepared fruit pieces aside in the mixing bowl. To prepare the grapefruit: Use the same method as described above, using only the outer part of the rind and the segments of fruit. Combine the finished fruit segments and sliced strips of peel with the prepared pomelo in your mixing bowl. To prepare the kumquats: Slice off the tip where the stem was attached. Next, slice the kumquat in half. Remove any little seeds. Next, each half of the kumquat into very thin strips. Combine the prepared kumquat with the prepared grapefruit and pomelo. To prepare the lemons and oranges: Slice off the blossom and stem end of the fruit. Slice the fruit into quarters. Slice off the pithy center of each quarter, where the membranes join together and the seeds are hiding. Lay out the pieces of fruit so that the skin side is facing you and slice the oranges and lemons into the thinnest pieces you can manage. Next: Combine the fruit and the water in a nonreactive container and let it sit for 24 hours.

- Day 2 (the easy part): Bring boiling water canner to a boil. Wash jars and lids in hot, soapy water. Put the fruit mixture into a large, nonreactive pot. Turn the heat on medium and bring to a simmer. Simmer the fruit for 20 minutes to soften the rinds. Pour in the sugar and stir to combine everything. Turn the heat to high, and cook, stirring occasionally, until the marmalade reads 220 on a candy thermometer or passes whatever gel test you like. Ladle the hot marmalade into hot jars, leaving 1/4" headspace. Process for 10 minutes.

90. Fizzy Strawberry Jellies

Serving: Serves 8 | Prep: | Cook: | Ready in:

Ingredients

- 500 grams TOTAL Greek Yoghurt
- 2 packets strawberry jelly
- 1 liter low sugar lemonade
- 400 grams English strawberries
- 1 handful fresh chopped mint

Direction

- Remove the green leaf and stalk from the strawberries, cut in half and divide equally between eight tumblers.
- Make up jelly to manufacturer's guidelines, but replace cold water with an equal quantity of the lemonade.
- Set in fridge for 4 – 6 hrs.
- When the jelly is set, spoon a dollop of TOTAL Greek Yoghurt on to the top of each glass and sprinkle over some chopped mint.

91. Fragrant Kumquat Marmalade

Serving: Makes about 1 cup | Prep: | Cook: | Ready in:

Ingredients

- 1/3 pound fresh kumquats (about 1 heaping cup, or about 16 kumquats)
- 6 ounces white fruity semidry wine (I like Cupcake Vineyards Sauvignon Blanc)
- 3/4 cup granulated sugar

Direction

- Prepare an 8-ounce jar with lid, or two 4-ounce jars with lids.
- Wash and drain the kumquats. Snap off the little green stems. Cut the fruit in half from north pole to south pole, and then cut each half into very thin half-moon shapes. You'll run into some seeds, so pitch them as you

work, with the tip of your knife. There may be some stragglers, but no worries, as you can catch them later on. And they're edible anyway, so seriously, don't worry.

- Place the fruit in a medium-sized saucepan. Pour the wine over. Stir in the sugar. Bring to a boil over medium-high heat, and boil for about 7 - 9 minutes. Turn off heat and move pan aside. Let sit for one minute as you get your jar ready. Using a wide-mouth funnel is really helpful here, because this stuff is H-O-T! Scrape your hot stuff into the jar. Let sit for a minute or so, then seal your jar according to your preferred method.
- My preferred method is to let jar cool some, and then stash in the fridge until I eat it all, which is pretty darn quick.

92. French Baguette, With Parmigiano Reggiano Cheese, Italian Organic Fig Preserve And Balsamic Glaze

Serving: Serves 14 | Prep: | Cook: |Ready in:

Ingredients

- 1   French baguette, sliced into 1/2 inch rounds
- 1   Di Bruno Bros. Parmigiano Reggiano cheese
- 1   jar, Italian organic fig preserves
- 1   bottle of Blaze (Balsamic Glaze)

Direction

- Preheat oven to 375 degrees. Place baguette rounds on parchment paper on baking sheet.
- Cut thin slices of cheese, and place one slice on each round. The cheese is a bit crumbly, but that's OK - you can place some of the crumbles on the bread.
- Top each round with a 1/2 teaspoon of fig preserve.

- Drizzle the balsamic glaze over each bread round.
- Place baking pan in the oven, and bake for about 10 - 12 minutes, or until the cheese starts to melt. Just keep an eye on it as you don't want to cheese to be too melted and the fig jam to start dripping down.
- Transfer rounds to a serving plate, and enjoy with your Italian wine!

93. Fresh Fig And Strawberry Jam

Serving: Makes 4 1/2 pint jars | Prep: | Cook: |Ready in:

Ingredients

- 1 pound fresh green figs, stemmed and cut up
- 2 cups quartered strawberries
- 2 cups vanilla sugar
- 3 tablespoons Harvey's Bristol Cream
- grated zest of one Valencia orange

Direction

- Place figs, strawberries, vanilla sugar and Harvey's in medium stainless steel or enamel saucepan. Cover and let stand for 1 hour stirring occasionally.
- Bring to a boil over high heat, reduce heat to medium and boil rapidly, uncovered until mixture will form a gel about 15 minutes, stirring frequently. Remove from the heat.
- Use the freezer test to see if it's gelling. Put a couple of small plates in freezer. After 15 minutes, put a spoonful of the jam on plate and return to freezer for two minutes. (Take jam off the heat while you wait so it doesn't overcook.) Then take the plate out and rotate it. The jam should move slowly as you rotate it. If it throws itself off the plate onto the floor, keep cooking and try again in five minutes with the other plate. You'll get a feel for this.
- To prepare the jars, fill a large stockpot with enough water to cover the jars and place the jars in the water. Start heating over medium.

About 10 minutes before you're ready to fill the jars, put the tops in. Fill the jars, leave about a half inch from the top for airspace, wipe the rim and side so the jars will seal well. Put the filled jars back in the hot water. Place the pot over high heat, cover and bring to a rocking full boil. Once it boils, set timer for 10 minutes. At the end of 10 minutes, turn off heat, take off top and leave jars in water for five minutes. Then lift out and place on heat safe surface. I put mine on a kitchen towel on a cake rack out of the way. Don't touch or dry jars for 12-24 hours. Be sure all are sealed. (You'll hear them pop and when you punch the tops they don't make a sound. If they don't seal for any reason, refrigerate them.

94. Fried Egg Toasts With Mascarpone, Apricot Jam, And Chives

Serving: Serves 1 | Prep: | Cook: | Ready in:

Ingredients

- 2 pieces Italian Bread
- 2 eggs
- 2 teaspoons Mascarpone Cheese
- 2 teaspoons Apricot Jam
- 1 Chives (Chopped)
- 1 teaspoon Olive Oil
- 1 Salt
- 1 Pepper

Direction

- Grab 2 Slices of Italian Bread and Toast
- On medium heat prepare a non-stick frying pan with olive and crack eggs into the pan and salt/pepper to taste.
- Fry the eggs to preference (soft or hard yolk), and remove from fire
- Spread Mascarpone cheese on toasted bread
- Place one egg on each piece of toast.
- Spread apricot jam on eggs

- Top with chives

95. Fried Green Tomato And Egg Sliders With Tomato Jam

Serving: Makes 8 sliders | Prep: | Cook: | Ready in:

Ingredients

- 1 1/2 pounds ripe tomatoes
- 1   small Vidalia onion (or other sweet onion)
- 1 tablespoon butter plus more for spreading on bread
- 5 tablespoons olive oil
- 3 tablespoons apple cider vinegar
- 1 cup sugar
- salt
- ground black pepper
- 2   green tomatoes
- corn starch, enough to coat tomato slices
- 1   bag seasoned fry mix
- 10   large eggs
- 1 cup buttermilk
- vegetable oil for frying
- 1   package King's Hawaiian Dinner Rolls (12/pkg)

Direction

- To cook the jam -- Coarsely chop the onion. Melt 1 tbsp. butter and 2 tbsps. olive oil in saucepan, add the chopped onion and cook over medium low heat. Stir every 3 – 5 minutes until caramelized and golden brown, about 20 minutes and up to 45 minutes. Adjust heat to prevent burning. Be patient and don't stir too often. Let the onion continue to turn color; you want the texture to be to the point it's almost melting. While the onions are caramelizing, cut the ripe tomatoes in half, crosswise. Scoop out seeds. Finely chop the fresh tomato. Add 2 tbsps. apple cider vinegar and the chopped tomato to the caramelized onion. As the tomatoes begin to release their juices, stir in 1 cup sugar and 1 tsp salt and bring to a boil. Stir constantly to dissolve sugar. Maintain heat at medium - low, stirring often. Occasionally stir until the spread is very thick. Adjust seasoning.

- To cook fried green tomatoes -- In a shallow bowl, beat 2 eggs and the buttermilk together with a fork. Place fry mix in a shallow bowl or plate. Pour corn starch into a separate shallow bowl or plate. Slice green tomatoes into slices about 1/3" thick to obtain 8 slices. Cut the slices from the middle of each tomato to obtain fairly uniform diameter. Pat dry with a paper towel. Dip each slice of tomato in corn starch, then dip into wet mixture shaking off excess, and then coat in fry mix. Place on a cookie sheet. Place the breaded tomato slices in a refrigerator to chill (helps breading to remain adhered) for about 1 hour. Heat oil in heavy skillet or frying pan to medium-high temperature. Avoiding crowding, place a few slices of tomato at a time in skillet frying for about 3 minutes on each side. Drain on paper towels and keep warm.
- Slice each bun in half and brush some melted butter both sides. In a sauté pan over medium heat, grill each side until just browned. Arrange bottoms of buns on a large platter. Place a fried green tomato slice onto each bun bottom.
- Cook eggs sunny side up and assemble -- Heat 2- 3 tbsps. olive oil in a non-stick skillet over medium-low heat. Crack no more than 3 eggs into the skillet at a time. Use your spatula to guide and form the whites and try to keep them uniform and from running out in large area. After about one minute slightly tilt pan away from you and spoon hot oil onto the whites only. Continue until the whites are fully set and white. Next, spoon a couple of spoonfuls of hot oil over the yolks to set them. Quickly smear a generous amount of tomato jam onto a slice of a fried green tomato (sitting on a bun) and place an egg on top of a jam-smeared fried green tomato. Season with salt and pepper. Repeat with remaining eggs.

96. Gilly's Rotisserie Chicken & Hot Pepper Jelly Sandwich

Serving: Makes 1 sandwich | Prep: | Cook: | Ready in:

Ingredients

- 2 pieces Your favorite sandwich bread - Toasted
- 1 tablespoon Hot Pepper Jelly
- 1 teaspoon Light Fat Free Mayo
- Sliced Rotisserie Chicken (Can be made with leftover turkey as well.)
- Fresh Tomato Slices
- Mozzarella Cheese (Can be substituted for provolone or any sliced cheese you have at the time)
- 2   Fresh Basil Leaves

Direction

- Set your oven to broil at 350.Pop your bread in the toaster, but use a lighter setting because we will be putting it in the oven (or toaster oven) in a few minutes.
- Slice the chicken, tomato, and cheese (if needed) and set them aside on a plate. Place your 2 basil leaves on the plate as well. (If you don't have fresh basil, dried basil will also work.)
- Grab a baking sheet and a piece of foil, remove the toast and place open face on the sheet. Spread the HPJ on one piece and the light mayo on the other. Build the sandwich by placing the chicken and tomatoes on the HPJ side, and place the basil and cheese on the mayo side. Broil the sandwich open faced for a few minutes until you see the cheese starting to melt.
- Remove from oven & let cool for a minute. Take the cheese and basil slice, place it on top of the chicken and tomato slice. Slice and serve!
- *Serve with a side you have leftover in your fridge, or any chip you desire in your cabinet. I personally love to slice this sandwich in half

and eat it with nothing else. It is delicious, savory, and warm. It's also my favorite go-to for when I'm tucked away in the house on a chilly fall day. (In the summer I make and pack it in a cooler. It's a perfect on the go sandwich and tastes delicious without heating up as well.)*

97. Ginger Peach Jam

Serving: Serves 12 half pint jars plus some for the fridge | Prep: | Cook: | Ready in:

Ingredients

- 12 cups peeled, pitted and chopped peaches
- 2 cups riesling wine
- 1/4 cup minced candied ginger
- 1 tablespoon microplaned fresh ginger
- 1 teaspoon cinnamon (Vietnamese is best)
- 1 to 2 cups sugar (this is going to depend on how sweet your peaches are)
- 2 - 1.75 ounces NO SUGAR NEEDED pectin
- 1 tablespoon butter
- juice from 2 lemons

Direction

- Sterilize your jars and put two spoons in the freezer. Bring the peaches and riesling to a boil in a big heavy pot. Add both gingers - I microplane the fresh ginger straight in there. Add the cinnamon. Simmer and stir for about 10 minutes until the peaches are soft. You may want to mash them a bit with a potato masher to break up the chunks. Stir in the lemon juice.
- Whisk the pectin into 1 c sugar. Add the sugar / pectin and bring the jam back to a boil. Taste it for sweetness and add more sugar if you need / want. Add in the butter and simmer / stir for another minute or so, then drizzle a bit of jam onto your frozen spoon. Run your finger through it, if the path stays clear your jam is done!

- Fill each jar to the first thread - this leaves 1/4 - 1/2 inch head room. Clean and dry the rim, place a dried top on (those were in hot water, right?) and secure them with a ring. Process / boil the jars for 10 minutes then remove them and let them sit undisturbed until completely cool - 12 hours minimum. That's it!

98. Goat Cheese Ice Cream With Honey And Fig Jam

Serving: Makes 1 quart | Prep: | Cook: | Ready in:

Ingredients

- 2 cups heavy cream
- 1 cup milk
- 1/3 cup honey
- 1/4 teaspoon salt
- 4 egg yolks
- 1/2 cup (4 ounces) fresh goat cheese, like Le Cornilly
- 1/2 cup fig jam

Direction

- Heat cream, milk, honey, and salt in a saucepan until just simmering. Meanwhile, in a light bowl, lightly whisk the egg yolks. Once milk mixture is simmering, slowly pour it into the yolks, while whisking constantly.
- Add the egg and cream mixture back into the saucepan and cook on low heat, stirring constantly, until the mixture thickens and coats the back of a wooden spoon, about 5 to 7 minutes. Remove from the heat.
- Crumble the goat cheese into a large bowl. Strain the warm custard through a fine mesh strainer onto the goat cheese and whisk until fully incorporated and smooth.
- Cover and cool in the fridge until thoroughly chilled, at least 2 hours or overnight.
- Freeze the mixture in an ice cream maker. Once it is frozen, transfer dollops of ice cream into a one-quart container, adding tablespoons

of fig jam as you go so that ice cream and jam are layered together. Run a butter knife through the mixture in a swirling motion two to three times to gently swirl the ice cream and jam.

- Seal the container and let the ice cream set in the freezer for at least 4 hours before serving. The ice cream will keep for a week in the freezer.

99. Goat Cheese Tart With Mango Habanero Jam

Serving: Serves 6 | Prep: | Cook: |Ready in:

Ingredients

- Flour, Salt, butter, water
- 1 1/2 cups Flour
- Pinch Salt
- 8 tablespoons Butter, cold chopped into small pieces
- 1/4-1/3 cups Ice cold water
- Goat cheese, ricotta cheese, egg yolks, salt and pepper, olive oil, onion, sugar, mango/habanero jam (or apricot jam with cayenne whisked in), pine nuts
- 12 ounces Goat cheese
- 1/2 cup Whole milk ricotta cheese
- 2 Egg yolks
- Salt and pepper to taste
- 1 tablespoon Extra virgin olive oil
- 1 Onion, halved and thinly sliced
- 1 tablespoon Sugar
- 1/2 cup Mango/Habanero jam, or apricot jam with 1/2 teaspoon cayenne pepper whisked in)
- 2 tablespoons Pine nuts, toasted

Direction

- Flour, Salt, butter, water
- To make the tart crust: Place flour, salt, and butter in the bowl of a food processor and pulse until the butter is in small pieces (just a

few seconds will do it). With the processor running, slowly add just enough cold water for the dough to begin to hold together. Turn dough onto a floured surface and knead briefly. Pat dough into a disk, cover with plastic wrap and refrigerate until the filling is ready.

- Goat cheese, ricotta cheese, egg yolks, salt and pepper, olive oil, onion, sugar, mango/habanero jam (or apricot jam with cayenne whisked in), pine nuts
- To make the filling: In a mixing bowl, mix the goat cheese, ricotta, egg yolks, salt, and pepper. Set aside. In a wide sauté pan over medium heat, drizzle 1 tablespoon olive oil. Place the sliced onions in the pan and cook, stirring frequently until onions begin to brown. Sprinkle the sugar on top and reduce the heat to the lowest setting. Slowly cook onions until they become deep brown and caramelized, stirring occasionally so they don't burn. This may take up to 20 minutes. Set onions aside.
- Preheat the oven to 375 degrees. To assemble the tart: On a floured board or countertop, roll the pastry dough into a circle, about 1/2 inch thick. Line a tart pan with the pastry and trim the edges to fit. Be careful not to stretch the dough or it may shrink when baking. Prick the bottom of the tart shell with a fork. Pre-bake the tart shell in a 375 ° F oven for about 15 minutes, or until the bottom of the shell just begins to brown. Remove the tart from the oven. If the bottom of the crust has puffed up, gently press it down with the base of a glass or measuring cup. Spread the caramelized onions onto the bottom of the tart shell, then spread the goat-cheese mixture on top of the onions. Smooth the surface with a spatula.
- Bake the tart at 375 degrees F for about 35-40 minutes. Filling should be just set and starting to brown on the edges. Cool. While the tart cools, toast the pine nuts in a pan over medium heat for about 3 minutes, shaking pan to keep them from burning. When the tart is completely cool, spread sweet and spicy Mango/Habanero or Apricot jam over the top.

Sprinkle toasted pine nuts on top. Serve at room temperature.

100. Goat Cheese With Tangy Clementine Jam And Fresh Thyme

Serving: Serves 4 to 8 | Prep: | Cook: | Ready in:

Ingredients

- 1 mini log goat cheese (110 grams)
- 3 pieces medium clementines (or other mandarin oranges)
- 1 tablespoon fresh thyme
- 2 tablespoons raw cane sugar
- 1/3 medium-sized hot chili pepper
- 1 teaspoon cornstarch
- 1 tablespoon water
- 3 slices farmer's bread

Direction

- Wash and pat dry the clementines.
- Shred the clementine peel with a shredder or peeler.
- Squeeze the clementines and pass the juice through a sieve.
- Chop the thyme and the hot chili pepper.
- In a small skillet, add clementine juice and peel, thyme, chili pepper, and sugar, and stir well.
- Bring to a boil, reduce heat, and let it shimmer for 5 minutes.
- Dissolve cornstarch into the water, add it to the skillet, and stir. It will take 2 to 3 minutes for the clementine juice to thicken.
- Remove from heat and let cool.
- Cut the bread slices into bites and the goat cheese into slices.
- Arrange each goat cheese slice on a bit of bread and add 1 to 2 tablespoons of the clementine jam on top.

101. Goat Ricotta Crostini With Spicy Onion & Garlic Jam

Serving: Serves a crowd | Prep: | Cook: | Ready in:

Ingredients

- 4 ounces Soft Goat Cheese at room temp
- 4 ounces Ricotta Cheese
- 3 Large Onions
- 10 Garlic Cloves
- 2 tablespoons Sugar
- 1 teaspoon Crushed Red Pepper Flakes
- 2 tablespoons Balsamic Vinegar
- 2 tablespoons Olive Oil
- 1 tablespoon Butter
- 1 - 2 Baquettes
- Bunch Fresh Chives (optional)
- Kosher Salt & Black Pepper to taste

Direction

- Slice onions in half from root to top then thinly slice.
- Heat olive oil and butter in skillet over medium heat, add onion slices and cook, stirring occasionally until well caramelized (20 minutes)
- Add garlic and cook for 3-4 minutes being very careful not to burn it. Season with kosher salt.
- Add sugar, red pepper flakes, and balsamic, partially cover and reduce heat to low. Cook, stirring every few minutes and adding water by a tablespoon or two when the liquid runs low. Cook for approximately 30 minutes, uncovered during the last few to reduce the mixture to a jam like consistency.
- While the onions are cooking, briskly mix the goat cheese and ricotta together. Season with kosher salt and black pepper to taste.
- Cool onion jam to room temp or place in the fridge.

- Right before the party, thinly slice and toast the banquette with a little olive oil and a sprinkling of kosher salt.
- Spread some of the cheese mixture on each crostini and top with a small spoonful of the onion jam, serve.
- If using the chives, cut into 3/4 inch lengths and place two chive batons in a crisscross fashion across the top of the onion jam.

102. Golden Plum Preserves Ice Cream

Serving: Makes about 1 quart of ice cream | Prep: | Cook: | Ready in:

Ingredients

- 2 cups whole milk
- 2 cups heavy cream
- 1 1/3 cups sugar
- 1 vanilla bean
- 10 egg yolks
- 3/4 cup prepared golden plum preserves

Direction

- Combine the milk, cream and sugar in a medium saucepan. Scrape in the seeds from the vanilla bean and add both the seeds and the bean to the saucepan. Bring to a simmer over medium high heat. Remove the saucepan from the heat; cover, and let stand for 30 minutes in order for the vanilla to infuse the cream.
- In a medium bowl, whisk the egg yolks to blend. Slowly, add the cream mixture, being sure to whisk constantly. Return the mixture to a clean saucepan and cook over medium high heat, stirring constantly, being sure to scrape the bottom and sides of the pan, until the mixture reaches a custard-like consistency and is thick enough to coat the back of a spoon.

- Prepare an ice bath in a large bowl. Set a medium sized bowl in the ice bath. Set a fine mesh sieve inside the medium bowl. Strain the custard through the sieve. Let cool completely, stirring occasionally. Once the mixture is cool, refrigerate until cold (preferably overnight).
- Pour the custard into an ice cream maker and freeze according to the manufacturer's instructions. Fold in the preserves and transfer the ice cream to an airtight container. Cover and freeze until the ice cream is hard.

103. Golden Raisin Scones With Apricot, Plum And Rose Petal Jam

Serving: Serves 8 | Prep: | Cook: | Ready in:

Ingredients

- Golden Raisin Scones
- 6 tablespoons cold butter
- 1 3/4 cups self rising flour
- 1 tablespoon very fine sugar
- 1 pinch salt
- 6 tablespoons golden raisins
- 1 egg, beaten lightly
- 2 tablespoons milk
- Apricot, Plum and Rose Petal Jam
- 6 small yellow plums
- 6 small apricots
- 1/2 cup sugar
- a generous sprinkling of dried rose petals
- 1 teaspoon vanilla extract
- 1 tablespoon lemon juice

Direction

- Golden Raisin Scones
- Preheat the oven to 425°F. Grease your baking sheet and line it with parchment paper.
- Sift your flour, sugar and salt into a bowl and rub in the butter with your fingertips until the mix is something like breadcrumbs.

- Mix in the raisins and then add the egg and milk and stir with a wooden spoon until your dough is soft.
- Shape the dough into a ball, press it down onto the cookie sheet and then cut into triangles.
- Brush the top of the scones with milk and then bake for 8-10 minutes, until they're golden brown.
- Apricot, Plum and Rose Petal Jam
- Peel, pit and chop the plums and apricots into small chunks.
- Put the plums and apricots into a pot, add the rose petals, sugar, lemon juice and vanilla extract.
- Bring it to a slight boil and then simmer, stirring occasionally. Cook down for about an hour.
- Fill jar, let cool to room temperature, then screw on lid and place in refrigerator.

| 104. | **Gooey PBJ Brownies** |

Serving: Serves 12 | Prep: | Cook: | Ready in:

Ingredients

- 2 1/3 cups all-purpose flour
- 2 1/3 cups light muscovado sugar
- 2/3 cup cocoa powder
- 1 teaspoon baking powder
- 1/2 teaspoon salt
- 7 1/2 tablespoons smooth peanut butter (thinner is better for this)
- 3/4 cup plus 3 tbsp water
- 3/4 cup plus 3 tbsp vegetable oil
- 2 1/2 tablespoons vanilla extract
- 1 3/4 ounces dark chocolate
- 6 tablespoons raspberry jam
- 3 ounces raspberries
- 2 tablespoons broken peanuts

Direction

- What you'll need: Preheat oven to 320°F | 8 x 12-inch baking pan | Parchment paper | Food processor or electric mixer
- Line the baking pan with the parchment paper, making sure there's a good overhang (this excess will act as handles to remove the brownie from the pan when it comes out of the oven).
- Add the flour, sugar, cocoa, baking powder, and salt to the food processor and whizz to combine. Add 2 tbsps. of the peanut butter, the water, oil, and vanilla. Blend until everything is well mixed (or put everything in a large mixing bowl and use an electric mixer). Break the dark chocolate into squares and add it to the mixture | Blend for another few seconds to mix in the chocolate.
- Use a spatula or metal spoon to empty the brownie mix into the baking pan and smooth it out so it goes all the way to the edges of the pan. Use a spoon to pour and drag swirls of the remaining peanut butter and the jam randomly over the top of the brownie, decorating the whole top with long swirls of jam. Push the raspberries and peanuts randomly into the mixture.
- Put the pan in the hot oven and bake for 45 minutes, until cooked but still squidgy in the middle (try to avoid the outsides drying out and getting too browned; you want to take it out sooner than you think—the middle will still be soft and maybe even wobbly, but it will cool down to a gooey perfection).
- Take the pan out of the oven and let it cool down almost to room temperature. Use the parchment paper to lift the brownie out of the pan and put it on a cutting board (you may need a friend to help with this to ensure it doesn't break in the middle). Cut into brownie portions and serve.

105. Gooseberry Jam

Serving: Makes roughly less than a pint | Prep: | Cook: | Ready in:

Ingredients

- 1 pint gooseberries
- 1.5 cups sugar, or to taste
- 1/2 lemon
- 7 mint leaves

Direction

- Fill a large pot with water. Place a glass jar on a rack in the pot or place a plate in the bottom of the pot---face up--- and submerge the glass jar, the lid and screw top. Bring to a boil and sterilize the jar for about 10 minutes. (The rack and plate prevents the jar from shattering if the bottom of the pot gets too hot.)
- While the water is being heated, wash gooseberries and pinch off stems. Mix berries, sugar and juice of half a lemon in a saucepan. (If you prefer less sugar, adjust the amount.) As the berries cook, mash them. Cook for about 10 minutes. Take off heat and infuse the jam with mint leaves for a few minutes. Then discard the mint.
- Fill the sterilized jar with the jam. Screw the top, but not super tight. Place back in the water bath and bring to a boil. Sterilize for 10 minutes. Remove the jar and let cool before placing it in the refrigerator.
- The jar is sealed if the lid is lowered in the middle. The lid will pop when you open the jar. Enjoy the jam right away, or save for later.

106. Grandma's Best Raspberry Jam

Serving: Makes 30 pints | Prep: 3hours0mins | Cook: 0hours45mins | Ready in:

Ingredients

- 14 pounds raspberries
- 8 boxes of pectin (Grandma uses SureJell)
- 2 cups lemon juice
- 32 ounces corn syrup
- 24 cups sugar

Direction

- Crush or puree raspberries.
- Heat the fruit in a large pot over medium heat until baby-milk warm (Grandma's words). You never bring it to a full boil.
- Add the pectin one box at a time, stirring slowly. This should take about 1/2 hour.
- Next add the sugar, corn syrup, and lemon juice. Stir well.
- Prepare your jars. The jars don't need to be hot but it helps that the lids are hot when you screw on rings.
- After jam thickens, let stand for 3 hours at room temperature. Then store in freezer.

107. Grapefruit Marmalade

Serving: Makes 6 half-pints | Prep: | Cook: | Ready in:

Ingredients

- 2 1/2 pounds grapefruit
- 6 cups water
- 5 cups sugar

Direction

- Place a small plate in your freezer — this is to test the doneness of the marmalade later!
- Use a peeler to peel the zest away from the grapefruit. Slice the zest into very thin strips — as thin as you can!
- Trim a small amount of the top and base away from the grapefruit. Place the grapefruit with this cut side down on the board so it's sitting on a flat surface. Starting at the top, cut the white pith away from the flesh. Continue

working your way around the grapefruit until the pith is gone.

- Cut the fruit into quarters, then slice the quarters into 1/4 inch-thick slices.
- Combine the sliced fruit, sliced zest, water, and sugar in a large pot. Bring the mixture to a simmer over medium heat. Stir until it reaches a simmer, then reduce heat to low.
- Attach a candy thermometer to the side of the pot, and continue to simmer until the mixture thickens and reads 220° F on a thermometer.
- Test the doneness by spooning a small amount of marmalade onto the frozen plate your prepared earlier. The marmalade should gel up very quickly to a set but spreadable consistency.
- Ladle the marmalade into clean, sanitized jars and attach the lids and rings. Process in a boiling water bath canner for 10 minutes. Turn the heat off of the canner, and let the jars sit in the water for 5 minutes more. Remove the jars carefully from the water and allow to cool to room temperature on a wire rack. It's important to not disturb the jars during this process—and it's ideal to leave them at least 10 to 12 hours before moving them. Once they're cooled, check the seals by pressing your finger on the top of the lid. It shouldn't move at all: If it does, the jar hasn't sealed properly. If it doesn't move, you're ready to open or store your jars! Store for up to 1 year in a cool, dark place. Once opened, the marmalade should be refrigerated and it will keep up to 3 months. If you don't want to can your marmalade, just let your marmalade cool to room temperature, then transfer the jars to the refrigerator. They'll keep in there for up to 3 months (the same shelf life as any opened jam/jelly/marmalade).

108.   Green Tomato Jam

Serving: Makes about 2 cups | Prep: | Cook: | Ready in:

Ingredients

- 3   large green tomatoes
- 1/2   medium onion
- 1/4 cup   apple cider vinegar
- 2 cups   water
- 1/2 cup   sugar
- 1 teaspoon   celery salt
- 1/2 teaspoon   crushed red pepper

Direction

- Cut the onion and tomatoes into large chunks and place them in a food processor. Puree to finely chop, leaving only a few large pieces.
- To a skillet, add the tomato puree to the rest of the ingredients. Turn the heat to medium and let the mixture come to a simmer, stirring every few minutes.
- Adjust the heat on the stove up or down so the mixture bubbles but isn't completely boiling. Stir every 10 minutes or so, and let the jam cook for 90 minutes to 2 hours, until the mixture is reduced with almost no liquid left in the pan and the tomatoes are dark golden in color.
- Let the jam cool slightly before transferring it to a container. Serve with bread, crackers, cheese, or any way you'd like. Enjoy!

109.   Grilled Flank Steak Sandwich With Sweet Onion Marmalade And Pear Horseradish Mustard

Serving: Serves 4 | Prep: -2hours0mins | Cook: 0hours15mins | Ready in:

Ingredients

- For the Flank Steak and Sweet Onion Marmalade
- 1   Flank Steak, 1 1/2 to 2 lbs
- 5 tablespoons   Worcestershire sauce
- 5 tablespoons   Ketchup

- 5 teaspoons Brown sugar
- 1/2 cup Red Wine
- 2   Large Vidalia onions, halved and sliced
- 3 tablespoons Canola oil
- 3 tablespoons Sugar
- 3 tablespoons Red Wine Vinegar
- 1/4 cup Water
- For the Pear Horseradish Mustard and Final Assembly
- 4   Ripe Pears, peeled and chopped
- 1/2   cinnamon stick
- 1   bay leaf
- 6   peppercorns
- 1/4 cup Red Wine Vinegar
- 1/2 cup Red Wine
- 1   10 ounce bottle of Grey Poupon Dijon Mustard
- 2 tablespoons Creamy Horseradish
- 4   Ciabatta rolls, split and cut side browned in an oiled pan
- Chopped lettuce for garnish

Direction

- For the Flank Steak and Sweet Onion Marmalade
- Marinate the flank steak in the Worcestershire, ketchup, brown sugar and red wine in the refrigerator for at least 2 hours or overnight.
- While steak is marinating, heat the 3 tablespoons of oil in a large skillet. Add the sliced onions and cook over moderate heat until the onions become soft. Add the sugar and cook stirring for a few minutes. Add the vinegar and turn the heat to low and cook until almost all of the liquid has evaporated. Add the water and simmer, stirring, until mixture is slightly thickened and onions are very tender, about 10 minutes.
- Prepare grill. Remove steak from marinade and grill it over hot coals turning once until it reaches your desired doneness. Medium rare to medium works best. Remove steak and let rest before slicing it into thin strips.
- For the Pear Horseradish Mustard and Final Assembly

- Wrap the cinnamon stick, bay leaf and peppercorns in a small piece of cheesecloth and tie with kitchen string. Add the chopped pears and cheesecloth bag to a large saucepan with the red wine vinegar and wine. Bring the mixture to a boil and reduce heat to simmer. Cook uncovered for about 20 minutes or until the liquid has reduced. Cool slightly and remove cheesecloth bag. Puree the mixture in a food processor. Add the pear puree to a large bowl along with the Dijon mustard and the horseradish. Stir to combine. The pear horseradish mustard keeps, covered and chilled for 1 month.
- Assemble the sandwiches. Spread the split and toasted ciabatta rolls with 1 tablespoon pear horseradish mustard per side (or to taste). Add the sliced steak and the onion marmalade. Garnish with lettuce. Enjoy!

110.   Grilled Fontina With Lingonberry Preserves

Serving: Serves 2 | Prep: | Cook: |Ready in:

Ingredients

- two   1/2 inch slices of a 4 x 4 piece of Danish fontina cheese
- 1 cup all purpose flour
- 2   eggs
- 1/2 cup whole milk
- 1 cup bread crumbs made from dried croissants
- 1/4 cup clarified butter
- lingonberry preserves

Direction

- Set up a breading station by placing the flour in a small casserole, whisk the eggs with the milk and pour them into a small casserole, and finally place the croissant crumbs into a small casserole. Line them up left to right starting with the flour then the egg wash and end with the crumbs.

- Cut each square piece of cheese into two triangles so you have four pieces total now.
- Dredge each piece of cheese into the flour making sure it is dusted with flour in all the crooks and crannies.
- Soak them in the egg was for a few seconds so the wash is absorbed by the flour. Otherwise when you remove it you will see the egg wash magically evaporate in spots leaving only flour.
- Now dredge the cheese into the croissant crumbs.
- Place them back into the egg wash, drain them, and then back into the croissant crumbs. It is really important that you double coat the cheese and make sure they are coated completely. You may even coat them a third time if you aren't sure. If they aren't completely coated they will leak the cheese and you will wind up with a hollow bread shell.
- Leave the cheese setting in the croissant crumbs. Place a 10 inch saute pan over medium high heat. Add the clarified butter.
- The butter is hot enough when you can drop some croissant crumbs in and they hesitate an instant and then start sizzling.
- Fry the cheese until brown and then carefully flip them with a spatula. It helps to tip the pan away from you so the oil runs to one side and then flip the cheese to the no oil side. Be careful not to splash the butter onto your hands.
- Brown the other side and serve with lingonberries on the side.

| 111. | Grown Up Birthday Cake |

Serving: Serves a birthday party | Prep: 0hours20mins | Cook: 0hours30mins | Ready in:

Ingredients

- yellow cake
- 2 1/2 cups AP flour
- 1/2 teaspoon salt
- 2 1/4 teaspoons baking powder
- 2 cups granulated sugar
- 4 eggs
- 1 teaspoon vanilla
- 1 cup white wine
- 1 cup olive oil
- 7 ounces raspberry jam, preferably homemade, but I used Bonne Maman
- bittersweet chocolate buttercream icing
- 1/2 cup unsalted butter, softened
- 1 cup confectioners sugar
- 1/2 cup Dutch processed cocoa
- 1/4 cup whole milk
- 1 teaspoon vanilla

Direction

- Yellow cake
- Preheat oven to 350° F.
- Butter and lightly flour 2 nine-inch cake pans.
- Sift together flour, salt, and baking powder. Set aside.
- In a standing mixer, blend sugar and eggs on med-high for a minute. Slowly mix in vanilla, wine, and oil.
- Gently fold dry ingredients into cake batter until smooth.
- Pour batter into prepared pans and bake for 25-30 minutes until cake tester comes out clean. Cool on wire racks.
- Spread jam on one layer; then top with the other. Frost top layer with icing (recipe below).
- Bittersweet chocolate buttercream icing.
- Blend butter and sugar. Fold in cocoa and gradually add milk until it starts to look like icing. Mix in vanilla.

| 112. | Habanero Corn Cob Jelly |

Serving: Makes 5 half-pint jars | Prep: | Cook: | Ready in:

Ingredients

- 12 corn cobs (cut off kernels and set aside for another use.
- 1 orange bell pepper, seeded and finely minced
- 4 orange habanero peppers, seeded and finely minced
- 2 quarts filtered water
- 3-4 cups sugar
- 2 tablespoons bottled lemon juice
- 1 envelope liquid pectin

Direction

- Place 2 quarts of filtered water into a large pot. Add corn cobs and bring water to a rolling boil. Boil, uncovered, for 30 minutes. Turn off the heat and remove the cobs.
- Strain the liquid through cheesecloth or a fine-mesh strainer into a large measuring cup. Note the amount of liquid, there should be approximately 3 1/2 cups. Measure an equal amount of sugar and set sugar aside.
- Pour the corn liquid back into the pot and add the minced peppers and lemon juice. Bring the mixture to a boil and cook for 10 minutes, stirring occasionally.
- Add the sugar and bring the mixture back to a rolling boil. Stir gently to dissolve sugar. Be careful not to stir too hard as this can create bubbles in your jelly. Add the liquid pectin and stir gently to incorporate. Boil for exactly one minute, then turn off heat.
- Pour jelly into hot, sterilized half-pint canning jars to within 1/4 inch from the top. Wipe the rims with a moist paper towel and place the canning lid and ring on the jar. Tighten the rings only until you meet resistance. Process in a hot water bath for 10 minutes.

---

113.   Habanero Jelly

Serving: Serves 12 - 4oz containers | Prep: | Cook: | Ready in:

Ingredients

- 1 cup finely chopped dried apricots
- 1/2 cup minced red onion
- 1/2 cup minced sweet red pepper
- 1/2 cup minced habanero peppers (wear gloves!)
- 1-1/2 cups cider vinegar
- 6 cups sugar

Direction

- Place all ingredients in a non-reactive deep pot. Bring to a boil, then turn off, cover and let the mixture rest overnight, to develop the flavor.
- Bring the jelly back to a boil that cannot be stirred down, around 230 degrees and boil hard for 10 minutes.
- Turn off the heat, skim as necessary (or add 1/2 tsp of butter to cut the foam) and stir well to distribute the solids.
- Place in jars, cover with lids and rings, then process in a boiling water bath for 10 minutes. From time to time, shake the jars as they cool, to keep the solids from floating to the top.

---

114.   Ham, Cheddar And Marmalade Toasties

Serving: Serves 2 | Prep: | Cook: | Ready in:

Ingredients

- 2 slices good quality ham, such as Black Forest
- 3 oz sharp English cheddar, sliced
- 1 to 2 T orange marmalade
- thinly sliced dill pickles or cornichons
- 2 T softened butter
- 4 slices of sandwich bread (I like hearty whole-grain or sourdough)

Direction

- Heat cast-iron skillet or griddle over medium heat.

- Spread bread slices with a very thin layer of butter and marmalade. Top two of the slices with ham, cheddar, and sliced pickles. Place the remaining bread on top and spread the outside with butter. Place in skillet buttered-side down and butter the other side. Cook on one side until cheese is partially melted and bread is browned, then flip and continue cooking until cheese is thoroughly melted and sandwich is golden and toasty.

115. Heirloom Tomato Marmalade

Serving: Makes about 4 cups | Prep: | Cook: |Ready in:

Ingredients

- 1 cup water
- 2 oranges, thinly sliced
- 1 lemon, thinly sliced
- 6 large heirloom tomatoes (about 4 pounds)
- 4 cups organic cane sugar
- 6 whole cardamom pods
- 3 whole cloves
- 1/2 teaspoon fine sea salt

Direction

- With a sharp knife, make an X on the blossom end of each tomato and cut the stem end out. Place in boiling water for 15 to 20 seconds. (Don't leave any longer or the tomatoes will start to cook) Plunge the tomatoes into a large bowl of ice water to stop the cooking process. Remove the peel. Cut in half and squeeze out the seeds.
- In a deep pot, cook water, oranges and lemons over medium heat until fruit is tender (15 0 20 minutes. Add the peeled tomatoes with the sugar, whole cardamom and cloves. Stir until sugar dissolves. Bring to a rolling boil, then lower the heat to a simmer and cook for 1 1/2 to 2 hours, or until the tomatoes are falling apart and beginning to thicken. (This may take

more time, depending upon the water content of the tomatoes.) Watch carefully to avoid scorching. Stir often.
- Remove from heat when mixture is the consistency of thick jam. Discard cardamom and cloves. Store in airtight jars, refrigerated, for two to three weeks.

116. Herbed Biscuit Bites With Ricotta Cream And Onion Jam

Serving: Makes about 40 1-inch bites | Prep: | Cook: | Ready in:

Ingredients

- 1 cup fresh ricotta
- 4 tablespoons heavy cream
- 1 cup flour
- 2 ounces finely grated Parmigiano Reggiano (I use a microplane grater)
- 1 1/2 teaspoons fresh cracked black pepper
- 1/2 teaspoon sea salt or kosher salt
- 1 teaspoon fresh rosemary
- 4 tablespoons unsalted butter, room temperature, cut into cubes
- 4 tablespoons white wine, or water
- 1 13 oz. jar onion jam (I use Stonewall Kitchen's Roasted Garlic and Onion Jam - it's the bomb)

Direction

- Preheat oven to 350 degrees F. Line a large sheet pan with parchment paper.
- FOR THE RICOTTA CREAM: In a mini food processor, whiz together the ricotta and the heavy cream until very smooth. Remove to a bowl and refrigerate.
- In the bowl of a food processor, combine the flour, salt, herbs, spices and cheese. Process for 30 seconds.
- Scatter the butter chunks over the flour and pulse the machine until mixture looks sandy.

- Drizzle the wine over the flour mixture, one tablespoon at a time, and pulse the machine a few times, until the dough begins to come together.
- Turn dough out onto a work surface and gather into a ball. Pat into a 3/8 inch-thick circle (or just under a half-inch.) Using a one-inch round biscuit cutter, cut rounds out and place on parchment-lined sheet pan.
- Bake biscuits for 15 minutes, or until bottoms begin to brown. Remove tray from oven and flip all the biscuits over. Return tray to oven and bake for an additional 5 or so minutes.
- Serve biscuits warm or cool, topped with a dollop of ricotta cream and onion jam. Also looks pretty with one rosemary needle resting on top.

117. Herbed Goat Cheese And Jam Crostini

Serving: Serves 8 | Prep: | Cook: |Ready in:

Ingredients

- 1 baguette loaf cut into thin slices(about 12 to 16)
- 1/4 cup olive oil
- 1 log of herbed goat cheese
- 1 cup Apricot and Rosemary Jam(I used Jam Lab's Apricot and Rosemary Jam)

Direction

- Cut the baguette into thin slices that are bite size. Brush olive oil on either side of each slice and grill them for about couple minutes each side, to get nice grill marks.
- Let them cool and crisp up. Add about 1 teaspoon of the herbed Goat Cheese on each slice.
- Smear each slice + Herbed Goat Cheese with a teaspoon of the Apricot and Rosemary Jam. Plate it beautifully with some apricots and Rosemary, Voila it is ready to eat! :-)

118. Hibiscus Pear Preserves

Serving: Makes 5 quarts | Prep: | Cook: |Ready in:

Ingredients

- 15 pears (about 5 pounds)
- 1 1/4 cups honey
- 8 3/4 cups water
- 5 lemons, juiced (or 3/4 cup plus 3 TBSP bottled lemon juice)
- 1 tablespoon dried hibiscus flowers

Direction

- Prepare your boiling water bath with 5 quart jars and lids.
- In a large pot, combine the honey, water and hibiscus flowers. I normally make a pouch for the hibiscus out of a coffee filter so I don't have to strain the liquid later. Bring to a boil and then let simmer at least 5 minutes while you prepare the pears.
- Peel, core and chop the pears.
- Remove the hibiscus flowers from the honey water mixture. Add the pears to the pot. Simmer for 3 minutes.
- Funnel the pears into the prepared jars and top with honey water mixture leaving 1/2 inch headspace. Add lids and rings and process in hot water bath for 15 minutes (10 if using pint jars).

119. Homemade Cranberry Jelly, In A Can

Serving: Makes 1 can | Prep: | Cook: |Ready in:

Ingredients

- 2 1/2 cups cranberries

- 1 1/2 teaspoons dry pectin (optional, but recommended)
- 1/4 teaspoon cinnamon (optional)
- 1/8 teaspoon nutmeg (optional)
- 1 pinch cloves (optional)
- 1 1/2 cups sugar
- 2/3 cup apple cider
- juice of 1/2 a lemon

Direction

- Place cranberries in a medium saucepan. Mix pectin and spices into the sugar, then add the sugar mixture to the cranberries and stir to combine. Add the cider and lemon juice.
- Cook over medium-high heat, stirring regularly. Once the cranberries have burst and the sauce has thickened, remove the pan from the heat. (If the sauce seems too thick, just add a splash of water or cider to thin it out.)
- Run the sauce through a fine sieve or food mill until all that's left are the bits of seeds and skins. Pour the strained sauce into an empty can. (It's best to use a can that's BPA-free and once held a neutral-tasting food, to avoid imparting any unwanted flavors.) Cover can with foil or plastic wrap and let set in the fridge, for at least 12 hours.
- When it's time to serve, run a butter knife around the sides of the jelly. If it still doesn't seem to want to slide out, crack open the bottom of the can with a can opener. (No need to try to take the bottom off—just a little bit of air should take care of the vacuum and let the jelly slide out easily.)

120.   Homemade Kaya (Coconut Jam)

Serving: Makes 1 cup (240 milliliters) | Prep: 0hours10mins | Cook: 0hours40mins | Ready in:

Ingredients

- 4 large egg yolks

- 200 milliliters (3/4 cup plus 2 tablespoons) full-fat coconut milk
- 30 grams (3 tablespoons) light brown palm sugar, finely chopped if crystallized*
- 65 grams (5 tablespoons) granulated sugar
- 3 fresh pandan leaves (you can find them in Asian stores; skip if you can't find them)
- 1 pinch fine sea salt
- (all ingredients should be at room temperature)

Direction

- Beat egg yolks with a fork until the yolks are combined (but don't beat them so much that they get foamy).
- Heat coconut milk together with the chopped palm sugar, granulated sugar, pandan leaves, and salt in a double boiler or over a bain-marie. I always use a medium-size pot, filled with about 1 inch of gently simmering water, and place a heat-proof metal mixing bowl (e.g. stainless steel) over the pot.
- Stir constantly with a rubber spatula as the coconut milk gets hotter. When the mixture comes to a boil (or at least nearly), remove the bain-marie (including the water pot) from the heat.
- With a ladle, gradually (!) pour half of the hot coconut milk mixture (about 1/2 cup) into the egg yolks while constantly stirring the yolks. It is very important to do this slowly and while stirring, otherwise the yolks curdle easily. Also, if you remove the upper bowl from the bain-marie to pour the mixture, be careful not to get burnt, because the steam is very hot. That's why I use a ladle.
- Put the bain-marie with the remaining coconut milk back on the stove and gradually add the egg-milk mixture while stirring.
- Stir until the mixture thickens, about 10 to 20 minutes, depending on the heat. Don't cook it over high heat, as the yolks will curdle. The final texture should be custard-like, similar to that of lemon curd. The kaya will still get thicker once it cools.

- Remove the pandan leaves and pour the kaya into clean jars. If you see any lumps or curdled egg, press the curd through a strainer first.
- Keep coconut jam refrigerated and use within 1 week.
- *Note: If you can't find light brown palm sugar, you can use 30 grams (3 tablespoons) dark brown palm sugar, or regular light/dark brown sugar instead.

---

121.   Homemade Strawberry Jelly

Serving: Serves 4 | Prep: 24hours15mins | Cook: 0hours25mins |Ready in:

Ingredients

- 5 cups strawberries
- 5 cups granulated sugar
- 1/4 cup lemon juice
- 5 tablespoons pectin (optional)

Direction

- Easy & delicious homemade strawberry jelly recipe for canning & preserving. Goes perfectly with Hanukkah Sufganiyot, Oznei Haman or a slice of bread.
- On a separate pan, heat the center lids to a simmer as well
- Mash the strawberries using a food masher (steel recommended) and add them to a large pot
- Pour lemon juice, sugar and pectin to the pot and start whisking till they dissolve in the mixture
- Boil the mixture for around 1 minute while stirring.
- Turn off the heat and skim off the appearing foam with a spoon
- Start filling the mason jars with jam one at a time with a wide-mouth funnel. Clean the residue from the jar's exterior.

- Place the center lids on the jars Tip: Make sure to leave a little space at the top of the jar
- Fill the canning pot with water, and boil for 10 minutes
- Turn off the heat, and let the jars cool off for a few minutes
- Using a jar lifter, remove the jars from the hot water and keep them out for 24 hours
- After 24 hours, check the lids for seal. If sealed properly, store the jars in a pantry or kitchen cabinet & Enjoy!

---

122.   Homemade Apricot Jam The French Way

Serving: Makes 4 medium jars | Prep: | Cook: |Ready in:

Ingredients

- 2 pounds fresh apricots (one kg)
- 4 cups granulated sugar (800 gr)

Direction

- Wash the apricots, cut them in half and take away the pits, then cut each half one more time.
- In a large pot, place the apricots along with the sugar. Place on medium heat until it starts to boil. During that time, mix gently so that the sugar does not stick to the bottom of the pot.
- Bring down the heat to low and let it simmer for about 35 minutes. Mix very gently about three times during the process. Do not mix too much or the jam may come out too liquid and the fruit could disintegrate.
- You know the jam is done when after placing a drop on a plate and tilting the plate, the jam does not run. So once it is done, immediately place the jam in tightly closed prepared glass containers (previously rinsed with boiling water).
- Let it cool down then place in the fridge. The jam is ready 24 hours later.

123. Honey Sweetened White Peach Jam With Lemon

Serving: Makes 2 half pints | Prep: | Cook: |Ready in:

Ingredients

- 2 pounds white peaches
- 8 ounces honey
- 1 lemon

Direction

- Prepare a small boiling water bath canner and 2 half pint jars. Place lids in a small saucepan and bring to a bare simmer.
- Pit, peel and chop peaches. Combine with honey in a small bowl and let sit until the honey dissolves into the fruit.
- Using a vegetable peeler, remove the zest from the lemon in strips. Stack zest pieces on a cutting board and julienne so that you end up with little slivers of lemon zest that resemble confetti. Add zest to peaches. Cut lemon in half and juice it into small bowl. Measure out three tablespoons and add to the fruit.
- Scrape the peaches, honey, and lemon zest and juice into a 12-inch stainless steel skillet and place over high heat. Cook, stirring regularly, until the peaches soften, the liquid reduces and the whole mixture becomes quite thick and spreadable, about 10 to 12 minutes
- If you like, during cooking, you can use a potato masher to help break down the peach pieces into more manageable sized bits.
- The jam is done when you can pull a spoon or spatula through it and jam doesn't immediately rush in to fill the space you've cleared. It will also become much splashier at the end of cooking.
- Remove pan from heat. Funnel jam into prepared jars. Wipe rims, apply lids and rings, and process in a boiling water bath canner for ten minutes.
- When time is up, remove jars from canner and let them cool on a folded kitchen towel. When jars are cool enough to handle, remove rings and test seals by grasping the edges of the ring and lifting the jar an inch or so off the countertop. If the lid holds fast, your seal is good. Sealed jars can be stored in a cool, dark place for up to one year.
- Alternately, if you prefer to skip the boiling water bath process, the jam can simply be funneled into a jar after cooking and refrigerated once cool. It will keep for 2-3 weeks in the refrigerator.

124. Hot Pepper Jelly Grilled Cheese

Serving: Serves 2 | Prep: | Cook: |Ready in:

Ingredients

- 1 packet Paramount Pita Squares
- 2 tablespoons hot pepper jelly
- 6 pieces crispy bacon
- 4 pieces cheese (cheddar, monterey or a mix)
- 2 tablespoons butter

Direction

- With a knife cut the edge of the pita and carefully open 2 pitas.
- Add a tablespoon of jelly, in a thin layer, to one half of each pita.
- Chop the bacon and add half to each sandwich.
- Add half the cheese to each sandwich, top with the other half of the pita.
- Add some of the butter to a pan and grill each side of the pita until golden brown. Enjoy with a cup of Roasted Red Pepper Soup.

125.   Hot And Sweet Pepper Funk Jam

Serving: Makes about a dozen or so jars | Prep: | Cook: | Ready in:

Ingredients

- 1   large red bell pepper, finely chopped
- 4 cups Different colored hot and sweet peppers (yellow, red, green, orange) Put peppers of the same color in the food processor together, then combine
- 4 cups white wine vinegar
- 3.5 packets Sure jel pectin
- 9 cups sugar
- 2 cups dried apricots (cut in quarters with a scissor)
- 1   large red onion, finely diced

Direction

- Heat vinegar in a heat-proof container in the microwave for 4 minutes. Pour over sliced apricots and soak until they are room temperature.
- Bring vinegar and apricots to a boil in a large jam pot (or Dutch oven - say 6 quarts).
- Add chopped peppers and onion to the vinegar/apricot mixture.
- Stir in sure jel pectin and return to a boil.
- Add sugar slowly, stirring constantly.
- Return to a boil and boil hard 1 minute, until jam sheets off the spoon.
- Pour into clean, sterilized jars and process 10 minutes in a boiling water bath. Keep until it's eaten - not long.

126.   Instant Pot Strawberry Jam

Serving: Makes about 3 cups | Prep: 0hours20mins | Cook: 0hours40mins | Ready in:

Ingredients

- 4 cups quartered fresh strawberries
- 2 1/2 cups sugar
- 1/4 cup lemon juice

Direction

- Combine strawberries, sugar, and lemon juice in the Instant Pot. Select SAUTÉ and adjust to NORMAL. Bring mixture to a full boil for about 8 minutes, stirring frequently. Press CANCEL. Secure the lid on the pot. Close the pressure-release valve.
- Select MANUAL and cook at high pressure for 8 minutes. When cooking is complete, use a natural release to depressurize. Press CANCEL. Remove the lid. Mash berries with a potato masher. Select SAUTÉ and adjust to NORMAL. Bring mixture to a full boil. Boil for 5 minutes or until mixture reaches gel stage (220°F) stirring frequently. Press CANCEL.
- Ladle into half-pint glass jars. Seal jars. Store up to 3 weeks in the refrigerator.

127.   Jam Cake With Black Walnuts

Serving: Serves 20 | Prep: | Cook: | Ready in:

Ingredients

- 2 cups sugar
- 2/3 cup lard
- 2 eggs
- 2 cups buttermilk
- 3 cups all-purpose flour
- 1 1/2 teaspoons cloves
- 1 1/2 teaspoons allspice
- 2 teaspoons cinnamon
- Pinch salt
- 1 teaspoon vanilla
- 2 tablespoons cocoa
- 2 teaspoons soda
- 3/4 cup jam
- 3/4 cup black walnuts

Direction

- Heat oven to 350 degrees.
- Cream sugar and lard.
- Add eggs.
- Beat well.
- Sift flour with cloves, allspice, salt, soda, cinnamon and cocoa. Add to sugar mixture alternately with buttermilk.
- Add jam and nuts.
- Makes three layers. Bake 25 minutes or until toothpick test shows it's done.

128.	Jam Tart (crostata) Dolci (dessert)

Serving: Serves 8 | Prep: | Cook: |Ready in:

Ingredients

- 2 recipes pasta frolla (short crust pastry) substituting 80 gms ground hazelnuts for 50 gms of cornstarch and 30 gms of flour of the double recipe
- 320 grams jam (apricot used here)

Direction

- Preheat the oven to 175C. Grease a pastry ring.
- Roll out half of the pastry.
- Line the pastry ring. Place the pastry ring on an ungreased parchment paper lined cookie sheet. Use a pastry scraper to help roll the dough around the rolling pin and then unroll into ring mould. Press the pastry into the mould, ensuring that the pastry fits into the bottom right corner of the tin so that when it cooks it doesn't slide downwards. Use your fingers to push the dough down into the ring and use a thumb to gently press it against the side ensuring that the dough is an even thickness. Use the rolling pin to roll across the top of the tin to remove excess pastry that extends beyond the top of the tart tin. Use a knife to cut any excess dough from the top of the tart using small cutting motions no larger than 3 cm at a time. Place the tin in the refrigerator for 10 minutes as this will help it to keep its shape when you bake it. Prick the bottom of the tart all around to ensure it doesn't balloon while baking. If using a ring mould, cut the excess paper around the mould.
- Use an offset spatula to spread the jam around the bottom of the tart.
- Roll out the remaining half of the pastry and cut it into strips.
- Place the strips across the tart, weaving them in and out of each other.
- Press the ends into the crust of the tart.
- Bake for 15-20 minutes or until evenly dark golden brown. Remove from the oven. Slide the pastry off the baking tray onto a wire cooling rack, slide out the paper.

129.	Jam Filled Cheese Turnovers

Serving: Serves makes 12 to 15 turnovers | Prep: | Cook: |Ready in:

Ingredients

- 1/2 cup unsalted butter, at cool room temperature (1 stick)
- 2 tablespoons heavy cream
- 1 cup shredded sharp Cheddar cheese
- 1 pinch salt
- 1 cup all-purpose flour
- Thick fruit jam, for the filling

Direction

- Cut the butter into 8 pieces and place, along with the cheese and cream, in the bowl of a food processor. Pulse briefly to blend. Add the flour and a pinch of salt to the work bowl. Pulse again until the mixture comes together to form a soft dough. Remove the dough from the processor and shape into a slightly flattened disc. Wrap in plastic wrap and refrigerate for at least an hour.

- When ready to bake, preheat the oven to 375°F, with the rack in the center position. Line a baking sheet with parchment paper. On a lightly floured surface, roll the dough out to a thickness a little less than ¼-inch. Cut circles with a 3½ or 4-inch cutter and place on the prepared sheet. Gather the dough scraps together gently and continue to roll and cut circles of the pastry. If the dough starts to soften, replace it in the refrigerator for a few minutes.

- Place a scant teaspoonful of jam in the middle of each dough circle and moisten the edges with a little water. Fold the dough over to form a half-round shape, and seal the edges with the tines of a fork. Make a couple of steam vents with the fork in the top of each pastry turnover.

- Place in the preheated oven and bake, for 15 to 20 minutes, or until set and handsomely golden in color. Allow to cool before enjoying as the jam filling will be very hot!

---

130.   Jam Filled Scones

Serving: Makes 8 | Prep: | Cook: |Ready in:

Ingredients

- 2-1/2 cups all-purpose flour
- 3 tablespoons sugar
- 1 tablespoon baking powder
- 3/4 teaspoon salt
- 1/2 cup unsalted butter, cold and chopped
- 3/4 cup heavy whipping cream, cold, plus more for the tops of the scones
- 1 large egg
- 1 teaspoon vanilla extract
- 6 tablespoons jam of your choice
- 3 tablespoons sparkling sugar, id desired

Direction

- Preheat the oven to 375 degrees. In a large bowl, combine the flour, sugar, baking powder, and salt. Use a pastry cutter or the back of two forks to cut the butter into the dry ingredients until pea-sized clumps are present throughout and the butter is well integrated. In a separate bowl, whisk the whipping cream, egg, and vanilla together. Pour the liquid ingredients into the dry ingredients and stir together until a shaggy dough forms. Dump the mixture out onto the counter and knead together just until a dry dough forms. You can add an additional 1-2 tablespoons of cream if your dough won't come together at all. Working quickly, divide the dough in two and pat each half into flat 8" dough rounds (see notes). Place one round of dough on a baking sheet and spread the jam evenly over top of it, leaving a ¾' border around the perimeter of the dough. Place the second round on top and pinch the edges together to seal the jam inside. Brush the scones with a thin layer of cream and sprinkle with coarse sugar, if desired. Bake in the preheated oven for 25-30 minutes, or until the tops and sides are golden brown. Allow to cool slightly before cutting to let the jam set. Cut into 8 equal slices and serve warm.

- Notes: To create two rounds of dough the same size, I line an 8" cake pan with plastic wrap and pat each half of dough into the bottom to create perfect circles. This isn't necessary but will help to keep your scones uniform. I try to choose a jam that isn't too sweet so that the scones aren't too sweet. If your jam is really sweet you can add the juice of half of a lemon to it to balance the flavor. This is entirely your choice!

---

131.   John DeBary's Preserves Sour

Serving: Makes 1 drink | Prep: 0hours1mins | Cook: 0hours0mins |Ready in:

Ingredients

- 2 ounces Irish whiskey
- 1/2 ounce fresh lemon juice
- 2 teaspoons peach preserves

Direction

- In a shaking tin, combine the drink ingredients. Add ice and shake for 15 seconds. Fine-strain into a chilled cocktail glass.

---

132. Katy's Cranberry And Jam Tart

Serving: Serves 8 | Prep: | Cook: | Ready in:

Ingredients

- 12 ounces fresh or thawed frozen cranberries
- 1 3/4 cups Sugar
- 1/2 cup apple juice
- 2 tablespoons lemon juice
- 3/4 cup jam (we love raspberry)
- 1 cup butter - room temp
- 2 large egg yolks
- 2 1/3 cakes flour
- 1 teaspoon baking powder
- 1/4 teaspoon salt

Direction

- Prep & cook time, including time to chill is 2 1/2 hours.
- You can make the jam mixture and the dough up to 3 days ahead; cover and chill separately.
- Sort, rinse and drain cranberries.
- Place berries in a 3 -4 qt sauce pan, over medium heat, stir berries with 1 cup sugar, apple juice and lemon juice until berries have broken down, released their juice & mixture is bubbly, about 10-15 minutes; stir in jam & cook for 1 more minute. Transfer to a bowl, cover and chill until cold.

- With a mixer beat butter with 3/4 cup sugar until smooth; beat in egg yolks, stir in flour, baking powder and salt until well blended. Divide dough into 2 slightly unequal portions. Wrap the larger portion in plastic and flatten into a rectangular shape. Press the smaller portion over bottom and up the side of a 9 inch fluted tart pan with removable rim. Chill wrapped dough and tart shell until firm.
- Spoon jam mixture into tart shell and spread level.
- Unwrap the second portion of dough; place on lightly floured surface. With lightly floured rolling pin roll out dough into a shape that is about 8 by 10 inches. With a pizza or fluted cutter cut dough into 8 1" by 10" strips. Arrange four strips over filling about 1 inch apart. Place remaining strips over tart at a 45 degree angle to the first set. Trim edges flush with the dough in the pan. Sprinkle top of tart lightly with sugar.
- Place the tart on a baking sheet and bake on the lower rack at 350 degrees, rotating 1/2 through baking time until top is golden; 35 to 40 minutes. Serve warm or at room temp.

---

133. Kumquat Marmalade With Champagne And Figs

Serving: Makes approx. 1 pint | Prep: | Cook: | Ready in:

Ingredients

- 3 1/2 cups champagne
- 1/2 cup honey
- 2 sticks cinnamon
- 4 cardamom pods
- approx. 40 kumquats
- approx. 20 dried figs
- 1/2 cup raisins
- 1 teaspoon vanilla extract
- 1 tablespoon rose water-optional

Direction

- In a medium-sized pot on the stove, bring the champagne and honey to a boil. Reduce the heat to a simmer, and add the cinnamon sticks and the cardamom pods.
- Roughly chop the kumquats and remove as many seeds as possible. You'll be able to remove more later, but if a few remain, they won't harm you. Add to the champagne and honey. Add the dried fruits and allow to simmer for about 30 minutes, or until the kumquats and dried fruits are very tender and the mixture is fairly thick. Remove and discard any visible remaining kumquat seeds, as well as the cinnamon sticks.
- Turn off the heat and allow the marmalade to cool. Process in a high speed blender or food processor to break up any large chucks of fruit and to pulverize the cardamom. Return to the pot and add the vanilla and optional rose water. Mix well, and then spoon into glass jar(s). Store in the refrigerator; it will keep for a week or two.

134. Kumquat Smoothie Jam

Serving: Makes a portion of jam | Prep: | Cook: |Ready in:

Ingredients

- 250g kumquats
- 1/2 – 1 cup sugar
- 1/2 teaspoon finely minced/grated ginger
- 2 cups water
- Crushed seeds of 4-6 cardamom pods

Direction

- In a spice/coffee grinder, blend the cardamom seeds with some sugar, to crush the seeds and maximize the flavour extracted.
- Wash the kumquats and remove the stalk/stalk bed. Slice the kumquats in half length-ways then separate the skin from the central fruit flesh and seeds being careful not to discard anything of the membrane and seeds - set them aside in a small bowl as they're pectin-rich, perfect for providing a great set.
- Put the kumquat skins and the water in a large non-reactive bowl. Then put the membrane and seeds in a cheesecloth spice bag or in a makeshift cheesecloth bag – add to the skins in water. Cover and let stand for about 12 hours or overnight.
- After the 'rest', gently squeeze the cheesecloth into the bowl with the skins and water, to release the translucent, thick pectin-rich juices. Repeat the squeeze until most of the juices have been extracted, then discard the membrane and seeds.
- Put the kumquat mixture in a blender or food processor and pulse a few times, till the skin is chopped up and you get a cloudy, orange mixture.
- Pour the fruit mixture into a heavy-bottomed, medium sized saucepan and add the cardamom sugar and the ginger, stirring to dissolve it.
- Bring to a boil on high heat, 1 – 2 minutes and then turn down heat to a simmer to prevent excessive caramelisation and preserve the colour. Allow it to simmer, checking for 'readiness' by visual inspection – skim off any foam, and gently stir occasionally. From the world of jam gelling, it is ready when the temperatures reach about 100 degrees C (or 215-220 degrees F) and a teaspoon of mixture dropped onto a cold plate gels.
- Remove the pan from the heat once it has set and let stand for about 5 minutes. Then use as you want or can, according to your favourite canning recipe.

135. Late Season Cherry Tomato And Vanilla Jam

Serving: Makes 1 to 1/2 cups | Prep: | Cook: |Ready in:

Ingredients

- 2 pints cherry tomatoes, stemmed and cleaned
- 1/2 cup sugar, preferably turbinado or evaporated cane juice
- 1/2 inch piece of vanilla bean split open lengthwise

Direction

- In a non-reactive saucepan, cook all the ingredients over medium-high heat until the tomatoes begin to break down and bubble.
- Continue to simmer over low heat, stirring often, until the tomatoes have lost most of their water and the jam begins to thicken. It should take 30-40 minutes, and the jam will continue to thicken as it cools.
- Let the jam cool to room temperature. Transfer into containers to freeze (I use 4-ounce plastic storage containers). To help prevent freezer burn (which I have not had a problem with), lightly press a small piece of plastic wrap onto the surface of the jam before putting on the container lid. Store in the freezer for 4-6 months.

---

136.   Lemon Earl Grey Jam

Serving: Makes 1 jam jar | Prep: | Cook: | Ready in:

Ingredients

- 2 lemons (organic preferred, as you will use the skin)
- 1 1/4 cups granulated sugar
- 1/2 tablespoon butter
- 1 bag of Earl Grey tea
- 2 tablespoons pectin (the gel form; if using powder use only 1 Tbs)

Direction

- Bring water to a boil in a small saucepan and cook one whole lemon for 10-15 seconds (this softens the skin); remove with a slotted spoon.

Slice the lemon in half, reserving one half for juicing. Juice the reserved half of your quick cooked lemon and combine with juice of one additional (uncooked) lemon, to roughly equal 1/2 cup.

- Slice the stem end off of the other half of the cooked lemon half and discard. Cut remaining fruit into segments - include the skin. Grab and discard any large seeds. Using a small food processor, puree the segmented lemon, skin and all.
- Combine processed lemon, reserved lemon juice, and sugar in a small saucepan and bring to a bubble, stirring constantly. When the mixture has reached the boil, insert your bag of Earl Grey tea (I wrap the rescue string around the wooden spoon I'm stirring with to keep track of it). Cook for 5 minutes, adding the butter about halfway through, and keep stirring constantly! It smells great so you won't mind standing by. After 5 minutes, remove the tea bag, remove from the heat, and stir in the pectin.
- Let cool and serve, over cream scones or other baked goods, or place in sterilized canning jar to store. Enjoy!

---

137.   Lemon Financiers With Blackberry Jam

Serving: Makes 16 - 24 financiers (depending of size of the mold) | Prep: | Cook: | Ready in:

Ingredients

- Lemon Financiers
- 1/3 cup rice flour
- 1/3 cup almond flour
- 3/4 cup confectioners sugar
- 3 egg whites
- 4 ounces butter, cut into cubes
- 1/2 teaspoon vanilla extract
- Zest of one lemon
- Blackberry Jam

- 1 pint blackberries
- Zest and juice of one lemon
- 3   thyme spirgs
- 1/4 cup honey

Direction

- Lemon Financiers
- Preheat oven to 340. Sift together rice flour, almond flour, and confectioner's sugar. Place into a large bowl. Make a well in the center. Froth egg whites with a whisk and place in the center of the well.
- Heat a small pan over high heat. Add butter and turn into beurre noisette. Allow the butter to melt and come to a boil. Constantly move the pan around until the milk solids have turned a golden brown color. Remove from heat and cool slightly before adding to the center of the well. Add vanilla extract and lemon zest. Whisk dough together to form a smooth paste.
- Butter a rectangular or boat shaped tartlet mold (I used a round one, so whatever you have around the house is fine.) Place on a baking sheet. Fill tart molds about 3/4 of the way full, using a portion scoop or a tablespoon.
- Place in oven and bake for 15 to 20 minutes or until the paste has set. Remove from mold and let cool on a wire rack.
- Once financiers have cooled, place jam (recipe to follow) in a piping bag using the smallest tip. Place tip into bottom of financier and pipe a small amount of jam into each cake, about 1/2 teaspoon. Garnish cakes with confectioner's sugar. Cakes are best eaten the day of.
- Blackberry Jam
- Place all ingredients in a small saucepan and cook over low heat for 20 to 25 minutes or until the blackberries have softened and the juice has thickened.
- Remove thyme sprigs and place the jam in a food processor or blend with an immersion blender until smooth. Place in the refrigerator and cool until ready to use.

138.   Lemon Marmalade

Serving: Makes about 5, 16-ounce jars | Prep: | Cook: | Ready in:

Ingredients

- 4 pounds lemons
- 8 1/2 cups sugar
- 1/4 cup fresh lemon juice

Direction

- Day 1: Thoroughly wash the lemons and slice them into 8 wedges each, being sure to remove any seeds. Store half the lemon wedges in an airtight container and place in the refrigerator until Day 2. In a large, nonreactive saucepan, cover the other half of the lemon wedges with 8 cups of water; let stand at room temperature overnight.
- Day 2: Bring the lemon wedges to a boil. Simmer them over medium heat, stirring every 30 minutes, until the liquid is reduced by half, about 2 and 1/2 hours. Pour the lemon wedges into a fine mesh sieve set over a large heatproof bowl. Let cool completely. Wrap both the sieve and the bowl in plastic wrap and let drain overnight at room temperature. Also on day 2, slice the remaining half of lemon wedges very thin crosswise. In a large nonreactive saucepan, cover the lemon slices with about 8 cups of water and bring to a boil. Simmer over medium heat for about 5 minutes, stirring occasionally. Drain the lemon slices in a fine strainer; discard the cooking liquid. Return the lemon slices to the saucepan and cover with 4 cups of water. Bring to a boil and simmer over medium heat, stirring occasionally, until the liquid is slightly reduced and the lemon slices are tender, about 45 minutes. Let stand at room temperature overnight.

- Day 3: Add the strained lemon-wedge liquid to the slices in the saucepan. Stir in the sugar and the fresh lemon juice and bring to a boil. Simmer over moderate heat until the marmalade darkens (do not stir), about 30 minutes. Skim off any foam as needed. Spoon 1 tablespoon of the marmalade onto a chilled plate and refrigerate until room temperature, about 3 minutes. The marmalade is ready when it thickens like jelly and a spoon leaves a trail when dragged through it. If the marmalade is not yet complete, continue simmering and testing every 10 minutes until it passes the test. Spoon the marmalade into sterilized canning jars, leaving about 1/4 inch of space at the top of each jar. Tightly screw on the lids. Using canning tongs, lower the jars into a large pot of boiling water and boil for 15 minutes. Remove the jars using the tongs and let stand until the lids seal. Store the jars in a cool, dark place for up to 6 months.

139.　　　Lettuce Jam

Serving: Makes 1 1/2 cups (360 ml) | Prep: 0hours0mins | Cook: 0hours0mins | Ready in:

Ingredients

- 6 tablespoons (90 ml) neutral vegetable oil
- 10 1/2 ounces (300 g) assorted lettuces (about 1 packed heaping quart), including outer leaves and damaged leaves
- 2 large shallots, sliced into 3/4-inch (6-mm) pieces
- 1 1/2 tablespoons capers
- 8 cornichons
- 3 tablespoons Dijon mustard
- Fine sea salt

Direction

- Place a large pan over high heat. When very hot, add 4 tablespoons (60 ml) of the oil. When the oil shimmers, add the lettuce. Let the lettuce cook, undisturbed, until the moisture has evaporated, about 2 minutes, then stir to redistribute. Do not burn the lettuce, but cook through and make sure the leaves become dry. This should take 3 to 4 minutes total. The greens will absorb the oil. Using a plastic spatula, scrape the lettuce onto a plate and chill in the refrigerator until very cold.
- While the lettuce are cooling, return the large pan to medium-high heat and add the remaining 2 tablespoons of oil. Add the shallots and cook until translucent, 2 to 3 minutes. Scrape onto the same plate as the lettuce and cool both completely.
- Combine the capers, cornichons, and mustard in a food processor and pulse to chop, leaving the mixture chunky. Add the greens and process until a creamy paste or dip consistency forms. Season to taste with salt. Store in an airtight container in the refrigerator for 2 to 3 days.
- Other greens that work in this recipe: mixed chicories, head lettuce.

140.　　　Lightly Spiced Plum Jam

Serving: Makes three 1/2 pints and one 1/4 pint | Prep: | Cook: | Ready in:

Ingredients

- 6 cups chopped plums (unpeeled)
- 2¼ cups unrefined, granulated sugar
- 1-2 cinnamon sticks
- 10 allspice berries, gently cracked
- grated zest of 1 orange
- juice of ½ orange

Direction

- Set up your canning pot, get the water heating and the jars sterilizing. Mix the plums and sugar in a non-reactive bowl and let sit 5-10 minutes.

- In a heavy-bottomed pot set over medium heat, put the fruit-sugar mixture. Stir consistently until the sugar has melted completely, about 5 minutes. Add in the remaining ingredients and stir to combine. Turn up the heat to medium-high, and stir/cook until the fruit starts falling apart and you've got a solid amount of juice surrounding it. You want to have it at a good boil!
- The jam should start thickening after 15 minutes, and at about 20 minutes, either test the temperature (you're looking for 217-218) or remove the plate from the freezer and dab about 1/4 tsp on it. If the jam firms up quickly, you're ready to can. If not, cook/stir for a couple more minutes.
- When your jam is done, ladle it carefully into your jars, slide a thin knife or chopstick or the like along the inside edges of the jar to let any air bubbles in the jam escape, screw on the lids and bands and process for 12-15 minutes. Then, remove the jars from your waterbath and set them aside to cool on a cooling rack covered with a dishtowel (to prevent slippage).

141.   Love Letter Jam

Serving: Makes 2½ pints | Prep: | Cook: | Ready in:

Ingredients

- To deal with the rose petals and make the rose syrup
- 3 ounces fresh red rose petals (do not use ones that have been sprayed with insecticide or the like); this is roughly 12 or 13 roses, headed.
- 3 tablespoons freshly squeezed Meyer lemon (or regular lemon) juice, divided
- 6 cups water, or more
- 1 cup granulated sugar
- To make the jelly
- 1 cup reserved rosewater

- 1 Meyer lemon, washed and diced (including peel except for large ends)
- 1 small, firm apple (about 4 oz), cored but left unpeeled, diced
- 1 box fresh red currants, about 5.3 oz
- 1½ cups granulated sugar (you might need a bit more, per your taste)
- ¼ cups granulated sugar, whisked with 2 tsp natural pectin

Direction

- To deal with the rose petals and make the rose syrup
- Wash the rose petals well, and trim off any white ends you come across. Drain the petals and place into a 4 qt, or larger, pot. Cover with fresh, cold water, add 1½ tablespoons lemon juice, bring to a boil, and then simmer for 30 minutes, stirring occasionally.
- When the water is red, and the petals have faded to a pale magenta, drain the petals, reserving 4 cups of the rosewater. Set the petals aside.
- In the same pan, combine 2 c reserved rosewater (from what you just drained and set aside), ½ c water, 1 c sugar and the remaining 1.5 tablespoons Meyer lemon juice. Boil 10 minutes, making sure sugar is dissolved. Remove from heat and stir in reserved petals. Let macerate 2 hours and then drain, reserving this rose syrup. At this point, you can dispose of the petals.
- To make the jelly
- If you're planning to can this jelly, get your canning pot set up- water boiling, jars out, etc.
- In a (separate) large pot, add another 1 c reserved rosewater, 1 c water, the diced lemon, diced apple, and the cheesecloth purse (if using; see note 2 above). Turn the heat to high. When boiling, add the currants, and the rose syrup you made earlier. Boil 10 minutes, remove cheesecloth purse, and add 1½ c sugar.
- Let the mixture cook until the sugar dissolves and a nice boil returns. Remove from heat and carefully strain through a fine-mesh sieve, ultimately returning the liquid to your pot. Put

all solids into a food mill set with the finest disk, place the mill over the pot holding the liquid, and crank until all additional juice is pressed out. Discard solids.

- Return this strained "jelly" to a boil, and whisk in about 1/4 of your sugar-pectin mixture. You might get a few small clots which you can strain out. At this point, you can do the freezer-plate test, or you can just go for it (the freezer-plate test is kind of hit or miss in my opinion).Ladle into jars and process in the boiling water bath for 10 minutes.

142. Low Sugar Plum Jam

Serving: Makes 2 cups | Prep: | Cook: |Ready in:

Ingredients

- 800 grams plums, pitted and quartered
- 250 grams sugar
- Juice of ½ a lime/lemon

Direction

- Place a heavy-bottomed pot over medium heat and toss in the plums. Stir, then clamp on a lid and cook until tender and the plums are falling apart, about 5-10 minutes (the timing will depend largely upon the ripeness of the plums). Push the plums down using a spatula and mush them as you go along.
- Once the plums are tender, add the sugar to the pot. Cook the jam over medium-high heat stirring frequently until the sugar is dissolved. Continue simmering for a further 10 minutes, skimming off any scum that rises to the surface (note: stir frequently at this stage as there is a risk of the sugar catching at the bottom).
- Continue cooking until the jam has thickened, another 5 - 7 minutes or so. (A good way to tell if it's done is to scoop some up in a ladle and pour it back into the pot. You want it to fall in clumps and not be too runny). If you think it's

not there yet, let it cook for a little while longer.

- Taste the jam; if you think it's too tart, add more sugar and cook until it dissolves completely.
- When ready, add the lime/lemon juice and ladle them into clean glass jars. Let them sit outside until they get to room temperature and then refrigerate.

143. Lychee Jelly Hearts

Serving: Makes a lot | Prep: | Cook: | Ready in:

Ingredients

- 1/3 cup lychee syrup, canned
- 1/3 cup water
- 2 packets gelatin
- 1/2 cup sugar
- 1/2 cup applesauce
- 1/2 cup lychee, minched/chopped fine
- 2 tablespoons red jelly, like raspberry or strawberry, optional, for color
- 2 teaspoons lemon juice

Direction

- Lightly oil 8X8 baking pan.
- In a bowl, sprinkle gelatin over 1/3 cup of water. Ignore for 5 minutes, let the gelatin soften.
- In saucepan, combine syrup with sugar, stir over medium heat until sugar has dissolved. Add in the applesauce and lychee bits, and red jam if using, and mix until well combined. Add in the gelatin mixture and bring to a boil. At this point you can vitamix it smooth, or keep the chunks if you want. Pour mixture into prepared baking pan, allow to cool to room temp and then transfer to fridge until firm, 3 hours.
- Cut into squares, or if you're being cutesy, use 1/2" cookie cutters. I had dw fashion small

hearts for me made out of strips of aluminum from a soda can.

- Dredge in some sugar to coat. BAM.
- Store in airtight container in fridge for up to a week

144.　　MELON JAM WITH STAR ANISE

Serving: Makes 1 cup | Prep: | Cook: | Ready in:

Ingredients

- 300 grams muskmelon, roughly chopped
- 4 tablespoons sugar
- 3　star anise
- 1/8 teaspoon salt
- 1 tablespoon lemon juice

Direction

- Add melon and sugar to a heavy bottomed pot and cook covered until the fruit has softened, about 5-6 minutes.
- Break down the fruit by pressing down with a potato masher. Add the star anise, salt, and lemon juice and continue to cook uncovered on a low flame for 10-15 minutes until the melon starts to get pulpy. Stir often, and keep an eye on it constantly as the sugar tends to stick to the bottom if left unattended.
- Check the consistency by taking a spoonful of jam and letting it drop back down into the pot. If it clings slightly to the spoon and falls in a clump, it's done. If it looks too wet still, continue cooking for a further 5 minutes.
- Once done, scoop out the star anise and discard. Ladle the jam into a glass jar and refrigerate.

145.　　Marbled Jam Cake

Serving: Serves 8 | Prep: | Cook: | Ready in:

Ingredients

- 1/3 cup oat flour (40g)
- 1/3 cup buckwheat flour (40g)
- 1/3 cup all-purpose flour (40g)
- 1 teaspoon baking powder
- 1/2 teaspoon baking soda
- 1/4 teaspoon salt (omit if you are using salted butter)
- 1/3 cup sugar (67g)
- large pinches grated nutmeg or spice of your choice
- 4 tablespoons unsalted butter, cold and cut into small cubes
- 1/4 cup quick oats (20g) or rolled oats (the latter will remain chewy in the completed cake)
- 1/2 cup plain yogurt (if you only have greek style, you'll need to increase the amount of milk)
- 1/8 to 1/4 cups whole milk (milk and yogurt can be interchanged, or replaced by buttermilk)
- 1 teaspoon vanilla extract (optional)
- 1/2 to 2/3 cups simple, runny, fruit-based jam or preserves, preferably with pieces of fruit

Direction

- Mix the flours, baking soda, baking powder, salt, spice and sugar together with a whisk in a medium bowl.
- Add the butter, and squeeze the cubes into the flour with your fingers, as you might with a pastry dough, until you have a mealy consistency.
- Add the yogurt, a splash of milk and vanilla extract. Stir to completely combine--it should be like thick cake batter, not watery but not as stiff as a muffin or biscuit dough. If you need to thin it, use the greater amount of milk.

- Use a few turns of a wooden spoon to fold in the rolled oats.
- Pour into a buttered 9" pie plate (a round cake tin works, too). The batter will rise considerably, so don't go for anything smaller unless it has high sides.
- Drop 3-5 generous dollops of your jam on top of the batter.
- Use a table knife to drag the jam strategically throughout the batter. Resist the urge to stir and blend. Use a few (ok, maybe several) carefully-planned drags to marbleize the jam into the batter, starting in the dollop of jam and moving the knife (or the pie plate) in simple arcs. Add smaller spoonfuls and streaks as you see fit.
- Bake in a 350 degree (preheated) oven for 35-40 minutes. The center should be firm and the jam fairly well hidden under the golden, risen cake.
- Let cool at least 1 hour. Yes, the cake will fall in places where the jam had been hot and bubbly.
- Slice and serve wedges with whipped cream or ice cream, or eat with a big spoon.

146.   Marmalade Bread Pudding

Serving: Serves 6 | Prep: | Cook: | Ready in:

Ingredients

- For the bread
- 10 tablespoons (6 oz) softened butter
- 10-12 slices of thick-cut, white bread
- 4 tablespoons marmalade
- 2 large oranges, zested and juiced
- 1 lemon, zested and juiced
- 1/3 cup superfine sugar
- For the custard
- 360 milliliters (12 fl oz) milk
- 2 eggs
- 2 tablespoons superfine sugar

- 4 tablespoons light cream

Direction

- Preheat the oven to 400 F and generously butter a large baking dish (about 2 litres) with some of the butter.
- Cut the crusts off of the bread then butter and spread with marmalade. Cut each slice into 4 triangles.
- In a small bowl stir together the orange juice, orange zest, lemon juice, lemon zest and sugar until the sugar has dissolved.
- Soak each triangle of bread in the syrup and arrange in the baking dish until it's completely full.
- In a large bowl whisk together the milk, eggs, sugar and cream. Pour this over the bread triangles in the dish. Spoon over any remaining syrup.
- Bake pudding for 30 minutes until browned and crisp on top.

147.   Marmalade Glazed Salmon On Pea Shoots & Spring Greens With White Wine And Lemon Cream Sauce

Serving: Serves 4 | Prep: | Cook: | Ready in:

Ingredients

- Salmon and Greens
- 4 pieces Salmon filet, each cut about 2 inches wide and weighing about 8 oz
- 4 cups loosley packed pea shoots
- 4 cups mixed tender, young spring greens~any mix of spinach, chard, arugula, turnip or radish greens
- 2 tablespoons orange marmalade
- 1 tablespoon lemon zest
- 2 tablespoons lemon juice
- salt and pepper
- 2 tablespoons grape seed or canola oil

- 1 tablespoon minced chervil
- White Wine and Lemon Cream Sauce
- 1 lemon, juiced
- 1/3 cup Chenin Blanc or other crisp white wine
- 2 sprigs chervil
- 1 sprig parsley
- 6 tablespoons butter
- 1/3 c thick heavy cream or creme fraiche
- 1 egg yolk
- salt

Direction

- Prepare your pea shoots and greens, wash them well. Trim top of pea shoots to about 3 inches, and pull leaves off remaining stem. Remove any thick stems from other greens and tear larger leaves into pieces that are about 3 inches.
- Mix 2 T marmalade with 2T lemon juice and set aside.
- Preheat oven to 450
- Start sauce: in a small saucepan combine lemon juice, wine, chervil and parsley. Bring to a simmer and reduce to about half. Remove herbs and then whisk in 3 T butter.
- Brush salmon all over with wine, lemon and butter mixture, and season with salt and pepper
- Finish sauce: temper egg yolk with a bit of the wine, lemon and butter mixture, and then whisk into remaining butter mixture in saucepan. Heat slowly, whisking, until mixture thickens and gets really thick and looks curdled. Turn off heat. Whisk in remaining butter and cream. Add salt to taste Keep warm, but don't reheat.
- Heat oil in large frying pan that has a lid (you'll be using this same pan for your greens), and place salmon in pan skin side up. Cook for 1 minute. Place salmon on baking pan, skin side down, and brush with marmalade mixture, then add a bit of salt and pepper to each. Bake in 450 oven for 15 or 20 minutes. Remove promptly from oven. Let rest for a minute while you cook the greens.

- Place pea shoots and greens in pan you used for the salmon. The water left on the greens from washing should be enough for wilting them, but if you dried them really well, then add a bit of water to the pan. Turn the heat on high, cover, and cook for about 45 seconds. Toss briefly, and cook for another 15 seconds. If you prefer, you may cook them down more, but I prefer them less cooked.
- To serve, pour some sauce on the plate, add greens, and top with salmon. Garnish with minced chervil and lemon zest.

148.　　　Melon Jam

Serving: Makes 600 ml or 2 1/2 cups jam | Prep: | Cook: | Ready in:

Ingredients

- 1 canary melon (or cantaloupe, roughly 2 pounds or 1 kg)
- 2 cups granulated sugar
- Juice of 1 lemon

Direction

- Cut the melon into slices and remove the seeds and skin (try not to cut too close to the skin as the flesh near here remains quite hard and crunchy). You should have about 2 pounds of fruit left. Chop the melon flesh into roughly 1-inch/2-cm cubes and combine with sugar and lemon in a bowl. Let macerate about 6 hours or overnight.
- Place a saucer in the freezer to use for testing the jam setting later.
- Pour the melon and all its juices into a large heavy-bottomed pot. Bring to a rapid boil and cook, on high, for about 25 minutes or until the jam is set. During this time, check it and stir it often to make sure it's not sticking or burning. If you think it is (or is close to) sticking or burning, check to see if the jam has set right away with the saucer test.

- To check if jam is set, place a blob of the hot liquid jam on the cold saucer. Wait a moment for it to cool then look at it. It should be wobbly; if you tilt the plate it should slide slowly; and if you poke it, most importantly, it should wrinkle slightly. If so, it's done. If you prefer a smooth rather than a chunky jam, you can mash the fruit or blend with an immersion blender off the heat. (I did the latter.)
- Remove from the heat and spoon into sterilized jars and either process the jars (boiling the closed jar and its contents for at least 10 minutes) or seal and keep refrigerated. If refrigerating (and once opened), use the jam within a couple of weeks.

---

149. Meyer Lemon Cured Preserves

Serving: Makes 8 lemons | Prep: | Cook: |Ready in:

Ingredients

- 8 organic meyer lemons
- 1 1/2 cups sea salt
- 1 1/2 cups granulated white sugar
- extra virgin olive oil

Direction

- Boil a large pot of water. Blanch the lemons in the boiling water for 10 to 15 seconds. Cool the lemons in a big bowl of cold water. Cut off the ends of the lemons (about 1/2 inch) and slice into 1/8-inch rounds. Remove the seeds as you go.
- Combine the sugar and salt in a large bowl.
- With sterilized mason jars, scoop the sugar mixture into the bottom of the jars so it is generously covered with the mixture. Place a slice of lemon into the jar and cover it completely with sugar mixture. Keep on alternating lemon slices and the sugar mixture until it fills the jar. Push down the slices to make room for more lemon slices as you go.

Fill the jars and top with olive oil (I used about 2 to 3 tablespoons of olive oil per 1 pint jar).
- Refrigerate for at least 2 weeks to 1 month before eating. The preserves should be soft. Remove any excess sugar and salt before using. I like to mince them before I put them into a dish. These lemons should last up to a year or longer in the fridge.

---

150. Meyer Lemon Key Lime Marmalade

Serving: Makes 3 pints | Prep: | Cook: |Ready in:

Ingredients

- 1 pound meyer lemons
- 2 pounds key limes
- 2 tablespoons grated, fresh ginger
- 2 pounds granulated sugar

Direction

- Slice the lemons, first in half (length-wise), then as thinly as you can (cross-wise). Place in a large, non-reactive pot. (I like to use an enamel-coated cast iron Dutch oven).
- Juice all of the limes into your pot through a wire-mesh strainer (keeps those seeds out!)
- Add enough water to the pot to just cover the lemons, then let them sit, covered, overnight.
- Put a plate with several teaspoons in the freezer - you'll need these later for testing the set of things.
- Bring your mixture to a hard boil for approximately 20 minutes - you're looking for the lemon rinds to start to get tender here.
- Replace whatever water you just cooked off, then add the sugar and ginger, making sure to stir it in thoroughly.
- Return to a gentle boil and reduce heat to maintain that slow, gentle boil. Stir occasionally, picking up the frequency as the water cooks out and you get closer to gel-stage (you don't want the stuff on the bottom to get

stuck and burn). Depending on the size of your pot, you may need to stir more frequently/vigorously to keep it from foaming over. Alternatively, you can lower the heat for less foam, but this will lengthen cooking time.

- When the foam starts to settle down and the liquid starts to darken, remove from heat and test the gel using one of your frozen spoons; spoon out a little bit, return the spoon to the freezer for a minute or two. Feel the bottom of the spoon - it should feel room temperature. If it's too hot, put it back in the freezer a moment longer. If the marmalade has the sort of set you like, you're done! Otherwise, put it back on for another 2-5 minutes and then test again.
- This should keep in the fridge for at least a week, but you can water-bath can it; I processed my half-pint jars for 10 minutes. I imagine it's shelf stable for at least a year, but I've not had the chance to find out, since we eat it too fast :-)

---

151.   Meyer Lemon Vanilla Bean And Ginger Karma Marmalade

Serving: Makes 4 or 5 half pints, or 8 or more quarter pints | Prep: | Cook: |Ready in:

Ingredients

- For Preparing the Lemons
- 4 cups water
- 1 1/2 pounds Meyer lemons
- For the Meyer Lemon Marmalade
- 4 cups granulated sugar
- seeds from 1 vanilla bean, scraped out
- 1 tablespoon fresh ginger grated with a microplane

Direction

- For Preparing the Lemons
- Halve the lemons crosswise. With a small paring knife, pick out all the seeds. Then, cut

the lemons halves lengthwise. With an amazingly sharp knife, thinly slice each quarter so that you have a cross-section of a crosswise slice. I generally am able to cut 5 or 6 slices per lemon quarter.

- Place the lemon slices in a copper jam pot, or a large Dutch oven that is equal in size. Allow the lemons and water to sit, covered, for 24 hours at room temperature.
- For the Meyer Lemon Marmalade
- Bring the lemon slices and water to a boil, and then immediately turn the heat down to medium low. Simmer the mixture until it is reduced to about 4 cups, stirring often. This may take anywhere from 30 to 45 minutes.
- Add the sugar, stirring constantly, and bring to a rolling boil over moderate heat. Adjust the heat as needed so the mixture reduces, stirring all the time. (Do not leave the marmalade either unattended or unstirred!) After about 8 minutes, add the vanilla bean seeds and the fresh grated ginger. Continue to stir until the marmalade is ready. This may take anywhere from 10 to 13 minutes total cooking time. Also, the color of the marmalade will deepen as it cooks.
- Ladle the marmalade into sterilized half pint jars. Process in a boiling water bath for 10 minutes, and wait for the PING sound when you remove the jars from the water bath. Any jars that do not PING should go into the refrigerator for immediate use. Allow the marmalade to sit undisturbed for a day. Enjoy!
- NB - The quarter pint jars are great for gift giving.

---

152.   Mint, Rose And Rhubarb Jam

Serving: Makes 1/2 - 1 jar of jam | Prep: | Cook: |Ready in:

Ingredients

- 1 rhubarb stalk, chopped into 1/4 inch pieces

- 3-4 sprigs fresh mint, stalks and all (reserve a few leaves for garnishing)
- 2 - 3 tablespoons rose jelly (Depends on the sweetness and strength of the rose jelly. If you can't find any in your local grocery store, just add another spoonful of honey)
- 1 - 2 tablespoons Honey
- 1/2 lemon, zested and juiced
- 1/2 orange, juiced
- 2 star anise
- 1 pinch salt

Direction

- Add all ingredients to a small/medium sized saucepan. Place over medium heat. (Yes, it really is that easy □)
- Stir frequently with a rubber spatula to help break down the rhubarb pieces ensure nothing sticks to the bottom and burns. You want to see a slow simmer. If it looks more like your pre-jam mixture is boiling, reduce the heat.
- When the jam has reached the consistency you prefer, take the pan off the heat and set aside to cool.
- Once cooled, strain out the solids. (If you love mint like me, I would recommend re-adding the cooked leaves.) Serve on toasted bread, freshly baked croissants, swirled through oatmeal, or anything else your heart desires in the morning to go along with your cup of coffee. Garnish with the reserved mint leaves, either whole or chopped.

---

153.   Mozzarella In Carrozza With Sun Dried Tomato And Roasted Red Pepper Jam

Serving: Makes about 2 cups jam and 2 sandwiches, or cut several small squares or triangles for appetizers | Prep: | Cook: | Ready in:

Ingredients

- For the jam:

- 1 cup sun-dried tomatoes, packed in oil and herbs, drained slightly
- 1 cup roasted red peppers, packed in water, drained slightly
- 2 tablespoons sherry vinegar
- 5 tablespoons granulated sugar
- 3 tablespoons strawberry jam
- 1 dash salt
- For the sandwiches:
- 4 slices bread (I like Wave Hill's small country boule)
- 4 slices fresh mozzarella, about 1/4-inch to 1/2-inch thick
- 1 large egg
- 1/3 cup cream or milk
- 1 pinch salt
- 1 tablespoon olive oil
- 1 tablespoon unsalted butter
- Fresh basil

Direction

- For the jam:
- In a mini-chopper, place the tomatoes and process. Don't purée them -- small chunks are good. Remove to a small sauce pot.
- Place the red pepper in the mini-chopper and repeat. Add them to the tomatoes.
- Add the rest of the ingredients to the pot and bring to a boil. Reduce the heat to simmer the mixture and continue cooking for 10 to 15 minutes, stirring frequently, until thickened.
- Pour into a sterilized 1-pint jar. Let cool, then store in refrigerator.
- For the sandwiches:
- Place the sliced mozzarella on 2 slices of bread, then top with the two remaining slices.
- In a shallow soup bowl or small casserole, beat the egg, cream, and salt with a fork.
- Lay the sandwiches in the custard and press gently with a spatula. Carefully turn sandwiches, and repeat until most of the liquid is absorbed. If using less-dense bread, like white sandwich bread, reduce the soaking time.
- In a medium nonstick skillet, melt the oil and butter over medium-low heat. Add the

sandwiches and cook for about 5 minutes, or until the bottom sides are nicely golden. Carefully turn the sandwiches with a spatula and cook the other side for another 5 minutes, or until bottoms are nicely golden and the cheese is melty. Add a bit more butter if needed.

- Place a folded paper towel on a dish and briefly place sandwiches on it to absorb some of the grease.

- The sandwiches can be kept warm in a low oven for about half an hour before serving.

- Serve the sandwiches hot. Place them on a warm serving plate and cut in half, or cut them into smaller pieces if serving as hors d'oeuvres. Place a couple spoonfuls of the jam on the side of the sandwich, or place the jam in a bowl for guests to serve themselves. Alternately, top each appetizer portion with a dollop of the jam. Sprinkle with basil, any way you like -- torn, ribbons, or whole.

- Buon appetito!

---

154. Mrs. Wheelbarrow's Focaccia With Apricot Jam, Caramelized Onion, And Fennel

Serving: Makes one 14- by 10-inch focaccia | Prep: | Cook: | Ready in:

Ingredients

- For the dough:
- 1 1/2 teaspoons active dry yeast
- 1 cup warm water
- 2 1/2 to 3 cups all-purpose flour
- 3 tablespoons olive oil, plus extra for the bowl
- 1 teaspoon chopped fresh rosemary
- 2 teaspoons kosher salt
- For the topping:
- 2 tablespoons olive oil, plus more for brushing
- 2 medium onions, halved lengthwise and sliced into thin half-moons

- 2 cups sliced fennel
- Kosher salt and freshly ground pepper
- 8 ounces apricot jam
- 4 ounces aged, crumbly goat cheese (but fresh is fine, too)
- Crunchy sea salt

Direction

- In a large bowl, sprinkle the yeast over the warm water and stir well. When small bubbles start to form on the surface, after 5 minutes or so, add 1 cup of the flour and stir well. Let rest for 10minutes.

- Add another cup of the flour, the oil, rosemary, and salt, and stir until you have a shaggy mass. Turn out onto a well-floured work surface and sprinkle the dough with about a tablespoon of flour. Allow the dough to rest and absorb the flour for about 10 minutes. Wash the bowl, dry well, and lightly oil it.

- Using a spatula or a bench scraper, gently lift, fold, and press down the dough, then give it a quarter turn. Continue this gentle kneading until the dough is smooth and elastic, about twelve turns, adding as little additional flour as possible. This is a wet, sticky, dough.

- Place the dough in the bowl and turn to coat in the oil, then cover with a tea towel and let rise for an hour. (Or, for a tangier focaccia, place the covered bowl in the refrigerator for up to 2 days for a slow rise. Bring to room temperature before proceeding.)

- Heat the 2 tablespoons olive oil in a large sauté pan over low heat. Add the onions and fennel, season with plenty of salt and pepper, and cook slowly until well browned and caramelized, 14 to 20 minutes. Remove from the heat.

- Preheat the oven to 450° F. Line a baking sheet with a piece of parchment. Brush the parchment with oil.

- Place the dough on the parchment-lined baking sheet and press out into a 14- by 10-inch rectangle. If the dough shrinks back and fights you, let it relax for 10 minutes, then press it out gently. It does not need to be perfect by any means. Dimple the focaccia allover with your fingertips (as though you were lightly playing the piano). Let rest for 20 minutes.

- Brush the focaccia lightly with olive oil. Using an offset spatula, spread the preserves to within 1/2 inch of the edges. Cover the preserves with the onions and fennel. Break up the cheese and dot it over the onions. Drizzle with olive oil and sprinkle with crunchy salt and pepper.
- Bake the focaccia until it is golden brown and the cheese is bubbly and toasty, 20 to 25 minutes; the internal temperature will register190° F.
- Serve warm or at room temperature.

155.	Mrs. Wheelbarrow's Jam Tarts

Serving: Makes 12 tiny tarts, six 3-inch tarts, or one 9-inch tart | Prep: | Cook: | Ready in:

Ingredients

- 4 ounces unsalted butter, softened
- 1/2 cup granulated sugar
- 1 large egg yolk
- 2 cups all purpose flour
- A big pinch of kosher salt
- 8 ounces any jam, preserves, or conserves

Direction

- In the bowl of a stand mixer fitted with the paddle attachment, or in a large bowl, using a hand mixer, beat the butter and sugar until light and creamy. Add the egg yolk and blend until combined. Add the flour and salt and blend until combined. Turn out the dough, gather it together, and form into a disk. Keep covered with a slightly dampened towel as you work.

- If making tiny tarts, set out twelve 1-by-2-inch molds. Pinch off pieces of dough the size of a walnut and press one into each mold. Place the mold(s) on a baking sheet. Alternatively, press the dough over the bottom and up the sides of a 9-inch tart pan with a removable bottom. Chill the crust for 30 minutes.
- Preheat the oven to 350° F.
- Prick the crust all over with a fork. This will keep the crust from ballooning up in the oven, although it still may rise a bit; don't worry, it will go back down. Bake tartlets for 8 to 12 minutes, 15 to 20 minutes if using a tart pan, until the crust is very lightly browned, about the color of sand. Watch carefully and do not overbake. Remove to a rack and cool completely.
- Using a toothpick, carefully release the tiny tart shells from the pans; or, remove the large tart shell from its pan. Warm the jam in a small saucepan and spoon it into the baked shells. Let the tarts cool before serving.
- Jam tarts are best when enjoyed within 3 days.

156.	Muh's Pepper Jelly

Serving: Makes about 5 pints | Prep: | Cook: | Ready in:

Ingredients

- 6 1/2 cups sugar
- 1 1/2 cups apple cider vinegar
- 1/4 cup ground red hot peppers (like poblano), seeds discarded
- 3/4 cup ground green bell peppers, seeds discarded
- 1 bottle fruit pectin, like Certo

Direction

- Combine the sugar, vinegar, and ground peppers in a saucepan. Boil for 10 minutes.
- Add certo and stir well.
- Pour into sterilized jelly jars and keep in the refrigerator for up to 6 months.

| 157. | Multigrain Marmalade Muffins |

Serving: Makes 16 | Prep: | Cook: | Ready in:

Ingredients

- 1/2 cup whole wheat flour
- 1/2 cup oat flour [ground oats]
- 1/2 cup spelt flour
- 1/2 cup buckwheat flour
- 1 teaspoon baking powder
- 1/2 teaspoon baking soda
- 1/2 teaspoon kosher salt
- 1 cup buttermilk
- 1/2 cup greek yogurt
- 2 ounces unsalted butter, room temperature
- 1 tablespoon honey
- 8 ounces marmalade
- 1 egg

Direction

- Preheat the oven to 350 degrees. Line two 12-cup muffin tins with liners [16].
- In a medium bowl, place the whole wheat flour, oat flour, spelt four, buckwheat flour, baking powder, baking soda and kosher salt [all dry ingredients]. Whisk thoroughly to aerate and combine.
- In a small bowl, whisk together the buttermilk and yogurt.
- In a large bowl, beat together the butter, honey and half of the marmalade [4oz] for about three minutes. Scrape down the sides of the bowl with a spatula and add the egg and beat until mixed in thoroughly. Add the last 4oz of the marmalade and beat until combined, about 1 minute. Scrape down sides of the bowl.
- Add a third of the flour mixture on low speed and mix until just combined. Add half of the dairy mixture, mix again until just combined. Repeat with another third of the flour, milk,

and flour, each time beating only until just barely combined.
- Scoop batter into muffin tins with an ice cream scoop or spoon, about halfway up. Bake 35-40 minutes, until golden brown. Remove to a rack to cool.
- Serve warm right out of the oven or toasted the next day.

| 158. | Mushroom Confit Polenta Tart With Tomato Fig Jam |

Serving: Serves 8 to 10 | Prep: | Cook: | Ready in:

Ingredients

- For the Jam:
- 1 tablespoon olive oil
- 1/2 cup minced onion
- 1/2 teaspoon kosher salt
- 1/4 teaspoon red pepper flakes
- 1 garlic clove, minced
- 1 tablespoon tomato paste
- 3 tablespoons minced dried fig
- 1 teaspoon unsweetened cocoa
- 1/4 cup balsamic vinegar
- 1 teaspoon organic sugar
- 1 (28-oz) can chopped San Marzano tomatoes
- For the filling:
- 2 medium onions, peeled and chopped
- 3 pounds baby portobello mushrooms, cut in quarters
- 1 tablespoon minced fresh rosemary
- 4 garlic cloves, peeled and smashed
- 3/4 cup olive oil
- 1/2 teaspoon kosher salt
- 1/2 teaspoon cracked black pepper
- For the crust:
- 1 tablespoon butter
- 2 tablespoons olive oil
- 1 small shallot, minced
- 2 garlic cloves, minced
- 1 teaspoon kosher salt
- 1 tablespoon organic sugar

- 1 1/2 cups chicken or turkey stock
- 1 1/2 cups polenta (coarse grain)
- 2 tablespoons heavy cream
- 3/4 cup grated Parmesan
- 1 egg, lightly beaten

Direction

- For the jam, in a medium saucepan heat oil over medium heat until shimmering. Add onion and salt; cook, stirring occasionally until softened and caramelized, about 12 minutes. Stir in red pepper flakes and garlic, cook until fragrant, about 30 seconds. Add tomato paste and fig; cook, stirring constantly 3 minutes. Stir in cocoa, balsamic and vinegar until well incorporated. Add tomatoes, reduce heat to low; cook uncovered, stirring occasionally, until mixture reduces to 1 cup, about 2 hours. Add salt and pepper to taste. Set aside until ready to use, or refrigerate up to 7 days.
- For the filling, preheat oven to 400 degrees Fahrenheit. In a large bowl combine onions, mushrooms, rosemary, garlic, olive oil, salt and pepper; toss to coat. Transfer filling to a rimmed baking sheet. Spread filling into an even layer and drizzle oil left in the bottom of the bowl over the filling. Place baking sheet in the oven. Bake 40 minutes or until mushrooms are tender and fragrant. Remove baking sheet from oven, let cool 15 minutes. Place filling in food processor and pulse until filling is roughly chopped, about 2 to 3 pulses. Add salt and pepper to taste. Set aside.
- Meanwhile, for the crust, butter a 9-inch round tart pan (or rectangular tart pan) with removable bottom, set aside. In a large saucepan heat olive oil over medium heat. Add shallots, garlic and salt; cook, stirring occasionally until soft, about 2 minutes. Add sugar and stock. Bring to boiling, reduce to simmer. Slowly whisk in polenta, stirring until smooth. Cook, covered, 20 minutes, stirring occasionally. Remove from heat, let cool 30 minutes, uncovered. Stir in cream and Parmesan until well mixed. Stir in egg. Press polenta into buttered tart pan to create 1/4-inch thick side and bottom crusts. Place tart pan on an unlined baking sheet. Place baking sheet in oven. Bake 12 to 15 minutes or until set and lightly browned.
- Remove pan from oven. Spoon mushroom mixture evenly over the polenta crust. Slice into wedges or rectangles and serve with tomato-fig jam.

---

159. My Blancmange With Fig Marmalade

Serving: Serves six | Prep: | Cook: | Ready in:

Ingredients

- Blancmange
- 1 cup milk
- 2 cups milk
- 1/4 cup cornstarch
- 1/3 cup sugar
- 1 teaspoon orange extract
- 1/2 blood orange peel
- 1 clove
- 1 pinch nutmeg
- 1 pinch salt
- Fig Marmalade
- 1 pound Figs
- 1/2 pound sugar
- 1 pinch salt
- Blood orange zest and peel
- 1 tablespoon brandy or whisky

Direction

- Blancmange
- Place 1 cup of the milk into a saucepan. Add orange peel and clove. Bring milk to a simmer over medium heat.
- Meanwhile, in a small bowl, whisk together the cornstarch, sugar and salt. Whisk remaining milk into the cornstarch mixture. When the milk in the pan begins to simmer, pour the cornstarch mixture into the saucepan in a thin steady stream. Whisk vigorously and

increase heat just a bit to bring the mixture to a gentle boil. Allow the mixture to boil for a little, continuing to whisk, then remove from heat. Remove the orange peel and clove. Stir in the pinch of nutmeg and the extract.

- Pour the pudding into six ramekins, covered with plastic wrap directly on the pudding so it doesn't get a skin. Refrigerate for at least 6 hours or overnight. Garnish with the fig marmalade.
- Fig Marmalade
- Wash the figs, break them open, and combine them with the sugar and orange peel in a bowl. Cover them and let them rest overnight.
- Next morning heat the figs with a pinch of salt over a moderate flame, stirring. Let them scorch until they come to a boil. Add the orange zest and brandy or whisky; reduce the heat, and simmer, skimming away the foam occasionally, until a drop on an inclined plate doesn't run. Serve warm or at room temperature.

---

160.   My Husbands Favorite Jam Tart

Serving: Serves 8 | Prep: | Cook: |Ready in:

Ingredients

- Hazelnut Pie Dough
- 1 cup flour
- 1/4 cup Hazelnut flour (ground hazelnuts)
- 1 tablespoon Light Brown Sugar
- 1/2 teaspoon Salt
- 8 tablespoons Unsalted Butter
- 1/8 teaspoon Cinnamon
- 1 Egg
- 1-2 teaspoons Ice Water
- jam and Frangipane Filling
- 1/2 cup seedless Raspberry Jam, heated
- 8 tablespoons Unsalted Butter, room temperature
- 1/2 cup Sugar

- 3.5 ounces Almond Paste
- 1 teaspoon Almond Extract
- 3 Eggs
- Pinch Salt
- 1/4 cup Almond Flour/Meal
- 1/4 cup All Purpose Flour
- 1/4 cup Sliced Almonds

Direction

- Make the dough. Pulse the hazelnut flour, all-purpose flour, brown sugar, salt and cinnamon in a food processor. Pulse in butter one tablespoon at a time. With machine running add egg. If dough is not yet sticking together add water a little bit at a time until dough just comes together. Flatten into a disc, wrap in plastic and put in fridge until firm.
- Roll out dough to fit a 4x14 rectangular tart pan. Fit into tart pan. Pull away scraps. Prick bottom of tart all over with a fork and put into freezer until firm. Preheat oven to 350 degrees. Line tart pan with parchment and fill with pie weights. Cook for 12 minutes. Take out pie weights and parchment and cook for 10 minutes longer. Set aside to cool.
- Make filling: In a bowl of a stand mixer beat butter, sugar and almond paste until fluffy. Add Almond extract and salt. Then add eggs one at a time until all incorporated, scraping down sides of bowl as needed. Add almond flour and all-purpose flour until all incorporated.
- Spread Jam on bottom of tart. Dollop spoonfuls of batter on top and spread evenly trying not to incorporate it with the jam. Sprinkle sliced almonds on top. Bake tart for 30 minutes until puffed and golden enjoy!

---

161.   My Meyer Lemon Marmalade

Serving: Serves 3 cups | Prep: | Cook: |Ready in:

Ingredients

- 16 Meyer lemons
- 4 cups organic cane sugar
- 1/2 cup chopped crystallized ginger

Direction

- Zest the lemons with small-holed zester. You will have little ribbons of pure zest. Squeeze and strain the juice. (Sixteen lemons yielded 2 cups of juice.)
- Combine the zest, sugar, juice and ginger in a heavy-bottomed pot. Bring to boil, lower heat and cook for one hour, stirring frequently.
- Remove from the heat, store in a non-reactive container and allow mixture to rest overnight on the counter.
- In the morning, reheat jam in heavy pot to 220 degrees on a candy thermometer.
- Fill sterile jars and store.

---

162. My Mother's Strawberry Jam

Serving: Makes 2 pints | Prep: 0hours45mins | Cook: 0hours35mins | Ready in:

Ingredients

- 4 cups hulled and quartered strawberries
- 2 1/4 cups granulated sugar
- Pinch salt
- Juice of 1/2 a lemon
- 1 1/2 teaspoons cold unsalted butter

Direction

- Put a small plate in the freezer.
- Combine the strawberries, sugar, salt and lemon juice in a medium, heavy saucepan. Set the pan over low heat and cook, stirring frequently, until the sugar dissolves and the mixture starts to bubble.
- Continue to cook over low heat for about 30 minutes, until a bit of the jam sets on the plate

you've been keeping in the freezer (when you tip the plate, the jam should run only very slowly).
- Turn off the heat and stir the butter into the jam—this will help to clarify the jam and get rid of the foam once it cools.
- Spoon the hot jam carefully into hot sterilized jars and either process the jars or seal and keep refrigerated. If refrigerating, use the jam within a week or two.
- Some sterilizing notes:
- Use glass jars with no chips or cracks and tight-fitting lids.
- To sterilize, wash both the jars and lids thoroughly with hot, soapy water. Bring a large pot of water to a boil and boil the jars and lids (don't boil metal lids or rubber seals) for 15 minutes. Alternately, after you've cleaned the jars and lids, arrange them (lids open sides up), without touching, on a baking sheet and put them in a 175° F oven for 30 minutes. To sterilize metal lids and/or rubber seals, put them in a bowl, pour boiling water over them to cover and let them soak for a few minutes.
- Sterilize all of your additional equipment (tongs for handling hot jars, funnels, ladles, etc.) by dipping them in boiling water for a few minutes.

---

163. My Aunt Jagica's Cookies With Jam

Serving: Makes about 40-50 double cookies | Prep: | Cook: | Ready in:

Ingredients

- 8 ounces butter
- 8 ounces shortening
- 8 ounces icing sugar
- 1 1/2 pounds flour
- 1 egg
- 2 egg yolk

- 1 tablespoon baking powder
- 1 teaspoon vanilla
- 1 lemon, zest
- jam of your choice (I use apricot jam)

Direction

- In the bowl beat the butter, shortening and sugar until smooth (2-3 minutes). Beat in the vanilla and lemon zest.
- Gently stir in the flour just until incorporated.
- Flatten the dough into 4 disks, wrap in plastic wrap, and chill the dough until firm but not hard (30 minutes).
- Preheat oven to 350F with the rack in the middle of the oven.
- Roll out the dough between two parchment papers.
- Use a cookie cutter of your choice to cut out the cookies. Make sure you put the same size cookies on the baking sheet for even baking.
- Bake for 6 - 8 minutes for smaller cookies, or until the cookies change colour.
- Using a small knife place a jam on a whole cookie, place a cookie with a hole over the whole cookie, repeat.
- You can use different jams.

164.   Nam Prik Pao (Chile Jam)

Serving: Makes about 1 pint | Prep: | Cook: | Ready in:

Ingredients

- 1 2-inch square tamarind paste
- 75 grams (about 2 1/2 ounces) dried Puya chiles
- 1 cup rice bran oil (or any high-heat-tolerant vegetable oil)
- 2 heads' worth garlic cloves, thinly sliced
- 5 medium shallots, thinly sliced
- 2 tablespoons Thai shrimp paste, broken into small chunks
- 1/2 cup chopped palm sugar
- 2 to 3 tablespoons fish sauce

Direction

- Combine the tamarind paste with 1/2 cup very hot water and break up the paste with a spoon or your fingers; soak for a few minutes, breaking up the paste a few more times if needed. Push the mixture through a mesh strainer with the back of a spoon; set aside the pulp that passes through the strainer, and discard what remains inside the strainer. Stem and seed the chiles.
- Heat the oil in a wok or large skillet over medium-high heat until hot but not quite smoking. Add the chiles, and cook, stirring, for 15 to 20 seconds, making sure they don't burn. Remove with a slotted spoon, and transfer to a plate.
- Add the garlic to the oil, and fry, stirring frequently, until just golden brown. (It will continue to brown after it's out of the oil, so don't go too dark now.) Transfer to the plate with the chiles. Fry the shallots until golden brown, and transfer to the plate. Turn off the heat, leaving the oil in the pan. Transfer the chiles, garlic, and shallots to a food processor; pulse, scraping down the sides as necessary, until the mixture turns into a paste (no need to make it totally smooth).
- Turn the heat under the pan to medium. Add the shrimp paste, and cook, stirring and breaking it up, for about a minute or two. Add the palm sugar, and cook, stirring, until it dissolves. Add the chile, garlic, and shallot mixture, the tamarind pulp, and 2 tablespoons of the fish sauce. Stir to combine, then turn the heat to low. Cook, stirring occasionally so the bottom of the pan doesn't burn, until the mixture thickens slightly, 2 or 3 minutes. Taste the mixture; if it still needs salt, add more fish sauce, a little at a time.
- You can store the jam (and the oil) in a jar in the fridge or freezer; use it in stir fries or soups, spoon it on top of rice or noodles, spread it on toast, or use it as the base for the dressing for Yum Yai Salad.

165. No Cook Raspberry Lime Freezer Jam

Serving: Makes 6 x 1 cup jars | Prep: | Cook: | Ready in:

Ingredients

- 4 cups crushed fresh raspberries
- 1 packet freezer pectin (45g)
- 2 limes, zested
- 1.5 cups sugar

Direction

- Stir sugar, zest and pectin in a large bowl.
- Add crushed raspberries and stir for 3 minutes. Note: easiest way to crush berries is pulsing in food processor.
- Spoon into 6 x 250ml (1 c) preserving jars. Wipe clean and add lid and ring. Close tightly.
- Let sit for 30 minutes so it thickens.
- Refrigerate - will last up to 3 weeks or Freeze - will last up to 3 months.

166. No Bake Orange Marmalade Cake

Serving: Makes 1 small loaf tin | Prep: | Cook: | Ready in:

Ingredients

- No Bake Cake
- 7 oz (2 bars) Godiva orange flavored dark chocolate
- 1/2 cup orange Marmalade (I used Keillers)
- 7-8 digestive biscuits crumbled into big pieces
- 1/4 cup confectioners or icing sugar (adjust as per your sweet tooth)
- 2 tbsp unsalted butter
- 2 tablespoons Ribena Blackcurrant syrup
- Optional Chocolate Ganache Icing
- 1 bar (3.5 oz) dark chocolate
- 2 tablespoons heavy cream
- 2 tablespoons unsalted butter
- 1/4 teaspoon Sea salt crystals
- slivers of candied orange peel

Direction

- Line a small loaf tin with cling wrap, leaving some extra wrap to hang over the edges
- Heat the marmalade, Ribena blackcurrant Syrup, and icing sugar (I chose to omit this since I prefer to under sweeten my desserts, but you may add it as per taste) on low heat till it melts into a thick syrup.
- Remove from heat, add the crumbled biscuits and mix well to coat the biscuits completely with the marmalade mixture. Allow to sit for 10 - 15 minutes for the marmalade mixture to soak in.
- Break the chocolate up into squares. Combine with the butter and heat in a microwave for ~ 1 minute. Stir well till the chocolate is completely melted, shiny & combined with the butter.
- Add the chocolate to the biscuit / marmalade mixture and stir to ensure that the biscuits are completely enrobed with in the chocolate.
- Pour the mix into the lined loaf tin. Smooth the surface with an offset spatula. Cover the surface of the cake with the overhanging cling wrap and leave in the refrigerator to chill for ~ 2 hrs.
- Heat the ingredients for the ganache icing (except for the sea salt and candied orange peel) in a double boiler and mix well until smooth & shiny.
- Once the cake has chilled, remove the cling wrap and drizzle with the ganache. Sprinkle with the sea salt crystals and the bits of candied orange peel.

167.   Nutty Thumbprint Cookies Filled With Figgy Pudding Jam

Serving: Makes 32 cookies | Prep: | Cook: | Ready in:

Ingredients

- ** For the Cookie Dough **
- 8 ounces (228 grams) pecan pieces
- 55 grams / 60 ml / ¼ cup superfine sugar, divided
- 2 cups (8.8 ounces / 250 grams) all-purpose flour
- 2 sticks (8 ounces / 226 grams) unsalted butter, cut into ½" cubes and chilled
- Good pinch of salt
- 1/4 teaspoon ground nutmeg
- 2 teaspoon / 10 ml vanilla
- 2 teaspoon / 10 ml water
- ** For the Filling **
- 80 grams / 2 ¾ ounces / ½ cup dried sour cherries
- 42 grams / 1 ½ ounces / ¼ cup coarsely chopped black mission figs
- 24 grams / 2 tablespoons / 30 ml granulated sugar
- 2 tablespoons / 30 ml brandy
- 1/8 teaspoon ground cloves
- ½ teaspoon ground mace
- ¼ teaspoon ground allspice
- 1/2 teaspoon nutmeg
- Optional:
- Confectioners' sugar for dusting the cookies, if you wish (I typically don't.)

Direction

- Prepare the dried fruit filling: Buzz to a paste the dried fruit and brown sugar in the food processor. In a small heavy saucepan heat the fruit with 1/3 cup of water, along with the brandy, mace, allspice and cloves. Cook over medium heat, stirring frequently, until the sugar is dissolved and the fruit thickens. Let it sit until ready to bake the cookies.
- Make the cookie dough: Pulse the pecans in the food processor with 2 tablespoons of the granulated sugar, 6 or 7 times, to chop. Remove the nuts.
- Put the butter, remaining 2 tablespoons of sugar and half the flour in the food processor. Buzz for about ten seconds. Add the rest of the flour; sprinkle on the salt and nutmeg, and then drizzle on the water and vanilla. Buzz for about 10 seconds. Add the nuts and process for another 5 - 10 seconds; pulse a few times if necessary fully to combine the ingredients. (You want the nuts still to be visible.)
- Roll the dough into four 8-inch logs. Tightly wrap in plastic wrap (cling film) and chill in the refrigerator for at least 2 hours, up to 3 days. The cookies will taste better if the dough is chilled for at least 24 hours.
- When ready to bake, heat oven to 325 degrees. Use a bench scraper or sharp knife to cut each log into 8 equal-sized chunks.
- Roll into balls and place on parchment-lined cookie sheets. Make a deep impression in the middle of each, using your thumb; fill with the spiced fruit spread. Bake for 24 minutes, turning the cookie sheets halfway through. Let cool on the cookie sheets, on a rack, for about 10 minutes before removing.
- You may have a tablespoon or two of the filling left over, depending on how large your thumbprints are. Use it like jam on buttered toast, or swirl a touch of mustard in it and put it on a grilled cheese sandwich.

168.   Oat Streusel Jam Bars

Serving: Makes 9x9-inch pan | Prep: 0hours20mins | Cook: 1hours0mins | Ready in:

Ingredients

- 3 cups rolled oats, divided
- 3/4 cup brown sugar
- 2 1/2 teaspoons kosher salt

- 1 cup unsalted butter, roughly chopped, plus more for greasing
- 1   (13-ounce) jar blackberry jam (about 1 heaping cup)

Direction

- Add 2 1/4 cups rolled oats to a food processor. Blend until a fine flour forms. Add the brown sugar and salt and pulse to combine. Scatter the butter evenly on top and pulse until a shaggy dough just starts to form. Add the remaining oats and pulse a couple times to incorporate.
- Remove 1 1/4 (loosely packed!) cups of streusel. Spread out the clumps (clumps are good!) on a plate and stick in the freezer to firm.
- Meanwhile, preheat the oven to 350° F. Arrange a baking rack in the bottom third of the oven. Line a 9- by 9-inch baking pan with parchment. The easiest way to do this is cut a roughly 12- by 12-inch square. Now cut slits inward from each corner — this will help the paper fold into place. Smear a bit of butter inside the pan. Place the parchment inside and smooth out with your hands.
- Press the remaining oat streusel into the lined pan, forming an even layer. Spread the jam on top. Take the streusel from the freezer — it should be very firm — and sprinkle on top.
- Bake — on a rack toward the bottom of the oven — for 50 minutes, rotating halfway through. Let cool for at least 30 minutes in the pan, then use the parchment to remove from the pan, and transfer to a rack to cool completely. Cut into 16 or 12 or 9 pieces, depending on how big or little you like your jam bars.
- These freeze well. I like to wrap them individually and grab on my way out the door.

Serving: Makes about 24 | Prep: | Cook: |Ready in:

Ingredients

- 11/2 cup Oat flour
- 1 cup Brown sugar (firmly packed)
- 1/2 teaspoon Salt
- 2 cups Oats
- 3/4 cup Cold Butter
- 11/2 cup Jam or preserves
- 1/2 cup Chopped pecans (optiona)

Direction

- Preheat oven to 375.
- Combine everything except the butter, jam and pecans in the bowl of the food processor. Pulse briefly to combine.
- Cut butter into chunks and add to processor. Pulse until mixture is crumbly.
- If you prefer you can cut the butter into the dry ingredients with our finger tips or a pastry blender.
- Reserve 11/2 cups of the crumbs.
- Press remaining crumbs evenly over the bottom of a 9x13 pan
- Spread jam over the pressed crumbs. Sprinkle with reserved crumbs and pecans.
- Bake for 25 minutes until lightly browned.
- Cool in pan and cut into bars

Serving: Serves 12 | Prep: | Cook: |Ready in:

Ingredients

- 4   layer cake pans
- 2 1/2 cups sugar
- 1 cup milk
- 3 1/2 cups all purpose flour
- 1 tablespoon baking powder

- 5 eggs
- 1 tablespoon vanilla flavoring
- 2 sticks of butter, cut into small pieces
- 1 jar of apple jelly

Direction

- To make the cake:
- Butter the cake pans or treat them with nonstick spray. Set aside.
- Combine all dry ingredients into the mixer. (You may want to drape a kitchen towel over the mixer for the next step.) Blend for five seconds.
- Stop mixer and add half the butter pieces. Blend butter in, then add the rest of the pieces. Keep mixer running and add eggs one at a time, beating each one in well before adding the next. Add milk slowly, then add flavoring
- Once all ingredients are blended, pour mixture into cake pans. Bake at 325 for 15-20 minutes per layer, or until layers are golden around the edges and a toothpick comes out clean. Allow layers to cool in pan, then turn out onto a clean dish towel or cooling rack.
- To assemble the cake:
- Place the bottom layer of the cake onto a serving platter. Spread apple jelly over the layer, then place the next layer on top of it. Continue until all the layers are used up. Frost cake with the rest of the jelly, then serve to an appreciative audience.

---

171. Olia Hercules' Watermelon Rind Jam

Serving: Makes two 450-milliliter (3/4-pint) jars | Prep: | Cook: | Ready in:

Ingredients

- 500 grams (1 pound) watermelon skin, tough thin green rind peeled and discarded, white skin finely chopped

- 300 grams (10 ounces) golden caster sugar (or substitute superfine sugar or demerara or turbinado, ground fine in the food processor)
- 4 limes, halved and thinly sliced (optional, see note in Author Notes above)

Direction

- Mix all the ingredients together in a container, cover with cling film, and leave in the refrigerator overnight.
- Cook the mixture in a non-reactive saucepan over low heat, making sure the sugar melts before it boils, for 50 minutes or until the watermelon skin turns translucent.
- Pour into 2 warm sterilized 450-milliliter (3/4-pint) jars, seal and let cool. Store in the refrigerator. It should keep unopened for several months.

---

172. Oma Jam

Serving: Makes roughly 4-5 cups jam | Prep: | Cook: | Ready in:

Ingredients

- 4 pints fresh Raspberries (3 1/4 c Berries once crushed)
- 1/4 cup fresh Lemon juice
- 4 1/2 cups Sugar
- 1 cup Karo Light Syrup
- 1 packet MCP Pectin

Direction

- Wash and rinse your jam containers and rinse the fruit
- Using a potato masher crush the berries - not too much - 2 cup batches at a time. There should be body in the mash and not too much juice. Once all batches are crushed combine fruit into one bowl.
- Gradually stir in the pectin into the fruit. Let the fruit stand for 30 minutes, stirring lightly every 5-10 minutes.

- Mix in the Karo Syrup so that everything is completely integrated
- Lastly, gradually add the sugar and stir gently until the granules are completely dissolved. Put your jam in your containers and let stand at room temperature for 24 hours. Jam can be used immediately, refrigerated for up to a month and frozen for up to a year.

173.   Onion Jam

Serving: Makes one cup | Prep: | Cook: |Ready in:

Ingredients

- 2   Bermuda onions
- 2-3 tablespoons Vegatable oil
- 2 tablespoons Pomegranate molasses
- 1 1/2 tablespoons Honey
- 1/2 teaspoon Tobasco or other hot sauce
- salt and pepper

Direction

- Peel and thinly slice onions. Saute over medium low heat in oil with salt and pepper until well caramelized. Deglaze pan with a bit of water or red wine.
- Add pomegranate molasses and honey and reduce to a jam like consistency. Add the hot sauce to taste. (Try not eliminate the hot sauce as it is an important counter balance to the sweetness of the other ingredients.)
- Note: Pomegranate molasses is available at most Middle Eastern markets and from numerous on line sources.

174.   Open Face Steak Sandwich With Red Onion Jam And Blue Cheese

Serving: Serves 2 | Prep: | Cook: |Ready in:

Ingredients

- Red Onion Jam
- 2 medium red onions, halved and thinly sliced lengthwise
- 2 tablespoons unsalted butter
- 1/8 cup (1 ounce) granulated sugar
- 1/8 cup (1 ounce) brown sugar
- 1/4 teaspoon kosher salt
- 1/8 teaspoon ground black pepper
- 1/3 cup (about 12) fresh, sweet, ripe cherries, pitted
- 1/3 cup red wine (Pinot Noir and Zinfandel work well)
- 1 tablespoons sherry vinegar
- 3/4 teaspoon fresh thyme leaves
- Steak Sandwich
- 2   slices of Na'an bread
- 2 cups arugula, washed and dried - enough for 2 sandwiches
- 2 tablespoons olive oil
- 1/2 tablespoon balsamic vinegar
- 1 pound flank steak
- 1 tablespoon brown sugar
- 1 teaspoon kosher salt
- 1 teaspoon dried thyme
- 1/2 teaspoon ground chipotle pepper
- 1/2 teaspoon ground black pepper
- crumbled blue cheese

Direction

- Red Onion Jam
- Melt the butter in a sauté pan over medium heat. Add the red onion and toss to coat. Once the onion begins to soften and melt into the sauté pan, add the sugars, salt and pepper. Toss well again and reduce the heat to medium-low. Cook for approximately 30 minutes, turning the onions occasionally. By then the onions should begin to caramelize. If not, cook longer. Tip: the more the onions are tossed around in the sauté pan, the slower they will caramelize. I toss mine around about every 5 minutes.
- When they begin to caramelize, add the wine, sherry wine vinegar and cherries. Continue to

- cook on medium-low heat another 15 minutes until the cherries are very soft, the liquid is absorbed / cooked off, and the onions are caramelized.
- Remove from the heat and toss in the fresh thyme leaves. Let cool to room temperature.
- Steak Sandwich
- Salt both sides of the flank steak and bring to room temperature, about 30 - 45 minutes. Using a paper towel, dab any moisture off the steak surfaces.
- Combine the brown sugar, salt, thyme, and ground peppers in a small bowl. Rub on the dry steak surfaces. Heat up the grill. Grill the steak over direct heat about 4 minutes per side for medium rare.
- Toast the Na'an bread on the grill. Toss the arugula in the olive oil and balsamic vinegar. Set aside.
- Assemble your sandwiches: Spread a good thickness of the red onion jam on the toasted bread. Place the arugula on top. Sprinkle some blue cheese on a cutting board and place the steak on top of it. Slice the meat against the grain. Sprinkle more blue cheese on top and layer the slices over the arugula.
- Pour the rest of the Pinot Noir or Zin in a couple wine glasses and relax.

175. Orange & Lemon Marmalade Cake

Serving: Makes 1 loaf loaf cake (10-inch pan) | Prep: | Cook: | Ready in:

Ingredients

- 2/3 cup lemon marmalade, divided
- 13 tablespoons butter, softened
- 3/4 cup sugar
- 2 teaspoons lemon zest
- 1/2 teaspoon orange zest
- 3 eggs
- 2 tablespoons fresh orange juice

- 1 1/2 cups all-purpose flour
- 1 1/2 teaspoons baking powder
- 3/4 teaspoon kosher salt
- 4 tablespoons confectioners' sugar

Direction

- Heat oven to 350 degrees. Grease a 10-inch loaf pan and set aside.
- Roughly chop any large chunks of lemon peel in the marmalade. In the bowl of an electric mixer, beat 12 tablespoons of the butter, the sugar, the lemon zest and the orange zest until light and fluffy. Beat in the eggs, one at a time, until incorporated. Beat in 1/3 cup marmalade and the orange juice.
- In a separate bowl, whisk together the flour, baking powder and salt. Add the mixed dry ingredients to the wet mixture until just combined.
- Scrape the batter into the greased pan. Bake until the cake is golden brown and a toothpick inserted into the center comes out clean, about 55 minutes.
- Remove the cake from the oven and allow to cool slightly, about 10 minutes. Remove the cake from the pan and set it right-side up on a drying rack. Meanwhile, in a small saucepan, heat the remaining 1/3 cup marmalade over low heat. When the marmalade is melted (but not burning) whisk in the confectioners' sugar and the remaining 1 tablespoon of butter. Pour the glaze over the top of the cake, allowing some of it to drizzle down the sides. Allow the cake to cool completely before serving.

176. Orange Marmalade Glazed Chops

Serving: Serves 2 | Prep: | Cook: | Ready in:

Ingredients

- For the Chops
- 2 pieces French pork chops

- 1 piece salt, to taste
- 1 piece pepper, to taste
- 15 milliliters olive oil
- 30 grams orange marmalade
- 45 milliliters balsamic vinegar
- For the French Green Beans & Olive Tapenade
- 400 grams French green beans
- 100 grams shallots
- 15 milliliters olive oil
- 1 piece salt, to taste
- 1 piece pepper, to taste
- 75 grams black olives, pitted
- 10 grams anchovies
- 15 grams shallots, thinly sliced
- 50 milliliters olive oil
- 1 piece salt, to taste
- 1 piece pepper, to taste

Direction

- For the Chops
- Season pork chops with salt and pepper on both sides.
- Heat olive oil in pan.
- Sear chops for 3-4 minutes on each side.
- Add in balsamic vinegar and orange marmalade.
- Reduce heat to simmer, cover, and cook for about 7 minutes.
- For the French Green Beans & Olive Tapenade
- Combine all ingredients for the tapenade in a food processor, and process until smooth. Set aside.
- Bring a pot of water to a boil.
- Add in the French beans and boil for a minute.
- Strain out and transfer to an ice water bath for about 2 minutes to stop the cooking process.
- Just before serving, sauté the chopped shallots and French beans in a little olive oil.
- Top off with the tapenade, give a quick stir, and take off the heat.
- Serve while hot.

177.   Orange Marmalade Tarts With Bittersweet Chocolate Ganache And Mascarpone Crème

Serving: Makes 16 4-inch tarts | Prep: | Cook: | Ready in:

Ingredients

- Orange Marmalade
- 6 organic California navel oranges
- 6 cups granulated sugar
- 8 cups water
- Shortbread crust, Bittersweet Chocolate Ganache and Mascarpone Creme
- For the shortbread crust:
- 1 3/4 cups unbleached all-purpose flour
- 1/2 cup rice flour
- 1/4 teaspoon salt
- 1 cup unsalted butter
- 1/2 cup granulated sugar
- 1 egg yolk
- For the bittersweet chocolate ganache:
- 1/2 pint heavy cream
- 8 ounces 60% cacao bittersweet chocolate, chopped
- For the mascarpone creme:
- 16 ounces mascarpone cheese
- 2 tablespoons Cognac (or more, to taste)
- 2 tablespoons granulated sugar

Direction

- Orange Marmalade
- Wash and dry the oranges. Slice the ends off of the oranges. With a mandoline, cut the oranges into very thin slices (as thin as you can get them). Place the sliced oranges, sugar and water into a heavy pan. Stir to combine. Place on high heat. Stirring frequently, let the mixture come to a boil. Once the mixture starts to boil, reduce the heat to medium and let it simmer until the temperature reaches 200 degrees on a candy thermometer. Continue stirring frequently while the mixture simmers. Cook until the mixture is reduced by half and looks thick and glossy, about 2 to 2 1/2 hours.

Turn off the heat and let stand while you prepare the shortbread crust, chocolate ganache, and mascarpone creme.

- Shortbread crust, Bittersweet Chocolate Ganache and Mascarpone Creme
- To make the shortbread crust: In the bowl of a stand mixer, place the butter, sugar and egg yolk and beat until combined. Add the dry ingredients and mix until the dough comes together into a ball. Turn the dough onto a lightly floured surface and roll to 1/8-inch thickness. Using a 4-inch circle cutter, cut dough and place into 3-inch tartlet pans. Press dough into the tartlet pan. If there is a little dough above the top of the tartlet pan, roll your rolling pin over the top of the pan to neatly cut the excess dough. Prick the crust randomly with a fork to avoid bubbles in the crust. Bake in a preheated 350 degree oven for 12-14 minutes or until lightly browned. Remove from oven and immediately put enough marmalade into each tartlet crust to fill almost to the top (about 1/8 cup). Set aside while you make the ganache.
- To make the bittersweet chocolate ganache: In a small saucepan, place heavy cream and heat just until very warm. Stir in bittersweet chocolate and remove from heat. Keep stirring until the chocolate is melted and the ganache looks smooth and shiny. Drizzle the ganache over each tart.
- To make the mascarpone creme: Place the mascarpone in the bowl of a stand mixer. Add the cognac and sugar and mix on low speed to combine. When ready to serve, place a dollop of the mascarpone creme on top of each tart. Garnish with a piece or orange peel from the marmalade. Enjoy!

178. Orange And Apricot Jam Squares

Serving: Makes 24 squares | Prep: | Cook: | Ready in:

Ingredients

- For the shortbread base:
- 200 grams butter, softened
- 100 grams castor sugar
- 150 grams flour
- 100 grams cornflour
- 1 teaspoon baking powder
- 1/3 cup smooth apricot jam
- For the topping:
- 100 grams butter
- 1/2 cup flour
- 1/2 cup brown sugar
- 1/2 cup desiccated coconut
- 1 teaspoon finely grated orange zest

Direction

- Preheat your oven to 170°C. Grease and line your baking tin.
- Start by making the base. Cream the butter and castor sugar together until pale and fluffy. Add the flour, cornflour and baking powder. Beat for a minute, then use your hands to bring the mixture together.
- Press the dough into the tin in an even layer. Spread the apricot jam over the shortbread base layer. Set the tray aside.
- Place all of the topping ingredients in a bowl. Use your fingertips to rub everything together until evenly combined. Crumble small clumps of the topping over the jam layer as evenly as you can.
- Pop the tin in the oven and bake for 40 minutes until the topping is golden. Allow to cool completely before removing from the tin and cutting into squares.

179. Orange Pumpkin Torte With Cranberry Jelly And Ricotta Mascarpone Whipped Cream

Serving: Serves 8-10 | Prep: | Cook: | Ready in:

Ingredients

- For the Cake
- 2 cups roasted pumpkin or any other kind of squash, preferably, or 15 oz. of canned pumpkin
- 4 eggs
- 1 cup vegetable oil
- 1 cup granulated sugar
- 1/2 cup brown sugar
- 1 navel orange, zested, and the zest divided into thirds, and juiced, with the juice set aside
- 1/2 teaspoon salt
- 1 teaspoon baking soda
- 2 teaspoons baking powder
- 1 1/2 teaspoons cinnamon
- 1 teaspoon grated fresh ginger
- 3 cups all-purpose flour
- 1 cup finely chopped walnuts (optional)
- 1/4 cup very finely chopped candied or crystallized ginger (optional)
- For the Fillings
- 1 cup sugar
- Orange juice, plus enough water to equal one cup
- Orange zest
- 1 12-ounce bag fresh cranberries, rinsed
- 1 cup heavy cream
- 1 pound whole milk ricotta cheese
- 8 ounces mascarpone cheese
- 1/2 cup granulated sugar
- 1/4 cup finely chopped candied or crystallized ginger (optional)
- 1/4 cup coarsely chopped walnuts (optional)

Direction

- Mash, then drain the roasted pumpkin or squash for 1/2 hour in a sieve lined with a paper coffee filter. Preheat oven to 350 degrees. Grease a 10"x"15" baking sheet.
- In a large mixing bowl stir together (by hand) pumpkin, eggs, oil and both sugars until blended. Add one-third of the orange zest and the remaining ingredients; stir until well-blended, but be careful not to over-mix.

- Spread batter into prepared pan and bake on middle oven rack for 35-40 minutes, or until a toothpick inserted in center comes out clean. Cool completely.
- Combine orange juice/water mixture, a third of the orange zest, the 1 cup sugar and cranberries in a medium saucepan. Bring to boil, then reduce heat and boil gently for 10 minutes, stirring occasionally. Let cool to room temperature.
- In a large bowl combine the ricotta, mascarpone, the 1/2 cup sugar, and remaining orange zest. Using an electric beater, whip the ricotta-mascarpone mixture until thoroughly combined and smooth.
- In a medium bowl, beat the cream until soft peaks form. Gradually fold the whipped cream into the ricotta until the mixture is smooth. Cover and refrigerate.
- To assemble torte, cut cake into four equal-sized rectangles. Place one rectangle onto a serving platter and spread with one-fourth of the whipped filling and drizzle with 1/4 cup cranberry-orange sauce; repeat with remaining layers, filling and sauce (refrigerate extra sauce for another use). Garnish torte with crystallized ginger and walnuts, if desired. Refrigerate until serving, and refrigerate any leftovers.

---

180. Pasta Flora Jam Tart

Serving: Serves 20 | Prep: | Cook: | Ready in:

Ingredients

- 400 grams gluten free flour
- 300 grams icing sugar
- 200 grams almond meal (ground almonds)
- 250 grams unsalted butter, cut in cubes room
- Pinch salt
- 1 teaspoon baking powder
- 50 grams brandy
- 2 eggs beaten
- 200 grams apricot jam

Direction

- Mix all the dry ingredients with the eggs and brandy.
- Add the butter at room temperature and knead lightly.
- Make into a ball, and put it in the fridge for half to one hour.
- Roll out half the dough to fit the bottom of the tart pan.
- Spread the jam evenly on top.
- Roll the remaining dough into strips to about 1cm thick and place on top of the jam at lattice pattern.
- Bake in a preheated oven at 160 Celsius for an hour.

---

181. Paula Wolfert's Herb Jam With Olives And Lemon

Serving: Serves 6; makes about 1 1/2 cups | Prep: | Cook: | Ready in:

Ingredients

- 4   large cloves garlic, halved
- 1 pound baby spinach leaves
- 1   large bunch flat-leaf parsley, stems discarded
- 1/2 cup celery leaves, coarsely chopped
- 1/2 cup cilantro leaves, stemmed
- 1/4 cup extra-virgin olive oil
- 12   oil-cured black olives, pitted, rinsed, coarsely chopped
- 1 1/4 teaspoons Spanish sweet smoked paprika (pimenton de la Vera)
- Pinch of cayenne
- Pinch of ground cumin
- 1 tablespoon lemon juice, or more to taste
- Salt and freshly ground pepper

Direction

- Put the garlic cloves in a large steamer basket set over a pan of simmering water and top

with the spinach, parsley, celery, and cilantro. Cover and steam until the garlic is soft and the greens are very tender, about 15 minutes. Let cool, then squeeze the greens dry, finely chop, and set aside. Using the back of a fork, mash the garlic cloves.

- In a medium cazuela set over a flame-tamer or in a heavy-bottomed skillet, heat 1 tablespoon of the olive oil until shimmering. Add the mashed garlic, olives, paprika, cayenne, and cumin and stir over moderately high heat for 30 seconds, or until fragrant. Add the greens and cook, mashing and stirring, until soft and dry and somewhat smooth, about 15 minutes.
- Remove from the heat and let cool to room temperature. Mash in the remaining olive oil. Refrigerate, closely covered, for at least 1 day and up to 4 days.
- To serve, return to room temperature. Stir in the lemon juice and, if it seems too thick, thin to a spreadable consistency with water or olive oil. Season with salt and pepper. Pack in a serving dish and serve with crackers or semolina bread.

---

182. Peach Jam With Lavender And Honey

Serving: Makes 5 cups | Prep: | Cook: | Ready in:

Ingredients

- 2 tablespoons Dried lavender flowers
- 1/2 cup water
- 4 cups slightly mashed peaches - from 8-9 peaches, peeled, pitted and diced
- 1/4 cup fresh lemon juice
- 3/4 cup orange blossom honey (room temperature)
- Pomona's Universal Pectin (or other low sugar powdered pectin)
- 4   12-oz jars

Direction

- If using Pomona's Pectin - prepare calcium water according to package directions and set aside.
- Bring water and lavender flowers to a boil in a small saucepan. Turn off heat, cover and let steep for 30 minutes. Strain lavender, reserving water.
- Put mashed peaches in a medium saucepan.
- Add lemon juice, lavender water, and 4 tsp calcium water from Pectin recipe, and stir to combine.
- Bring peach mixture to a boil.
- While waiting for peaches to boil, mix together honey and 3 tsp Pectin Powder.
- When fruit is at a boil, add pectin-honey mixture and stir vigorously 1-2 minutes to dissolve pectin. Return to a boil, and immediately remove from heat.
- Fill jars with jam, cover and refrigerate for up to 3 weeks.

183.   Peach Marmalade

Serving: Makes 1 cup | Prep: | Cook: | Ready in:

Ingredients

- 6 Granny Smith apples, cut into cubes (leave skin on and include the pits)
- 1/2 lemon, juiced
- 6 ripe peaches, peeled and cut into quarters
- 1/3 cup honey

Direction

- Combine the apples and lemon juice in a medium pot. Add 1 quart water. Cover, place over high heat, and boil over high heat for 40 minutes.
- Strain the juice through a sieve and discard the pulp. Return the juice to the pot, set over high heat, and boil for 10 minutes.
- Add the peaches and honey and cook over high heat for about 20 minutes. To test if the marmalade is done, drop a spoonful onto a

plate. As it cools, you can see if it has reached the thick consistency of marmalade. If it is too thin, let it boil down for a few more minutes and then check again.
- Pour the marmalade into a jar, let cool and secure the lid. It will keep for about 2 weeks in the refrigerator.

184.   Peanut Butter & Jelly Crunch Bread

Serving: Serves 10 | Prep: | Cook: | Ready in:

Ingredients

- 2 cups Flour of choice
- 1/8 teaspoon Baking soda
- 1 teaspoon Salt
- 2 teaspoons Baking powder
- 3/4 cup Peanut butter powder
- 1 Egg
- 1 cup Milk
- 1/3 cup Warm water
- 1/4 cup Honey
- 1/4 cup Brown sugar
- 1/2 cup Dried fruit of choice, diced fine
- 1/4 cup Nuts of choice, chopped fine

Direction

- Preheat oven to 325 degrees. Line a bread pan (8"x4" or 9"x3") with parchment paper or coat bottom and sides with non-stick spray, and place a piece of parchment on the bottom of the pan.
- Combine the dry ingredients in a medium-sized bowl and set aside.
- Place the milk, honey, warm water and sugar in a smaller bowl and mix to work in the honey. Then, add egg and combine.
- Pour the liquid mixture into the dry mixture, and combine thoroughly with a spatula or heavy spoon.
- Place half the mixture in the pan, then add a layer of nuts and dried fruits, reserving 2

tablespoons of the fruit and 1 tablespoon of the nuts.

- Pour the remaining bread batter on top of the mixture and spread evenly. Top with reserved fruit and nuts.
- NOTE: This bread takes about an hour to bake, so to prevent burning on the top, loosely covered it with foil or parchment before placing in the center of the oven.
- Bake until a toothpick comes out clean, which is between 45 minutes and one hour. Start checking at 45 minutes.
- Cool to warm if serving or completely if freezing, slice with a serrated knife for best results. Serves 10 good-sized pieces, or wrap individual slices and freeze for later use.

---

185. Peanut Butter & Jelly Mug Cake

Serving: Serves 1 | Prep: 0hours4mins | Cook: 0hours1mins | Ready in:

Ingredients

- 1/4 cup peanut butter
- 1 tablespoon brown sugar
- 1 egg
- 1/4 teaspoon baking powder (see Note below)
- 1 pinch salt
- 1 tablespoon grape jelly (or whatever you have on hand)

Direction

- In a 12-ounce mug, whisk peanut butter, brown sugar, egg, baking powder, and salt together until smooth. Then plop in the jelly, swirling it into the batter with a knife.
- Microwave mug cake on high for 45 to 60 seconds, or until just set.
- Note: If you want a fudgier, gooier cake, then leave out the baking powder.

---

186. Peanut Butter & Jelly Overnight Oats

Serving: Serves 2 | Prep: | Cook: |Ready in:

Ingredients

- 1 cup old-fashioned rolled oats
- 0.25 cups peanut butter + more for serving
- 2 tablespoons chia seeds
- 2 tablespoons pure maple syrup + more for serving
- 1.5 cups vanilla almond, soy or coconut milk
- Pinch coarse salt
- 0.25 cups strawberry fruit preserves
- 0.5 cups fresh strawberries, sliced
- 0.25 cups slivered almonds

Direction

- In a medium mixing bowl, whisk together oats, peanut butter, chia seeds, pure maple syrup, milk and salt. Transfer to a jar with a lid and refrigerate overnight. Stir in fruit preserves, more peanut butter and more maple syrup, to taste, and top with fresh strawberries and slivered almonds.

---

187. Peanut Butter & Jelly Sandwich

Serving: Serves 1 | Prep: | Cook: |Ready in:

Ingredients

- 3 tablespoons peanut butter
- 2 tablespoons jelly, your own personal choice, I use plum jelly
- 2 pieces of sandwich bread, either white or wheat

Direction

- Put 3 tablespoons of peanut butter in a bowl or plate.
- Add the 2 tablespoons of jelly to the peanut butter.
- Mix the peanut butter and jelly about 20 strokes until both is mixed smooth.
- Put the mixed peanut butter and jelly onto a slice of bread.
- Smooth out the peanut butter mixture on the slice of bread and then place the other piece of bread on top.
- You can either slice the sandwich in half cross-ways [/] or right down the middle. It's great with a side of sliced cheese and a glass of milk!

---

188.   Peanut Butter And Jam Scones

Serving: Serves 8 | Prep: | Cook: |Ready in:

Ingredients

- 2 1/4 cups whole wheat pastry flour (or all-purpose)
- 1/4 cup brown sugar
- 1 tablespoon baking powder
- 1/2 teaspoon baking soda
- 1/2 teaspoon salt
- 1/4 cup unsalted butter, cold, cut into small cubes
- 1/3 cup peanut butter
- 2 tablespoons milk or cream, plus more for finishing
- 1/2 cup plain yogurt
- 1/2 - 2/3 cups jam or jelly (or chocolate chips)
- 1 tablespoon coarse sugar (turbinado or demerara)
- 2 tablespoons crushed peanuts

Direction

- Preheat the oven to 375°F.
- Combine flour, sugar, baking powder, baking soda, and salt in a mixing bowl. Using a pastry cutter or two knives, cut in the butter until the

mixture looks sandy. Mix the peanut butter in with your hands until large clumps form. Add the milk and yogurt. You want a soft but not sticky dough. Add more milk a tablespoon at a time if the mixture is too dry.

- Turn the dough onto a lightly floured Silpat or sheet of parchment paper and pat it into an 11×9-inch rectangle, about 1/2-inch thick. Spread the jam over the dough. Fold one long side of the dough toward the center, then fold the opposite side over that to form 3 layers, as if you're folding a business letter. Press lightly on the top of the dough to seal it. To discourage the dough from breaking as you lift it, fold the Silpat in and then peel it back to separate it from the dough. (Thanks for the tip Heidi!) Slide onto a baking sheet.
- Brush the top with milk or cream and generously sprinkle with sugar and peanuts.
- Bake for 30-35 minutes, until the scone is firm to touch and dark golden on the bottom. Allow to cool for 10 minutes on the baking sheet, then transfer to a wire rack. Slice into squares to serve.

---

189.   Peanut Butter And Jelly Crispy Brown Rice Bars

Serving: Makes 18-20 bars | Prep: | Cook: |Ready in:

Ingredients

- 4 tablespoons unsalted butter
- 10 ounces marshmallows
- 1 cup peanut butter
- 1 teaspoon vanilla extract
- 6 cups brown puffed rice cereal
- 1/2 cup raspberry preserves
- 1 teaspoon vanilla sea salt (or your favorite finishing salt)

Direction

- In a deep saucepan over medium heat, add the butter. Once melted stir in the marshmallows and stir with a wooden spoon until melted. Add the peanut butter and vanilla, remove from heat, and stir to combine. Stir in the puffed brown rice cereal and make sure all pieces are evenly coated.

- Spoon half of the mixture into a greased 9×9-inch pan and press down with parchment to create an even, flat base. Pour the jam on top and spread an even layer across. Spoon the other half of the peanut butter and crispy rice mixture on top of the jam and push down with the parchment until evenly flat. Place in the refrigerator to cool completely, about 35 minutes. Cut into pieces and serve. Makes 18-20 bars, depending on how large you would like them.

190. Peanut Butter And Jelly Croissants

Serving: Makes 4-6 | Prep: | Cook: |Ready in:

Ingredients

- Syrup + Peanut Filling
- 100 grams sugar (syrup)
- 60 grams water (syrup)
- 1 teaspoon pure vanilla extract (syrup)
- 60 grams round roasted peanuts
- 20 grams almond flour
- 10 grams all-purpose flour
- 80 grams icing sugar
- 80 grams unsalted butter, room temperature
- 1 large egg, lightly beatened
- Assembly + Finishing
- 4-6 day-old good quality all butter croissants
- 4-6 tablespoons good quality or homemade strawberry jam
- 4-6 tablespoons crushed roasted peanuts to top
- 2-4 fresh strawberries, quartered for garnish
- icing sugar for dusting

Direction

- Syrup + Peanut Filling
- Syrup: In a small saucepan, heat sugar and water until dissolved, take off heat, let cool, and add vanilla extract. Set aside until ready to use.
- Peanut Filling: In a medium mixing bowl, cream together butter and icing sugar. Add egg in three additions, mixing thoroughly after each addition. Mix in flour and nuts until fully incorporated. Cover bowl with plastic wrap, chill until ready to use.
- Assembly + Finishing
- Set a rack in the middle of your oven, preheat to 375 degrees F / 180 C.
- Cut croissants in half, like you would for a sandwich.
- Brush the insides (top and bottom) with syrup twice so they soak up thoroughly. You might have some syrup left, depending how big your croissants are.
- Spread about 2 tablespoons of peanut frangipane onto the bottom half of each croissant. Top with about 1 tablespoon of jam, make sure to cover whole surface area of the croissants.
- Sandwich the croissants with the top half. Spread the leftover peanut frangipane on the tops, sprinkle with crushed peanuts.
- Bake in the preheat oven for about 15-20 minutes, until the tops have browned nicely. Cool croissants before garnishing.
- Spoon a little jam on the tops, garnish with strawberries. Finally lightly dust with icing sugar to finish.

191. Peanut Butter And Jelly Picnic Cheesecake (Vegan)

Serving: Serves 12-14 | Prep: | Cook: |Ready in:

Ingredients

- Crust
- 1/2 cup graham crackers finely grounded

- 1/2 cup pretzel sticks coarsely grounded
- 1/4 cup sea salt potato chips with ridges, coasely grounded
- 3 tablespoons Sucanat or unrefined raw sugar
- 4 tablespoons coconut oil (room temp/melted)
- 1 tablespoon Almond or other nondairy milk
- Cheesecake Filling, Layers and Topping
- 1 1/2 cups raw cashews (soaked overnight and drained)
- 3/4 cup full fat coconut milk (use creamier portion at the top of the can if possible)
- 1/2 cup creamy peanut butter of choice
- 1/3 cup melted coconut oil+ 1 teaspoon for chocolate dipped potato chips
- 1/3 cup light brown agave nectar
- 1/4 cup fresh lemon juice+4 tablespoons juice reserved for berry jelly preserves
- 1 teaspoon vanilla extract
- 1/2 teaspoon sea salt
- 2 cups whole potato chips with ridges (1 cup for topping, 1 cup for filling)
- 1/2 cup vegan dark chocolate chips (for dipped potato chip topping)
- 12 ounces fresh blackberries, washed (for preserves)
- 6 tablespoons Sucanat or unrefined raw sugar (for preserves)
- 2 teaspoons white chia seeds (for preserves)
- 2 tablespoons warm water (to dilute preserves for topping)
- 2 tablespoons roasted chopped peanuts (for topping)

Direction

- Crust
- Grease spring form pan with coconut oil.
- Put 1/2 cup graham crackers (3 sheets roughly) into food processor. Grind crackers to a fine crumb. Next throw chips into food processor and then pretzels. I processed all three crust ingredients separately to get the right texture. For pretzels and potato chips I just did a few pulses for larger, coarser crumbs.

- Mix ground graham crackers, pretzels and chips together in a bowl with coconut oil and 1 tablespoon of almond milk. Once all ingredients are mixed, spoon them into the spring form pan. Press mixture evenly with hands or back of a large spoon to compact and form crust. Put crust in freezer for an hour to solidify.
- Cheesecake Filling, Layers and Topping
- Remove chilled crust from freezer. Blend raw cashews (drain first) coconut milk, coconut oil, peanut butter, lemon juice, vanilla extract, and sea salt (optional) in a food processor. Be sure to process ingredients for several minutes until mixture is completely smooth. You may need to take breaks and scrape the sides down of the container to make sure all the cashew bits are ground. Use a knife or spoon to spread evenly.
- Take the cheesecake mixture you just blended from the processor and pour out approximately half of it onto the cheesecake crust. Use a knife or spoon to spread evenly. Return mixture to the freezer for approx. 45 minutes so the 1st layer batter can harden a bit. While waiting for the mixture to harden, you can make the jelly preserves and chocolate dipped potato chips.
- To make Jelly Preserves: Heat a medium size stock pot to medium high. Put berries into pot and cook until softened. Reduce the heat. Add lemon juice and sugar and cook for 2-3 more minutes. Use a large fork or potato masher to break the mixture down further and help dissolve the hard parts of the berries. Remove pot from heat. Add 2 teaspoons of white chia seeds to the berry mixture. Mix the ingredients thoroughly. Return to fridge to cool for at least 15 minutes.
- To make Chocolate dipped potato chips: Place ¾ of the total amount of chocolate into a heat safe bowl and place over the top of a pan of simmering water. If you have a double boiler, use that. Heat stirring occasionally until the chocolate has melted, then continue to heat the chocolate to 110 degrees F (43 degrees C) stirring occasionally. As soon as the melted

chocolate reaches temperature, remove it from the heat and stir the remaining chocolate chips in. Continue stirring until the chocolate has cooled to 90 degrees (32 degrees C) Use tongs or your hands to carefully dip potato chips in one at a time. Place on dipped chips on parchment paper. Cool until set in the refrigerator.

- When the time is up, remove the cheesecake from the freezer. Take remaining 1 cup of potato chips (not dipped) and lay them on flat on top of the 1st layer of the cheesecake cake. You may have to break up chips so they lay flat. Then pour a thin layer of the jelly preserves on top of the chips. Smooth out with a knife. Return cake to freezer for 15 minutes.
- Remove cake again from freezer. Spoon the remaining cheesecake batter on top of the jelly layer. Smooth out with a knife. You can remove the spring form pan but first run a warm knife along the edges of the ring so the ring comes off easily. At this stage, you can add the jelly/peanut/chip topping if you like.
- For Topping: Place remaining jelly preserves into a plastic squeeze bottle. Add warm water to help dilute and shake vigorously. If mixture clumps up, you can use a toothpick to clear the hole of the squeeze cap. Sprinkle roasted peanuts and drizzle preserves on top of the cake. Take chocolate dipped chips out of the fridge and stagger chips along the outside of the cake slightly overlapping.
- Cover and return cheesecake to freezer for 2 more hours.
- Defrost cheesecake ideally for 10 to 15 minutes before serving. Slice the cake with a serrated knife dipped in hot water. Enjoy!

---

192. Peanut Butter And Jelly Pie

Serving: Makes one 9-inch pie | Prep: | Cook: | Ready in:

Ingredients

- For the crust:
- 3/4 cup all-purpose flour
- 1/2 cup graham flour
- pinch salt
- 8 tablespoons very cold unsalted butter, cubed
- ice water, as needed
- egg wash, as needed
- For the filling:
- 1 cup cold heavy cream
- 1/2 cup confectioners' sugar
- 1 1/4 cups smooth peanut butter
- 8 ounces cream cheese, at room temperature
- 1/2 cup sugar
- 2 teaspoons vanilla extract
- 1/2 cup good quality jelly

Direction

- Preheat the oven to 425° F. Prepare a 9-inch pie plate.
- In a large bowl, whisk the all-purpose flour and graham flour to combine. Add the cubed butter into the flour to coat each piece. Use your hands to shingle the butter between the palms of your hands or using your fingers. Continue until the pieces of butter are about the size of walnut halves.
- Make a well in the center of the flour mixture, and add ice water. I start with 3 tablespoons for a single-crust pie, and then continue adding 1 tablespoon at a time until the dough comes together. Wrap the dough and chill it well, at least 30 minutes.
- On a lightly floured surface, roll out the dough to 1/4- to 1/8-inch thick. Roll the dough onto the rolling pin and gently transfer to the pie plate, unfurling the dough off the pin and into the plate. Press firmly to make sure the crust reaches all the way to the bottom of the plate, but don't poke any holes in the dough. Trim the dough to have a 1/2-inch overhang all the way around, and chill it for 15 to 30 minutes.
- Tuck the excess dough under at the edges, working all the way around and pressing lightly to help the dough "seal" to the outer

edge of the pie plate. Crimp the edges as desired. Freeze the crust for 15 minutes.

- Place a piece of parchment over the pie crust and fill with pie weights. Bake until the crust is lightly golden brown, 15 to 17 minutes. Remove the parchment and pie weights, and brush the base of the dough with egg wash. Return to the oven and bake until fully baked, 5 to 10 minutes more. Cool completely.
- In the bowl of an electric mixer, whip the cream to soft peaks. Add the confectioners' sugar and whip to medium peaks. Set aside.
- In the bowl of an electric mixer, cream the peanut butter, cream cheese, and granulated sugar until light and fluffy, 4 to 5 minutes. Add the vanilla and mix to combine.
- Fold the whipped cream into the peanut butter base. Pour the filling into the cooled crust. Smooth into an even layer. Refrigerate the pie until the filling is quite firm, 30 minutes.
- Spread the jelly in an even layer on the top of the pie. Keep chilled until ready to serve.

193.   Peanut Butter And Jelly Sandwich Cookies

Serving: Makes 13 | Prep: | Cook: | Ready in:

Ingredients

- 1 cup peanut butter, plus additional for making the sandwiches
- 1 cup brown sugar
- 1 egg
- 1 teaspoon vanilla extract
- 1 teaspoon baking soda
- For Filling
- peanut butter
- strawberry or raspberry jam

Direction

- Preheat the oven to 350. Line two large cookie sheets with parchment paper.

- Combine all of the cookie ingredients in a large bowl and stir well. Scoop out teaspoon sized balls of cookie dough and space them two inches apart on the cookie sheets. Using a fork dipped in sugar gently press the cookies down. Rotate the fork and press again to make the classic peanut butter cookie pattern. The dough is quite sticky so it is important to keep re-sugaring the fork to keep it from sticking.
- Bake the cookies for 10-12 minutes, or until lightly set and browning around the edges. The tops should still be light.
- Remove pans from the oven and let cool for a couple of minutes. Transfer cookies to a cooling rack and let cool completely.
- Turn half of the cookies over and spread the bottoms with a thin layer of peanut butter. Top with a teaspoon of jam and spread almost to the edges of the cookie. Top with remaining cookies.

194.   Peanut Butter And Jelly On Whole Wheat Ice Cream

Serving: Makes 1 qt | Prep: | Cook: | Ready in:

Ingredients

- 1 loaf whole wheat bread, split
- 10 ounces cream
- 1/3 cup honey
- 1/3 cup granulated sugar
- 2 tablespoons corn syrup
- 4 teaspoons corn starch
- 3 tablespoons cream cheese
- 1 cup peanut butter
- 1 cup jam of choice
- salt

Direction

- Preheat oven to 300. Take four slices of the loaf of bread and cut them into 1/4 inch cubes. Pour melted butter on top, sprinkle salt and toss. Spread on baking sheet and toast until golden brown and dry. They should be buttery croutons. Cool and set aside.

- Take the rest of the bread loaf and place it in a medium sized pot. Pour the milk over the bread and heat on med/low heat until the milk starts to simmer. Remove the pot from the heat and cover. Let the bread steep in the milk for at least 3 hours (overnight is totally fine). The bread will have soaked in a lot of the milk.

- Push the milk/bread mixture through a fine mesh strainer, or cheese cloth, to extract as much milk as possible. You want two cups of the liquid. If you end up with more than two cups, you can reduce the milk a little by bringing it up a simmer. If you end up with less than two cups of milk, you can add milk until you reach two cups. The point is that the milk taste like your bread, think cereal milk.

- Take the two cups of milk and place in pot with eight ounces of cream, honey, sugar, corn syrup and 1 tablespoon of salt. Heat over medium heat until mixture starts to simmer, making sure that all of the sugar has melted. Let simmer for five minutes.

- Make a slurry with the cornstarch and last two ounces of cream by whisking them together. Slowly stir the slurry into the milk mixture and bring back to a low bowl while stirring. Let simmer for an additional three minutes.

- In a separate bowl place the cream cheese. Pour a little bit of the hot milk mixture on the cream cheese and whisk together. Slowly add more of the milk until all of the milk and cream cheese is combined and there are no traces of lumps of cream cheese. Pour ice cream base into a plastic gallon back and cool in an ice bath. Chill in fridge overnight. Churn ice cream according to manufacturer's directions.

- Mix the toast croutons into the churned ice cream. Scoop a 1/2 inch layer of the ice cream into your container, then spread a layer of peanut butter on top. Make another layer of ice cream then spread a layer of jam. Repeat this until all ice cream is used. Take a butter knife and dip all the way down in the ice

cream and swirl the knife slightly to blend all the layers together. Freeze for three hours and enjoy!

---

195.   Peanut Butter And Raspberry Jam Galette

Serving: Serves 8 | Prep: | Cook: | Ready in:

Ingredients

- For the pastry dough: makes 2 crusts.
- • 1cup (2 sticks) unsalted butter, chilled
- • 2 cups white rice flour, plus more for work surface
- • 1 cup fine ground corn meal
- • 3/4 teaspoon salt
- • 2/3 cup cold sour cream
- • 2 large egg yolks
- • 1 tablespoon sugar
- • Zest of 1 large lemon
- For the filling:
- • 3/4 cup creamy Peanut Butter
- • 3/4 cup Seedless Raspberry Jam
- • 1 cup fine ground Pecans or Walnuts
- • 1/3 cup organic light brown sugar
- • 1/2 teaspoon cinnamon
- • 1 teaspoon organic vanilla extract

Direction

- Cut butter into 1/4-inch cubes. Place in an even layer on a plate and transfer to refrigerator to chill.
- Place the rice flour, cornmeal, salt, sugar and lemon zest in the bowl of a food processor, and pulse several times to combine. Add the butter, and egg yolks, process, until the mixture resembles coarse meal, about 10 seconds. Add sour cream and process until the dough just holds together (do not process for more than 30 seconds).
- Turn out dough onto a work surface. Divide in half, and place each half on a piece of plastic wrap. Flatten each to form a disk. Wrap, and

refrigerate at least 1 hour or up to 1 day before using.

- For the Galette you will need only one half of the dough, the other half I keep in the freezer.
- To make the filling; ground nuts with the light brown sugar and cinnamon. In a medium bowl mix jam and peanut butter, add the nuts and vanilla and stir well to combine all ingredients.
- Preheat oven to 375 degrees.
- On a lightly floured work surface, roll out dough to a 14-inch round, about 1/8-inch thick. Transfer the dough to a shallow glass pie baking dish.
- Arrange the filling on top of dough. Fold border over the filling, overlapping where necessary. Brush edges of dough with egg, sprinkle with sugar. Transfer to refrigerator and chill 15 to 20 minutes.
- Bake until crust is golden brown and the filling starts bubbling, 55 to 60 minutes. Transfer baking dish to a wire rack to cool the galette. Serve warm or at room temperature.

196. Peanut Butter And Jam Cookie Sandwiches

Serving: Makes 6 cookie sandwiches | Prep: | Cook: | Ready in:

Ingredients

- 1 cup peanut butter
- 1.4 cups creamed honey
- 1/4 cup protein powder or dry ingredient of choice
- 1/4 cup sugar free jam

Direction

- Preheat oven to 275 degrees.
- Blend together peanut butter and honey, make sure it's well blended.
- Mix in egg.

- Add protein powder or dry ingredient of choice, mix well.
- Roll into balls and place on cookie sheet a couple inches apart, press balls down with the bottom of a jar or cup to flatten.
- Bake in oven for around 8 minutes until edges are slightly darker brown cookies will be soft but firm up as they cool.
- When cool spread jam on the bottom of one cookie and top with another. Let sit for 5 minutes (if you can resist) to let jam soak into the cookie a bit.

197. Pear Pineapple Ginger Jam

Serving: Makes 10 1/2 pint jars | Prep: | Cook: | Ready in:

Ingredients

- 12 pears, cleaned, cored, peeled and sliced into 1" pieces
- 1 3" stub of ginger, peeled
- 1 whole pineapple, cleaned, cored and cut into 1" cubes
- 1 cup lemon juice (app. 4 big lemons juiced)
- 4.5 cups organic sugar
- 1.5 tablespoons vanilla extract
- 3 tablespoons crystallized ginger, finely chopped
- 1 tablespoon orange flower water

Direction

- Toss all the ingredients into a pot on the stove. Simmer over medium-low heat until tender, stirring occasionally, about 10 minutes.
- Reduce heat to low; simmer until mixture drops thickly from spoon, stirring often, about 1 hour.
- Remove the ginger carefully.
- While still hot, pour the jam into 10 sterilized 4-ounce jars and water-bath them according to your own canning process. I water-bathed

these jars for about 20 minutes, and then carefully removed the jars to rest on a towel until cool (overnight).

- Label the jars and give away liberally! (This jam is gorgeous on bread with a pat of butter, or stirred into granola and yogurt, or alongside a nice cheddar with crackers.)

---

198. Pear And Black Pepper Preserves

Serving: Makes about 7 half-pint jars | Prep: | Cook: | Ready in:

Ingredients

- 3 pounds very firm, pears such as Bartlett or Kieffer
- 1 3/4 cups sugar
- 1 cup wildflower or other mild honey
- 2-inch knob of fresh ginger
- 2 lemons
- 1 1/2 teaspoons freshly ground black pepper

Direction

- Peel, quarter, and core pears. Slice the quarter crosswise into 1/4-inch thick slices. You should have about 8 cups.
- Peel your lemon and julienne the zest. Halve and juice the lemons and reserve the juice.
- Peel the ginger, thinly slice it lengthwise, and then julienne it to be a similar shape to the lemon julienne.
- In a preserving kettle layer pears, sugar, honey, lemon zest, and ginger, finishing with a layer of sugar. Cover with foil and let stand overnight on the kitchen counter.
- The next day, place a plate and 3 spoons in your freezer.
- Remove the foil from the pears, stir in 1/3 cup of lemon juice and bring the mixture to a simmer over medium to medium-low heat. Cook very slowly until the pears are tender and translucent and the syrup is thick, about 1

to 1 1/2 hours. Be careful not to burn them. Add a little water if they begin to stick to the bottom of your kettle before the pears are tender.

- When the pears begin to look translucent, test the consistency of the syrup by placing a bit on one of your cold spoons and putting it back in the freezer for another minute or two. You want a consistency just thicker than maple syrup but not as thick as honey. If your pear syrup is not thick enough, cook another 10 minutes and test again.
- Gently stir in the black pepper just before you pull the preserves off the stove. Ladle hot preserves into hot sterilized jars and top with 2-piece canner lids. You can store your preserves in the refrigerator (or freezer if you use freezer safe jars), or you can process them for 5 minutes in a boiling water bath canner for pantry storage.

---

199. Pelion Orange Marmalade (Greek Recipe)

Serving: Serves 6 | Prep: | Cook: | Ready in:

Ingredients

- 2 kilos oranges
- 3 lemons
- 1.5 kilos sugar appro

Direction

- Wash and boil the oranges and lemons whole for 50 minutes.
- Drain the fruit. When cold cut them open and throw away the pips.
- Put all the fruit in batches in the blender and blend to the point that you have very small pieces, not completely mushed.
- Weigh the fruit again and add to it the same amount of sugar approx. 1.5 or 2 kilograms.
- Turn the oven on at 150 degrees Celsius.

- Pour everything in a large tray so the fruits spreads out evenly Place in oven and bake for 90 minutes.

200.   Pepper Jelly Drumsticks

Serving: Serves 2 | Prep: | Cook: | Ready in:

Ingredients

- 1/4 cup pepper jelly
- 1 teaspoon Dijon mustard
- 1/2 teaspoon Chinese mustard (optional)
- 1 teaspoon soy sauce
- 1/2 tablespoon butter
- 6 chicken drumsticks
- salt and pepper to taste

Direction

- Combine first five ingredients in a small saucepan and whisk together over medium heat until bubbling; remove from heat
- Prepare medium high grill and season chicken with salt and pepper
- Brush chicken with glaze, start grilling, and brush chicken again after turning over on grill; cooking about 10 to 12 minutes per side
- Put remaining glaze on the stove, bring to a boil and simmer for one to two minutes; glaze chicken once more when it comes off the grill

201.   Pepper Punch Plum Jam

Serving: Makes 4 half-pints | Prep: | Cook: | Ready in:

Ingredients

- 3 cups sugar, divided
- 1/4 cup water
- 1 medium habañero pepper, washed and sliced into thin rings (wear gloves when handling the pepper)
- 1 medium jalapeño pepper (about 4" long)
- 5 cups washed and chopped plums (you can use a mix of types; about 7 plums)
- 1 cup peeled and chopped peaches (about 1 large peach)
- 2 teaspoons chopped crystallized ginger
- 1/2 - 3/4 teaspoons coriander seeds, lightly toasted

Direction

- Fill your waterbath canner with water, cover and place over high heat on stove. Place four half-pint jars (with lids and bands) nearby. When the water is at a boil, you can sterilize the jars by submerging them in the pot. You can also prep the lids this way by putting them in the boiling water for 2-3 minutes and then removing them. You needn't sterilize or prepare the bands.
- In an 8" skillet set over medium-high heat, pour the ½ cup sugar and ¼ cup water. Stir to combine and continue stirring regularly until the sugar has melted. Add the habanero rings and candy them by cooking for 6-10 minutes. They'll start to look like a coating of sugar syrup is encasing them. Using tongs, remove the candied rings to a plate and set aside. Pour the habanero syrup into a small glass measuring cup or vessel. Set aside- you'll use some of this in the jam.
- Around the burner of a gas stove (or you can use a grill), place a sheet of foil (this makes for easier clean-up). Turn the burner on, and, using tongs, hold the jalapeño in the flames, rotating it regularly. You want to burn the skin and roast the inside. When the pepper's skin is evenly blackened, put it in a Ziploc and seal shut. After five minutes or so, remove it and then slough off the skin. This should be an easy task now. Dice the roasted jalapeño and set aside.
- In a jam or other large, heavy-bottomed, non-reactive pot set over medium-high heat, toss together the chopped plums, peaches and 2½ cups of sugar. When the sugar has melted, turn the heat up to high and add 2 tablespoons

of your reserved habanero syrup, your diced/reserved jalapeño and the chopped ginger. Stir to combine well.

- Using a spice grinder or a mortar and pestle, grind the toasted coriander seeds and add to the jam. Add at least half of your reserved candied habanero rings to the jam. Taste the jam. Keeping in mind that the heat of the peppers (the degree of spiciness) will fade some as the jam cools, add more habanero rings or syrup to taste. After 20 or 25 minutes, the temperature of the jam should be at about 218. It will sheet off the back of a wooden spoon, look thick and boil in a lava-like way.

- Carefully ladle the hot jam into your prepared jars, run a chopstick or slim knife around the edges to release any air bubbles, apply the lids and bands, and process in your waterbath canner for 12 minutes. Remove and let cool, undisturbed, for a few hours.

202.   Pineapple Ginger Preserves

Serving: Makes 2 half-pints | Prep: | Cook: |Ready in:

Ingredients

- 4 cups peeled and chopped pineapple
- 2 cups unrefined, granulated sugar
- 1 ounce fresh ginger, peeled and grated
- generous 1/4 teaspoon dried mustard
- zest of 1/2 an orange

Direction

- If you'll be canning this, set up your waterbath. Get the water boiling and your jars at the ready. In a heavy-bottomed, non-reactive pot set over medium-high heat, toss together the pineapple chucks and sugar. When the sugar has melted, add in the ginger, dried mustard and orange zest and stir to combine. Increase the heat to high- you want this at a nice boil.

- Stir frequently, and after 10 minutes, start checking the temperature. This should hover around 220 when done. When it's ready, ladle carefully into your prepared jars, apply the bands and lids, and process for 12 minutes. Serve with cream cheese and crackers, or in any other of a number of ways.

203.   Pistachio Mascarpone And Blackberry Jam Stuffed French Toast

Serving: Serves 4 | Prep: | Cook: |Ready in:

Ingredients

- 1/4 cup shelled unsalted pistachios
- 1/2 cup mascarpone cheese
- 2 tbsp + 1 tsp   pistachio paste
- 1 cup whole milk
- 3 large eggs
- 2 tablespoons honey, warmed in the microwave
- 1/4 teaspoon kosher salt
- 1/4 teaspoon vanilla extract
- 1/4 teaspoon orange zest
- 1 cup blackberry jam or preserves
- 4 1-1.5 inch thick day old challah bread slices
- 4 tablespoons butter (1 per piece of toast)

Direction

- For the Pistachio Mascarpone: Preheat oven to 350°F. Shell pistachios if not already shelled and spread out on a baking sheet. Toast for about 6 minutes, or until aromatic. Cool, chop finely, and place in a small bowl. Increase oven temperature to 375°F.

- Combine mascarpone, pistachio paste and chopped pistachios in a medium bowl and mix until ingredients are completely incorporated. Set aside.

- For the French Toast: In a shallow baking dish, whisk milk, eggs, honey, vanilla, orange zest, and salt until frothy and combined. Set aside.

- For each challah piece, use a paring knife to carefully slice a pocket into the bread. Slice into the bottom side of each piece, lengthwise, and cut nearly through to the other side of the bread, making sure to leave the sides intact. Use your fingers to open the pocket and create space for the filling.
- With a butter knife, carefully fill each pocket with a 1/4 of the pistachio mascarpone. Next, spread as much of the blackberry jam on top of the mascarpone as you can, making sure the fillings are spread throughout the entire slice of bread while still being able to close the pocket you created. Set aside and continue with 3 remaining slices.
- Soak the filled challah pieces in the custard for 30 seconds per side, and place on a plate to rest.
- Melt one tablespoon butter in a large nonstick skillet over medium low heat. One by one, cook challah slices for 2-3 minutes per side, or until golden brown, adding more butter to the skillet before adding another piece of stuffed bread. Place cooked French toast pieces on a rimmed baking sheet and finish cooking through in the oven for 5 minutes.
- Cut each piece in half and finish with a dusting of powdered sugar, maple syrup, or both. Serve immediately.

204.   Plum Jam With Rosemary And Ginger

Serving: Makes 1 1/2 cups | Prep: | Cook: | Ready in:

Ingredients

- 1 1/2 cups Plums, peeled and cut into 1/2" chunks
- 1 cup Blueberries
- 3 teaspoons freshly grated ginger
- 2 sprigs fresh rosemary
- 1/4 cup sugar
- 1 tablespoon white balsamic vinegar

Direction

- Add all ingredients into a 9" skillet at medium low heat until it simmers, turn down heat to retain a simmer for 10 minutes.
- Remove rosemary sprigs and continue to simmer an additional 10 minutes until the mixture coats the back of a spoon
- Remove pan from heat and let cool to room temperature. Spoon into lidded glass container and store in refrigerator up to a week

205.   Plum Jam With A Little Bite To It

Serving: Makes 7 half pints of plum jam | Prep: | Cook: | Ready in:

Ingredients

- 7 cups coarsely chopped plums - Santa Rosa, Friar, or other plum of your choice.
- 4 cups sugar
- 2 star anise pods
- 1/2 teaspoon crushed red pepper flakes
- 1/2 to 1 jalapeno pepper, finely chopped
- 1/2 cup lemon juice

Direction

- In a large glass bowl, combine all the above ingredients and stir well. Cover with plastic wrap, and let sit for a few hours.
- In the meantime, prepare a water bath and glass half pint jars and lids and seals.
- While jars are in the hot water bath, bring the plum mixture to a boil in a large, non-reactive pot (I use a Le Creuset) over high heat, stirring the mixture occasionally. Allow to boil hard for about 3 minutes, and then turn the heat down to medium to medium high. After about 12 minutes, the jam should be ready to can. (You can dip a metal spoon into the jam, and if the jam forms a "drape" off the spoon, the jam is ready to be canned.)

- I use a jam funnel to ladle the jam into the jars. Leave 1/2" headroom. After cleaning jars, lid and light screw on tops and process for 10 minutes. When you remove the processed jars, wait for the PING. No PING, put the jam straight into the refrigerator. Otherwise, you can store for long term use.

206. Plum Pucker Jam And Elephant Ears

Serving: Serves 2 cups | Prep: | Cook: |Ready in:

Ingredients

- Plum Pucker Jam
- 2 pounds Plums
- 1 Inch of pealed ginger, sliced thinly
- 3 tablespoons Honey (more depending on tartness of the plums)
- 1/4 teaspoon Cinnamon
- Non-stick spray
- Elephant Ears
- 1 Sheet of puff pastry (thawed according to directions)
- Thin layer of the Plum Pucker Jam
- Cane sugar for sprinkling

Direction

- Plum Pucker Jam
- Pre-heat oven to 450°F. Spray a backing sheet with non-stick spray. Half and pit the plums. Place the plums cut side down on to the baking sheet. Place the thin slices of ginger under the plums. Bake plums till mushy (about 30 to 40 mins). Take the plums, ginger and juices place in a mixing bowl. Add cinnamon and honey, mix. Here you can add more honey if you think that your jam is too tart. You can use a blender or immersion blender to puree the jam to you desired consistency.
- Elephant Ears

- Follow the directions for the puff pastry baking, and pre-heat oven to that temperature.
- Unfold pastry sheet on a floured surface. Lightly roll out pastry and spread a thin layer of the plum jam. Fold the edges toward the center (about 2 folds) and fold over on to each other. Cut the roll into 1/4 inch thick sections. Place on a backing sheet covered with parchment paper and sprayed with nonstick spray. Sprinkle with cane sugar. Bake until golden brown on the edges. After that get ready for some lip puckering!!

207. Plum And Star Anise Jam

Serving: Makes about 3 cups | Prep: | Cook: |Ready in:

Ingredients

- 2 pounds fresh, ripe plums (preferably red-fleshed), pitted and cut into big chunks
- 3/4 cup light brown sugar, packed
- 1 piece of star anise
- pinch of sea salt

Direction

- Combine all ingredients in a large saucepan. Cook over medium heat until mixture begins to bubble, stirring often. Lower to a simmer and cook for 30-40 minutes, continuing to stir occasionally to keep fruit from scorching. The jam is ready when the fruit is mostly broken down and a good amount of the liquid is evaporated. The jam will continue to thicken as it cools.
- Allow to cool to room temperature. Remove the anise, taking care to find any stray arms of the star that might have fallen away. Store the jam in an airtight container in the refrigerator for up to two weeks, or freeze in small containers for up to a few months.

208. Plum Jam With Tea Biscuit

Serving: Serves a crowd | Prep: | Cook: |Ready in:

Ingredients

- Plum jam
- 1.5 kg plums (stoned and left in one piece or cut in half)
- 0.5 kg sugar
- 0.5 teaspoons salt
- Classic butter tea biscuit
- 2 cups flour
- 2 teaspoons baking powder
- 1/2 cup cold butter
- 2 tablespoons sugar
- 1/2 teaspoon salt
- 3/4 cup cold milk plus some for brushing

Direction

- Plum jam
- In a bowl add sugar and salt to the plums and place in the fridge overnight.
- Next day, preheat the oven to 150 C (300 F) and put the plums into a roasting pan and place in the middle of the oven.
- Roast the plums for 1 hour before you mix.
- Place back in to the oven and keep roasting for additional 30-40 minutes. Plums will have a nice chunky texture (the way I liked).
- Still hot, scope jam in warm glass jars (2 jars 2 cups each), place a lid on and flip the jar upside down.
- Classic butter tea biscuit
- Mix all dry ingredients together and cut butter until crumbly.
- Add milk to dry ingredients and mix by hand until formation of soft dough. Rest the dough for a few minutes.
- Place the dough on the table and spread with hands until desire thickness, 1 inch approximately. Cut into serving size, brush some milk over top.
- Bake 400F for 15-16 minutes or until golden brown.

209. Poached Eggs With Tomato Balsamic Jam And Aioli

Serving: Serves 4 | Prep: | Cook: |Ready in:

Ingredients

- Tomato Jam and poached eggs
- olive oil to coat pan
- 2 cups chopped tomato, (use whatever kind of tomato you like include juices seeds everything)
- 1 shallot chopped
- 1 tablespoon balsamic vinegar
- 1 baguette
- 4 eggs
- Basil to garnish
- Aioli
- 2 egg yolks
- 1 large clove of roasted garlic
- 1/2 cup Minus 2 tbs vegetable oil
- 1/4 cup olive oil
- 2 tablespoons unsalted butter at room temperature
- 1 tablespoon lemon juice
- 1/2 teaspoon sea salt
- white or black pepper to taste
- Optional - 1/2 tsp lemon zest (if you like it lemony)

Direction

- Tomato Jam and poached eggs
- To make the tomato jam, heat your fry pan coated with olive oil, add the chopped shallot and saute until the shallot is translucent.
- Add the chopped tomato let it cook until tomato becomes soft. Add the balsamic vinegar continue cooking for a few minutes it should resemble a jam in consistency, Salt and pepper to taste.
- Cut your bread in half lengthwise Spread some aioli on the bread then spread with the tomato jam. Close the baguette and wrap in

foil place in warm oven (170-200 degrees) until eggs are done. You can also toast your bread in the oven, spread with the aioli or butter and place under the broiler until nicely browned. Then spread with the tomato jam. Whatever your preference.

- Poach your eggs. If you don't have an egg poacher just use a fry pan filled 3/4 full with water, salted. Break your egg into a ramekin and carefully add each egg to the boiling water. I let them cook about 3 minutes yolk will be very soft.
- Remove bread from oven open it up and place your eggs on top of the tomato jam, drizzle with aioli and chiffonade the basil and garnish.
- Aioli
- To roast the garlic take several cloves with the skin on lay on aluminum foil, drizzle with olive oil, make a packet with the foil. Place on baking sheet and bake in a 350 degree oven for approximately 10-15 minutes. Add to the blender the two egg yolks, lemon juice, butter, salt, pepper and garlic and optional lemon zest, blend until smooth. With blender on slowly add the oil until it becomes creamy and thick. Adjust seasoning and citrus to taste.

---

210. Polpettone With Onion Shallot Jam Over Creamy Root Vegetable Purée

Serving: Serves 4, 2 polpettone each | Prep: | Cook: | Ready in:

Ingredients

- Onion-Shallot Jam and Creamy Root Vegetable Purée
- Good olive oil to generously film pan
- 2 yellow onions, peeled, fine dice
- 4 shallots, peeled, fine dice
- 4 ounces white wine
- Sea or kosher salt to taste

- 2 large parsnips, peeled, diced
- 4 carrots, peeled, diced
- 3" piece fresh horseradish, peeled, diced
- 1 quart Heavy cream
- Sea or kosher salt and white pepper to taste
- Polpettone and Filling
- 1/2 cup sun dried tomatoes, rehydrated and drained
- 8 ounces fresh mozzarella, 1/2" dice
- 3" piece fresh horseradish, peeled, fine dice
- Juice of 1 lemon (not Meyer - too sweet) & zest of 1/2 of it
- Sea or kosher salt and pepper to taste
- 2 pounds ground turkey
- 1/2 cup Panko, preferably fine, unseasoned
- 1 large egg
- 1 teaspoon sea or kosher salt
- 1/2 teaspoon pepper
- 1 teaspoon dried oregano or 2 teaspoons fresh, chopped
- 2 cups Panko
- Green garnish of your choice

Direction

- Onion-Shallot Jam and Creamy Root Vegetable Purée
- Prepare onion jam. Generously film bottom of a heavy-bottomed pan or skillet with some good olive oil over medium heat. When warm, add onions and shallots along with a couple of good pinches of salt. Cover pan, and when contents begin cooking nicely, reduce heat. Continue cooking, stirring often (if some bits brown, that's fine, just not too much). When it looks as if much of the water has been cooked away, stir in the white wine. Cook until a sweetly rich, silky concentration is reached. Remove from heat. You'll reheat just before serving.
- Alternatively, make twice as much. Store the extra in a container in your refrigerator. Add it to soups, salad dressings, omelettes, grilled cheese sandwiches, or anything you think could benefit from some sweet silken richness.
- While jam is reducing, begin cooking the root vegetables. Add cream to a heavy-bottomed

stainless steel pot (aluminum will react badly with the lactic acid in the cream causing an off-taste and gray color). Add the vegetables, cover pot and begin heating over medium heat. Bring to a gentle simmer, then reduce heat a bit. Cook, stirring somewhat often, until vegetables can be VERY easily pierced with the tip of a sharp knife. Remove from heat. You will reheat, purée, and season just before serving. It's much easier to reheat in the rough state.

- Polpettone and Filling
- Prepare filling to set aside and permit flavors to blend. Place rehydrated sun-dried tomatoes, diced mozzarella, horseradish, lemon juice and zest in bowl of food processor. Pulse just until ingredients are relatively uniform in size - very small, but not a puréed paste. Scoop into a bowl and season to taste with salt and pepper.
- Mix polpettone. Place ground turkey, Panko, egg, salt & pepper, and oregano in a mixing bowl. If you've got gloves, use 'em. Mix ingredients with your hands until completely blended.
- Preheat oven to 350 degrees. Line a baking sheet with parchment.
- Shape and fill polpettone. Again wearing gloves, pick up a sort of small tennis-ball size of turkey mixture. Gently shape it into a ball. Press a large indentation into it with a thumb. With a spoon, scoop a generous amount of filling into it. Pinch it closed, then gently roll the polpettone between your palms to create a small football. Set on parchment. Repeat until all turkey mixture is gone.
- If you have filling left over, because not all of us visualize the same small-tennis-ball size, and "generous" can have different meanings, do not despair. Put it in a ziplock bag and freeze it. Use it in ravioli filling, in omelettes - you get my drift.
- Before baking, pour 2 cups Panko into a baking dish. Gently pick up each polpettone. Place in Panko, and with your hands gather it up around sides and end of polpettone. Turn it

over and repeat on other side. Repeat until all polpettone have been coated.
- Bake polpettone until gently browned and instant-read thermometer inserted into the center reads 165 degrees, about 20 minutes.
- While polpettone are baking, reheat root vegetables. When nicely hot, remove from heat and purée right in the pot with an immersion blender (if you don't have one, this would be an excellent reason to get one - and I don't take on new appliances quickly). Season to taste with salt and pepper. It should take your breath away, by the way. Also reheat the lovely onion-shallot jam.
- To serve, spread a puddle of the root vegetable purée in the center of each plate. Set two polpettone in it and top with the onion-shallot jam. Garnish with green of your choice - chopped fennel fronds, Italian parsley, basil chiffonade. Have a lovely dinner!

---

211.   Port Wine Jelly

Serving: Serves 4 jars of 250ml | Prep: | Cook: | Ready in:

Ingredients

- 1 bottle of good Ruby Port wine (750ml)
- 5 tablespoons fresh lemon juice
- 2 3/4 cups sugar
- 2 ounces powder fruit Pectin

Direction

- Wash and sterilize the jam jars and lids for 5 minutes in boiling water. Remove and drain upside down on a clean kitchen towel.
- In a pan (not aluminum), mix the Port wine with the lemon juice and the pectin (used in food as a gelling agent particularly in jams and jellies). Whisk to dissolve and bring to a boil.
- Add the sugar and bring back to a boil. Count 2 minutes after boiling point is reached and remove from the heat. If any foam forms remove it before putting jelly in the jars. The

jelly will still be liquid at this point but after it cools it jellifies due to the pectin.

- While the jelly is still boiling hot, fill the jars leaving 1/2 inch below the rim. Screw the lid, invert the jar for 15 minutes. Re-invert jar so it is straight, clean the outside surface and allow to cool. Put a label and store in a dark cool place.

212. Proscuitto, Goat Cheese, And Fig Pear Balsamic Jam Rolls

Serving: Makes 24 rolls | Prep: | Cook: |Ready in:

Ingredients

- Fig Pear and Balsamic Jam
- 1.5 pounds figs, stems removed and coarsely chopped
- .5 pounds pears, peeled and pit removed and coarsely chopped
- 1 cup brown sugar
- .5 cups balsamic vinegar
- .25 cups fresh lemon juice
- Proscuitto, Goat Cheese, and Fig, Pear, Balsamic Jam Rolls
- 1 cup fresh arugula
- 3 teaspoons fresh lemon juice
- 3 tablespoons extra virgin olive oil
- Pinch of freshly ground black pepper
- 12 pieces prosciutto, cut in half crosswise
- .5 cups goat cheese (chevre)
- .25 cups fig, pear, balsamic jam

Direction

- For the jam, combine the figs, pears, brown sugar, and balsamic in a large saucepan.
- Bring to a simmer over medium to high heat. Then lower the heat to maintain a gentle simmer and cook.
- Break up the large pieces and stir periodically until the jam thickens.

- Remove from the heat and squeeze about a tablespoon of lemon juice, stir. Taste and add more lemon juice if desired.
- Spoon the jam into a container with a lid.
- Using sterilized jars, spoon into jars, seal jarm and process in boiling water for 10 minutes. Let cool and lids should seal.
- For the prosciutto rolls, place arugula in a medium bowl. In a small bowl, whisk the lemon juice, evoo, salt, and pepper. Toss the arugula in the dressing until lightly dressed (you may not need all of the dressing).
- Spread one tablespoon of goat cheese across one of each piece of prosciutto. Top each with 1/2 tsp. fig, pear, and balsamic jam. Divide the dressed arugula evenly across each of the pieces of prosciutto. Starting from the end covered with the filling, carefully roll each piece of prosciutto. Serve

213. Pumpkin Buckwheat – Spelt Pancakes With Pumpkin Plum Jam

Serving: Serves 2 | Prep: | Cook: |Ready in:

Ingredients

- For pancakes
- 1/2 cup spelt flour
- 1/4 cup buckwheat flour
- 150 grams natural yoghurt
- 1 egg
- 3 tablespoons pumpkin puree
- 1 teaspoon baking powder
- 1 teaspoon baking soda
- 2 tablespoons erytrithol or xylithol
- 1 tablespoon coconut oil
- 1 teaspoon cinnamon, cardamom and ginger
- For jam
- 5 plums
- 3 tablespoons pumpkin puree
- 1 teaspoon cinammon, ginger and cardamom
- 1 tablespoon maple syrup or honey

Direction

- Blend all the pancakes ingredients. Fry on the dry non-stick pan, putting a portion using a spoon. Fry for around 2 min. each side.
- In the meantime prepare jam – put diced plums with pumpkin puree into the small pot and fry until soften. Add spices and optionally a bit of honey or maple syrup. Blend everything.
- Serve pancakes with plum jam and maple syrup.

214.   QUICK AND EASY RASPBERRY JAM

Serving: Makes 8 cups | Prep: | Cook: | Ready in:

Ingredients

- 2 pounds fresh raspberries
- 1 1/3 cups sugar
- 4 tablespoons instant pectin

Direction

- Give raspberries a quick wash and then crush one layer at a time in a large bowl or puree in a blender and set aside.
- In a separate bowl, stir the sugar and pectin together. Slowly add fruit and whisk together for 3 minutes until all the ingredients are incorporated.
- Pour raspberry jam mixture in to freezable containers making sure to leave at least 1/2 inch head space to allow for the liquid to expand once in the freezer. Let jam stand 30 minutes before placing containers in the freezer.
- To finish off your jam for gift giving, order one of these personalized food labels using a pre-made template on our website or create your own.

215.   Quick Blueberry Jam

Serving: Makes a little less than a cup | Prep: | Cook: | Ready in:

Ingredients

- 1 cup fresh blueberries
- 1/3 cup sugar
- 1/16 teaspoon kosher salt
- 1/2 teaspoon lemon zest
- 1 teaspoon lemon juice
- 2 tablespoons water

Direction

- Place all ingredients in a pan. Turn heat to medium. Bring the mixture to a boil, stirring every minute or so. When it comes to the boil, reduce the heat to a simmer. It will start to release neon juices and the fruit will begin to soften. Cook up to 30 minutes. Up to you. The longer you go, the smoother and more jam-like it will be. Store in the fridge and eat within a few days.

216.   Quince Jelly Tart With Cinnamon Cream Cheese

Serving: Makes one 10" tart | Prep: | Cook: | Ready in:

Ingredients

- 1 Martha Stewart Foolproof Pie Crust
- 8 ounces cream cheese at room temperature
- 1/4 cup brown sugar
- 1/2 teaspoon cinnamon
- 1 egg at room temperature, lightly beaten
- 1 teaspoon vanilla extract
- 1-3/4 cups quince jelly, stirred-up for easy spreading
- 1 tablespoon sugar for sprinkling

Direction

- Prepare one Martha Stewart Foolproof Pie Crust per instructions. When sufficiently chilled (about four hours), remove the two halves from refrigerator and roll one half out to fit into the tart dish. Trim excess dough from top edge of tin and use to fill in any thin areas around the walls of the crust. With a fork, poke holes in the dough all around the bottom of the tart.
- Heat oven to 350 degrees F
- In a mixer fitted with a paddle attachment, whip together cream cheese, brown sugar and cinnamon until light and fluffy (1-2 minutes), scraping down sides one time. Add egg and vanilla and mix until just combined.
- With a spatula, evenly spread cream cheese mixture in the tart shell.
- With a clean spatula, gently pour quince jelly evenly around the top of the cream cheese, taking care not to mix the two.
- Roll out second half of dough to about 1/8" thickness and with a 2" circle cookie cutter, cut out approximately 18 circles. Starting at one edge of the tart, and carefully working your way around in a circle, place the circles of dough with one edge touching the outer crust and one edge barely overlapping the last circle. Continue with a second row of circles and finish with one circle in the center.
- Sprinkle sugar over the top of the dough circles.
- Bake on the center rack for 30 - 35 minutes or until the top of the tart is golden brown. Let cool completely and serve at room temperature.

217.   RUSTIC WHITE PEACH & CITRUS BLUEBERRY JAM TART WITH MAPLE CRUMBLE

Serving: Serves 8 | Prep: | Cook: |Ready in:

Ingredients

- Puff Pastry Crust
- 2 1/4 cups all purpose flour or pastry flour
- 1/4 cup coconut sugar
- 4 tablespoons cold butter
- 3/4 cup cold water
- Toppings
- 1 cup blueberries
- 1 cup cold water
- 2 tablespoons maple syrup
- 1 lime (zest & juice)
- 1 orange (zest & juice)
- 2 sprigs of mint
- 1 tablespoon water/cornstarch mix
- 2 white peaches sliced thin
- 1/4 old fashioned oats
- 2 tablespoons raw sugar
- 2 tablespoons room temp. butter
- 1/4 teaspoon cinnamon

Direction

- 1. In medium sized bowl, add the flour, coconut sugar, and butter. With a fork, break up the butter into small bits. Then pour in the water and mix together till a dough forms. Set aside wrapped in the fridge.
- In a medium size sauce pan, add the blueberries, orange juice & zest, lime juice & zest, water, maple syrup, and mint. Boil on high for 5 minutes and reduce to low heat for another 5 minutes. Add in the cornstarch water mix and set aside.
- Preheat the oven to 375'F. Take the dough out of the fridge and on a floured surface, roll to 1/4 inch thickness. In a butter/greased fluted pan, lay and press the dough into the pan. Poke the sides and bottom with a fork. Bake in the oven for 10 minutes.
- While waiting for the dough mix the oats, raw cane sugar, maple syrup, butter, and cinnamon together in a small bowl.
- Pull the crust out of the oven and lay the jam down first in an even layer. In a circle, lay the peaches on top. Around the edges, sprinkle the crumble. Bake the tart for another 30

minutes. Allow to cool for 10 minutes to set up before serving.

218. Rapturous Morel Marmalade

Serving: Serves 10-12 | Prep: | Cook: | Ready in:

Ingredients

- Rapturous Morel Marmalade
- 8 ounces Fresh or Rehydrated Morels
- 4   Bacon or Pancetta Slices
- 2 sprigs Fresh Thyme
- 1/2 cup Veal Stock
- Salt & Pepper to Taste
- 1 cup Carrots, Diced
- 1 cup Shallots, Diced
- 1 cup Port Wine
- 1/2 cup Red Wine Vinegar
- 3 tablespoons Brown Sugar
- 1 teaspoon Black Pepper
- Salt to Taste
- Goat Cheese Polenta
- 4 cups Unsalted Chicken Stock
- 1 cup Polenta
- 1/2 cup Goat Cheese
- Salt & Pepper to Taste
- 1 tablespoon Freshy Thyme Leaves

Direction

- Rapturous Morel Marmalade
- In a large sauté pan, cook the bacon till lightly crisp. Remove the bacon and add morels, pinch of salt, and 2 tbs of butter. Cook till the mushrooms develop a nice brown crust. Add veal stock and thyme, simmer rapidly till the stock is more or less evaporated, leaving the mushrooms moist with the tiniest amount of liquid. Set aside.
- In a separate large pan heat 3 tbsps. butter. Saute the shallots and carrots with a pinch of salt till softened, about 10 minutes, stirring frequently. Stir in the sugars, vinegar, port

wine, kosher salt and pepper. Cook over medium heat until the liquid has reduced.
- Chop the sautéed mushrooms and bacon bits. Add to the warm sauce and combine gently but thoroughly over low heat till warmed. Check for black pepper, it should be fairly peppery. Serve with goat cheese polenta and crème fraîche. Be warned – highly addictive!!
- Goat Cheese Polenta
- Bring the chicken stock, 2 tbsps. butter, pepper, thyme, and salt to a boil in a heavy-bottomed pot. Sprinkle polenta slowly while constantly stirring the liquid. Reduce the heat to a gentle simmer, and constantly stir the polenta till it pulls away from the sides of the pan. The polenta is cooked when it is creamy and no longer grainy. It should take about 20-25 minutes to get the right consistency. (I cook polenta for at least an hour when I want it extra creamy as I serve it with my short ribs).
- Stir in the goat cheese and taste the seasonings. Pour immediately into a butter glass pan. When cool, cover and refrigerate overnight.
- Cut the polenta into any shape you wish. I usually cut them into bite size since I serve this at my cocktail parties. Heat a big skillet with some olive oil. Pan fry the bites till golden brown on each side. Top it with Morel Marmalade and crème fraîche. Serve warm.

219. Raspberry Chia Seed Jam

Serving: Makes 1 cup of jam | Prep: | Cook: | Ready in:

Ingredients

- 2 cups raspberries (fresh or frozen)
- 2 tablespoons honey
- 1   lemon, zested and juiced
- 1 tablespoon chia seeds (black or white)
- 1/2 teaspoon natural vanilla
- 1 pinch sea salt

Direction

- In a medium pot add everything except for the chia seeds (raspberries, honey, lemon juice, lemon zest, vanilla and salt). Place on stovetop over medium heat and stir to combine. Once mixture warms up and berries begin to get mushy (within a few minutes), mash with the back of a wooden spoon until all evenly broken down.
- Leave for 5 minutes on medium then reduce to low-medium for another 10 minutes, stirring once in a while.
- Remove from heat, add chia seeds and stir to evenly combine. Leave to cool. Pour into jar and refrigerate. Keeps for 3 to 4 weeks in the fridge.

until the raspberries are very tender and have released their juices.
- Take 1 full cup of the mixture and pour it through a fine mesh sieve. This filters out some of the seeds- so the jam is lightly seeded. Add the deseeded mixture back into the pan.
- Add the sugar and stir over low heat, until the sugar has dissolved. Increase the heat and bring the mixture to a boil. Boil rapidly for about 10-15 minutes, or until the jam passes the wrinkle test or reaches 220 degrees Fahrenheit on a candy thermometer.
- Allow the mixture to cool at least three minutes off the heat. Divide mixture into the sterilized jars. Process in a water bath for 10 minutes.

220. Raspberry Lemon Balm Jam

Serving: Makes 5-6 half pints | Prep: | Cook: | Ready in:

Ingredients

- 2 pounds Red Raspberries
- 4 1/2 cups Granulated Cane Sugar
- 1   lemon, juiced
- 1   bunch, Lemon Balm, flowers removed

Direction

- 12-14 hours before you want to jam, combine the Lemon Balm and the sugar. Rub the leaves and stalk into the sugar, until it is fragrant. Allow to sit for an entire day, covered.
- After the sugar has rested, pick out the lemon balm stalks and any errant leaves that might be in the sugar. Prepare a water bath, and sterilize six jars, lids, and rings (or use Weck rubber seals). Sterilize any other equipment you plan to use- like funnel, measuring cup, etc.
- Pour the raspberries in a large non-reactive pot (I use a 10 quart stainless steel jam pan). Gently heat the fruit on low, pressing the fruit against the pan. Cook for about 10 minutes,

221. Red Pepper Jam!

Serving: Makes about 1 1/2 cups | Prep: | Cook: | Ready in:

Ingredients

- 2   red bell peppers, finely chopped (about 2 1/2 cups)
- 3   large tomatoes (2 cups when grated)
- 5   cloves garlic, minced (1 solidly packed tablespoon when minced)
- 1/2   yellow onion, finely chopped (2/3 cup when chopped)
- 1 cup sherry vinegar
- 1/2 cup granulated white sugar
- 1/2 cup brown sugar
- 2 teaspoons freshly squeezed lemon juice
- 1/8 -1/4 teaspoons ground cayenne pepper
- 1/8 teaspoon Kosher salt
- 1/8 teaspoon ground black pepper

Direction

- Put a very wide-mouthed pot on the stove. I used a Le Creuset large casserole pot that's about 12" in diameter. This is important, otherwise the mixture won't boil down very well.

- Cut the tomatoes in half and grate them on a rough grater to remove the skins. You should get about 2 cups grated tomatoes when done. Throw them in a wide mouthed pot with the rest of the ingredients and bring to a boil.
- Reduce to an active simmer and cook until thick and syrupy (about 45 minutes). Let cool to room temperature before using to let the jam thicken and the flavors to meld. Refrigerate, assuming it lasts longer than 1 meal.

222.   Rhubarb Vanilla Jam

Serving: Serves 1/2 pint | Prep: | Cook: | Ready in:

Ingredients

- 8 3/4 ounces rhubarb
- 1 cup granulated sugar
- 2 tablespoons water
- 1 vanilla bean

Direction

- Chop the rhubarb into small pieces and place in a heavy saucepan with the sugar and water.
- Split the vanilla bean and scrape out the seeds with the flat side of a knife and drop into the pan. Add the bean.
- Stir the mixture over medium heat until the sugar is dissolved, stirring to scrape the bottom. Continue cooking over medium heat, stirring and breaking up the fruit with the back of the spoon. Cook for about 20 minutes until the jam is thick, just shy of spreadable, as it will thicken when it cools.
- Remove the vanilla bean and discard. Carefully spoon the hot jam into a half-pint jar and leave unsealed to cool. When cool, screw on the lid and refrigerate.

223.   Ricotta And Cherry Jam Crostata (crostata Di Ricotta E Visciole)

Serving: Serves 8 | Prep: | Cook: | Ready in:

Ingredients

- For the pastry crust:
- 2 cups (250 grams) of flour
- 1/2 cup (100 grams) of fine sugar
- 1 stick (½ cup or 125 grams) of cold butter, diced
- 1 whole egg plus 1 egg yolk
- finely grated zest of 1 lemon
- For the filling:
- 9 ounces (250 grams) sour cherry jam
- 1 pound (500 grams) firm ricotta (preferably sheep's milk)
- 1 whole egg plus 2 yolks
- 1/2 cup (100 grams) fine sugar

Direction

- For the pastry crust, combine the flour and sugar in a bowl. Add the butter and rub into the flour until the mixture appears crumbly (alternatively, pulse together in a food processor). Add the lemon zest, the egg and yolk and combine until the pastry just comes together into a smooth ball. Rest the pastry in the fridge for 30 minutes or overnight.
- In the meantime, prepare the ricotta filling by beating the ricotta, eggs and sugar until smooth and creamy.
- When the dough has rested, take about two-thirds of the dough and, on a floured surface, roll this to about 1/8 inch thickness to cover a 26cm or 10 inch pie dish. Trim the edges.
- Spread the jam over the pastry dough. Pour the ricotta mixture over this and smooth out the surface.
- With the remaining third of the pastry dough, roll on a well-floured surface to 1/8 inch thickness and cut into strips about ½ inch

wide, if you want a lattice top. Layer the strips in a crisscross pattern over the top and secure the ends on the edges of the pastry with a dab of water or the leftover egg white. If doing this without a top, save this dough for another use in the freezer.

- Bake the crostata at 350ºF for 25 minutes or until lightly golden and the centre of the crostata feels springy.

224.   Roasted Grape & Huckleberry Jam Galette

Serving: Serves 8 | Prep: | Cook: | Ready in:

Ingredients

- 1   pie crust, homemade or store bought
- 2 cups seedless red grapes, sliced
- 1/2 cup sugar
- Pinch salt
- 1/2 lemon, juiced and zest
- 3 1/2 tablespoons cornstarch
- 2 tablespoons Huckleberry jam
- 1 tablespoon Honey
- 1   egg
- Heavy cream, if needed

Direction

- Preheat the oven to 400 degrees. Roll the dough (either store-bought or homemade) out into a 12-inch round (it can be ragged). Transfer to a rimmed baking sheet lined with parchment paper and chill while preparing the filling.
- For the grape filling: Toss together the grapes, all but a tablespoon of sugar, the salt, the lemon juice and zest, honey, and the cornstarch. Pile fruit on the dough circle, leaving one 1/2-inch border. Gently fold the pastry over the fruit, pleating to hold it in (sloppy is fine).
- In a small bowl, whisk together the egg and cream. Brush pastry generously with egg and

cream mixture. Sprinkle remaining sugar on the crust. Bake for 35 to 45 minutes, until the filling, bubbles up vigorously, and the crust is golden. Cool for at least 20 minutes on wire rack. Serve warm or at room temperature.

225.   Roasted Grape Agave Jam

Serving: Makes 2 cups of jam | Prep: | Cook: | Ready in:

Ingredients

- 3 cups red, seedless grapes
- 2 teaspoons extra-virgin olive oil
- 1 pinch of salt
- 2 tablespoons agave nectar

Direction

- Pre-heat the oven to 450 degrees F. Line a baking sheet with parchment paper.
- Toss the grape with the evoo, sprinkle with salt.
- Bake for 15-20 minutes. Let the grapes cool completely on the baking sheet.
- Transfer to a small bowl, and using a potato masher, gently mash the grapes until they achieve a slightly chunky, yet pureed like consistency. Mix in the agave.
- Serve on homemade buttermilk biscuits.

226.   Roasted Jam

Serving: Makes about 2 pints | Prep: 0hours10mins | Cook: 0hours30mins | Ready in:

Ingredients

- 3 pounds (1.36 kg) fruit of choice, not peeled, pits/stems removed, and sliced or chopped (can be overripe, underripe, or perfect – doesn't matter!)

- 3/4 cup (149 g) granulated sugar (can be more or less, depending on how your fruit tastes)
- 1 lemon, juiced
- 1 handful flavorings (such as a few pinches of salt or dried spices, vanilla bean seeds, a splash of booze, etc.)

Direction

- On a baking sheet, toss the fruit with the sugar, lemon juice, and any flavorings. Let macerate while the oven preheats.
- Preheat the oven to 375°F. Transfer the baking sheet to the oven and roast until the fruit is very soft and the juices have thickened a bit (they may even start to turn dark at the edges of the tray). Cooking time will depend on the type of fruit—smaller, softer fruits like berries will take 15-20 minutes, larger, firmer fruits like stone fruit may take 20-30 minutes.
- When the fruit is very soft and tender, remove it from the oven. While it's still hot, use a potato masher or large fork to mash all the fruit on the tray. Transfer to a jar or other storage container and cool to room temperature, then refrigerate or freeze until ready to use.

---

227. Roasted Pears With A Lemon, Quince (Jam) And Brandy Sauce

Serving: Serves 4 | Prep: | Cook: | Ready in:

Ingredients

- 2 large, just-ripe pears
- 2 tablespoons butter, cut into tiny bits
- 1 heaping tablespoon brown sugar
- 1/3 cup brandy
- 2 tablespoons quince jam
- Zest of one lemon, finely grated
- 1/4 teaspoon grated nutmeg
- 4 egg yolks
- ½ cup heavy cream, scalded

- A small handful of toasted almond slices or pecans which have been toasted and then chopped, optional, for garnish

Direction

- Heat oven to 375 degrees Fahrenheit.
- In a shallow baking dish large enough to accommodate all of the pear halves, distribute the bits of butter and even sprinkle the brown sugar. Halve, peel and core the pears; place face down in the baking dish. When the oven is hot, roast the pears in the middle of the oven for 20 - 25 minutes, spooning the pan juices over them about half way through.
- Meanwhile, make the sauce: In the top of a double boiler over very gently simmering water (or bowl fitted over, but not touching, simmering water in a standard saucepan), stir together the sugar, lemon zest and nutmeg. Add the brandy and the jam and whisk together to blend thoroughly.
- Add the egg yolks, one at a time, whisking briskly all the while. After blending in the last yolk, start stirring with a wooden spoon, and continue to stir, constantly, until the sauce thickens and coats the back of the spoon. Don't worry about any slightly harder bits around the edges of the bowl; just bring them back into the sauce and continue to stir.
- When the sauce is thick, whisk in the hot cream until thoroughly blended. Strain through a fine-mesh sieve.
- Spoon generously over the roasted pears. Garnish with the sliced almonds or chopped pecans, if you like.
- This recipe was created by Food52 member Antonia James.
- NB: This is best served warm. It holds well for 3-4 days if refrigerated, and can be reheated in a microwave on medium-low power, stirring well after every half minute or so, or in the top of a double boiler. You'll need to thoroughly whisk it to smooth it out before serving.
- You can also make this with apricot jam, but then of course, it won't be quince sauce. It will, however, be just as delicious. ;o)

228.   Roasted Strawberry Balsamic Jam

Serving: Makes 1 ¼ cup jam + ¾ cup syrup | Prep: | Cook: | Ready in:

Ingredients

- 2 pounds strawberries, hulled and cut into halves
- 1/2 cup sugar
- 1 1/2 tablespoons good quality balsamic vinegar

Direction

- Place strawberries in a bowl, add sugar, and stir to mix thoroughly.
- Let berries sit and macerate while you heat your oven to 250 degrees.
- Once oven is heated, pour berries and their juices into a 9 x 13 baking dish, and spread out so they are in a single layer. Pour balsamic vinegar over berries, place baking dish in the oven, and bake for 2 hours. Check berries every 30-40 minutes and give them a quick stir.
- After 2 hours, remove berries from oven - they should look very dark red and a little dried out. There will also be a lot of syrup. Mash berries with a fork or a potato masher, then use a sieve to strain off the liquid syrup until jam reaches your desired consistency (don't forget to save the extra syrup!). Store jam in the refrigerator, and use within a couple of weeks.

229.   Roasted Tomato Jam

Serving: Makes about 3 cups | Prep: 0hours20mins | Cook: 2hours0mins | Ready in:

Ingredients

- 2 cups sugar
- 3 pounds ripe beefsteak tomatoes, cored and thinly sliced (1/4 inch)
- Large pinch salt
- Grated zest of 1 lemon
- Juice of 1 lemon
- 1   cinnamon stick
- 1/2 teaspoon fennel seeds, lightly crushed
- 2   dried red chiles

Direction

- Pour 1/3 of the sugar over the base of a 12-inch braising pan or other baking dish. Layer half the tomatoes, overlapping the slices, in the pan. Sprinkle with the salt, 1/3 cup sugar, and top with the lemon zest, lemon juice, cinnamon stick, fennel seeds, and chiles. Top with the remaining tomatoes, followed by the rest of the sugar. Let sit for 30 minutes. Heat the oven to 400 degrees F.
- Place the pan, uncovered in the oven and let cook for 1 hour. The tomato juices should simmer actively. Check every 20 minutes, spooning the juices over the top tomatoes, and removing the chiles if they char.
- Continue roasting and checking every 20 minutes -- the tomato juices should begin to gel at 2 hours, but it could happen a little sooner or later. Test the juices by spooning a little onto a plate, letting it cool, and running your finger though it. If it holds the line, the jam is ready. Remove the jam from the oven and let cool. I eat this jam fresh so I put it into jars and keep it in the fridge.

230.   Roasted Vegetable, Goat Cheese, And Spinach Quesadilla With Spicy Tomato Jam

Serving: Serves 2 | Prep: | Cook: | Ready in:

Ingredients

- 2 large whole wheat tortillas (I used a sprouted whole grain)
- small eggplant, cut in ¼ inch slices
- 1 small patty pan, yellow or zucchini squash, cut in thin slices
- 1 pepper (green, red or Italian frying pepper) cut in big chunks and seeded
- 2 tablespoons olive oil
- 1 clove garlic, minced
- 1 teaspoon sea salt
- 4 leaves fresh basil, torn
- 2 ounces fresh goat cheese (chevre)
- 2 tablespoons grated parmesan or romano cheese
- 2-3 tablespoons spicy tomato jam (or scant 1 Tbsp harissa)

Direction

- Place the vegetables on a flat oiled baking sheet. Brush the veggie slices with a mixture of the olive oil, garlic and salt.
- Roast at 400 until tops are browned, about 30 minutes. Flip, brush again, and roast another 20-30 minutes. Remove from pan and cool slightly.
- Heat a large skillet over medium heat and add one tortilla (no oil needed in the pan) Arrange the vegetables on top in a layer, sprinkle with chopped basil.
- Top with goat cheese, then a layer of the baby spinach, then sprinkle with the parmesan cheese.
- Spread the second tortilla with the tomato jam and then place the second tortilla on top, jam facing down. And cook until bottom tortilla is browning and getting crispy, pressing down with your hand or a spatula to make things stick together.
- Carefully flip the quesadilla to brown the other side. Remove to a plate and cut into four wedges (I use a pizza cutter for this).
- Eat one or two wedges hot today, and eat the rest cold or reheated tomorrow for lunch

231. Rosemary Fennel Cookies With Marmalade

Serving: Makes about 50 | Prep: | Cook: | Ready in:

Ingredients

- Marmalade
- 2 oranges (bergamot if you can find them)
- 3/4 cup sugar
- 1 cup water
- 1 pinch salt
- Rosemary-Fennel Cookies
- 1 cup (2 sticks) unsalted butter, softened
- 3/4 cup sugar
- 1 egg
- 1 teaspoon vanilla extract
- 2 1/2 cups all-purpose flour
- 3/4 teaspoon sea salt
- 1 teaspoon fennel seeds, crushed

Direction

- Marmalade
- Cut the oranges into eighths lengthwise and remove the seeds and the white pith, then slice these wedges as thinly a possible.
- Place sliced oranges in a small saucepan, cover with water and bring to a boil. Let boil for 5 minutes, then drain. (This step of blanching helps remove some of the bitterness and keep the bright color of the oranges. You can skip it if you like.)
- Return oranges to the saucepan and add the sugar, cup of water, and salt. Bring to a boil and cook until the marmalade begins to set, about 30 minutes. You can test for doneness by dabbing a little onto a plate that's been left in the freezer. After five minutes, run your finger through the dab of marmalade: if it wrinkles up, it's ready; if not, continue cooking.
- Remove marmalade from the heat and let cool completely. (Marmalade can be made several days in advance. Keep in the refrigerator until needed)
- Rosemary-Fennel Cookies

- Using an electric mixer, beat butter and sugar on medium speed until pale and fluffy, about 2 minutes.
- Mix in egg and vanilla until fully incorporated.
- Add flour, salt, rosemary and fennel and mix until combined, scraping down the sides of the bowl as necessary.
- Divide dough in half, shape into disks, wrap in plastic and refrigerate until firm, at least 1 hour.
- Preheat oven to 375 F. Remove one disk from the fridge, and lightly dust the countertop and the dough with confectioner's sugar. Roll out dough to about 1/8" thickness. Cut out cookies using a 2" round cutter (or any shape you like). Cut a hole in the center of half the cookies using a second, smaller cutters. Gather and re-roll scraps. Repeat with second disk.
- Place cookies about 1/2" apart on baking sheets lined with parchment paper. Bake for 10-15 minutes, until the edges are golden, rotating the baking sheets halfway through. Transfer baked cookies to a rack and let cool completely.
- Spread a thin layer of marmalade on each round cookie and sandwich it with a ring cookie.

232.   Ruby Red Raspberry Jam

Serving: Serves a few jars | Prep: | Cook: | Ready in:

Ingredients

- 3.3 pounds prepared Raspberries
- 1.7 pounds sugar
- 1/4 cup medium lemon – juice (1 medium lemon)
- "No Sugar Needed" Pectin

Direction

- What to do ahead: Sterilize jars and lids. Prepare some old newspaper to put under your jars when filing them. Read the instructions of the Pectin and check you have enough for your jam.
- Weigh the sugar. Put half the sugar in a non-reactive pot.
- Rinse the raspberries very quickly and put on kitchen paper towel to drain for 1 minute. Add the raspberries to the pot and cover with the remaining sugar. Stir to coat the raspberries with sugar and cover with a clean cloth. Let stand at room temperature for 8 hours, stirring occasionally, so the sugar dissolves completely before cooking. You will have a lot of syrup, unlike the mix fruit + sugar and cook method.
- For no-seed jam: Pass the raspberries through a food mill fitted with a fine screen and weigh the raspberries after deseeded.
- Bring the raspberries and sugar to a low simmer and cook for 15minutes, stirring constantly to prevent burning. During this boiling stage, skim off the foam, using a big spoon.
- Check the directions of your No-Sugar Needed Pectin Packet and measure the pectin needed for the weight of raspberries. To this quantity add 25% more of Pectin (see Note 3) and dissolve all of this pectin in the lemon juice.
- Add the lemon juice / pectin to the pan and allow the berry-pectin mix to boil on medium heat for 1 minute.
- Fill sterilized jars immediately (it's really important that the jam is still very hot) to 1/4 inch of tops, wipe clean the rims and close immediately with a sterilized tight fitting lid. Turn the jars up-side down for 20 minutes. Turn them back over and allow to cool.
- Clean jars, label them at least with the date and store in cool dark place.
- Note 1: Always make only one batch at a time. If you double or triple the recipe's contents you often end up with a softer jam.
- Note 2: If you want, sterilize the jam in the jars. Place the filled jars in a water bath. Boil for 10 minutes after the water has returned to a boil. Remove the jars to cool on a cooling rack.

- Note 3: Pectin – About Pectin: I did some research on brands sold in the US. The one that is most similar to the one I use nowadays is Sure-Jell "No Sugar Needed" Pectin. Because I cut down on sugar, I prefer to add 25% more of pectin to the jam and be sure that it sets, rather than having a runnier jam and having to "remake" the jam.

233.   Russet Potato And Jam Cake

Serving: Serves 20 | Prep: | Cook: | Ready in:

Ingredients

- 200 grams russet potatoes
- 250-300 grams flour
- 10 grams baking powder
- 200 grams powdered sugar
- 1 teaspoon cinnamon
- 1/4 teaspoon ground cloves
- zest from a whole lemon
- juice from 1/2 lemon
- 1 pinch salt
- 40 grams lard
- 1 egg
- 175 grams jam of choice

Direction

- Preheat the oven to 180 degrees C. Cook the potatoes with their skin on until a fork can easily pierce the potatoes. Drain them and leave to cool down. Peel the skin and pass the potatoes through a potato ricer or grate them on the small holes of a box grater.
- In a separate bowl, mix 250 g of flour with powdered sugar, baking powder, spices, salt, and the lemon zest. Add the flour mixture to the potatoes, and then add the lemon juice, lard, and the egg.
- Stir the mixture with a wooden spoon until everything comes together and you can continue kneading the dough with your

hands. You should end up with a slightly sticky dough. If your dough is too sticky, add more flour until you can easily handle it (add 25 g of flour at the time).
- Divide the dough into two equal parts. Grease and flour the bottom of a 9" round cake pan and press one half of the dough into the pan. Spread the jam over the dough in a thick layer. Roll out the remaining half of the dough and make a lattice over the jam. Use any remaining dough to form a log and line the cake.
- Bake the cake for 45 min or until the top starts to brown. Let the cake cool for 10 min, release it from the pan and leave on a cooling rack until it completely cools down. Sprinkle with powdered sugar before serving.

234.   STRAWBERRY CHIPOTLE JAM GLAZED SALMON TACOS

Serving: Serves 2 | Prep: | Cook: | Ready in:

Ingredients

- For the salmon:
- 1 6-8oz filet of salmon, wild-caught if possible
- 1/4 teaspoon corn starch, organic + GMO free if possible
- 1/4 teaspoon brown sugar
- 1/4 teaspoon salt
- 1 heaping tablespoons strawberry jam
- 1/2 chipotle pepper in adobo sauce, minced
- scant 1/4 cups soy sauce
- 1 tablespoon butter
- For the tacos:
- 4 corn tortillas
- 1 cup prepared black beans
- 1 avocado, sliced
- 1/4 cup chopped cilantro
- 1/2 cup leafy lettuce
- Lime crema
- Extra lime wedges for serving

Direction

- Preheat oven to 300 degrees. Pat salmon filet dry with paper towels. Combine corn starch, salt and sugar and rub into the dry salmon filet. Corn starch and sugar encourage browning and create a sticky surface for your glaze to adhere to. While this step isn't critical, it will help things turn out nicely.
- In a small sauce pan over medium heat, whisk jam, minced chipotle pepper if using and soy sauce until the jam is loosened up. Reduce to low heat and whisk regularly until the sauce is fragrant and reduced, 3-5 minutes. Remove from heat and allow to cool. It will thicken up considerably and this is a good thing.
- Heat butter over medium-high heat in a non-stick skillet (avoid cast-iron here... salmony smells will seep in and nobody wants that). Once butter is melted and just begins to brown, send salmon to the skillet, fleshy side down. Cook until the filet is nicely browned, about 5 minutes, then flip. Pour half the glaze over top, and cook for an additional 2-3 minutes. Send your fish the preheated oven, transferring to an ovenproof pan if your skillet isn't oven safe. Cook for 10 minutes.
- After removing salmon from the oven, let it rest for 5 minutes. This is perfect taco assembly time. Line up your tacos however you fancy. I prefer a smear of lime crema on the bottom of my tortilla, then black beans, then lettuce, then fish, then avocado, but let your personal taco intuition lead you.
- Flake salmon apart with a fork, then gently toss the pieces with the remaining glaze. Distribute between tacos and eat! Life-hack: use kabob sticks to hold your tacos in upright positions! One of dinner's biggest challenges, solved.

---

235.   Sarah K's Greengage Jam

Serving: Makes 2 jars | Prep: | Cook: | Ready in:

Ingredients

- 36 greengage plums
- 1.5 cups sugar
- 2 tablespoons Fresh ginger root extract
- 4 cloves powdered
- Juice of 1 lime

Direction

- Pit the washed and dried plums. Add to a saucepan along with the juice of 1 lime and ginger extract and simmer until completely cooked.
- Using an immersion blender puree the plums (peels and all, the peels were pretty thin for these plums).
- Return to the stove, add the powdered cloves and cook down until some amount of water has evaporated. Measure out the volume and add an equal amount of sugar. Increase heat so that the sugar melts and the jam starts boiling rapidly, keep stirring to prevent the bottom from scorching. Test by checking if the jam slowly drips in flakes from the wooden spoon used to stir the mixture.
- Ladle the jam into 2 sterilized jam jars, leaving about 1/4 inch at the top. Wipe any jam dripping on the rim of the jar. Fit the lid and loosely screw on the ring till it's just tight. Resist the temptation to tighten!
- Bring a large deep saucepan of water to boil (over the top of the lids). Gently place the jars into the boiling water and let it sit for about 5-7 minutes. Remove from boiling water, wipe dry and tighten the ring completely and allow to cool.

---

236.   Savory Corn And Basil Muffins With Ricotta And Tomato Jam

Serving: Serves 30 muffins | Prep: 0hours0mins | Cook: 0hours0mins | Ready in:

Ingredients

- For the tomato jam:
- 2 pounds tomatoes
- 1 cup packed brown sugar
- 2 cloves garlic, grated or finely minced
- 1 1-inch piece of ginger, grated or finely minced
- 1/2 teaspoon kosher salt
- 1/4 teaspoon ground cinnamon
- 1/4 teaspoon red pepper flakes
- For the muffins:
- 3/4 cup packed brown sugar
- 4 tablespoons unsalted butter, melted
- 3 large eggs
- 2/3 cup sour cream
- 1/3 cup olive oil
- 1 cup milk
- 2 2/3 cups all-purpose flour
- 1 cup stone-ground cornmeal
- 2 teaspoons baking powder
- 1 1/2 teaspoons baking soda
- 1 1/2 teaspoons kosher salt
- 1/2 teaspoon freshly ground black pepper
- 4 ears of corn, kernels only
- 3 tablespoons freshly chopped basil
- 2 cups ricotta cheese
- 1 handful basil, chiffonade (sliced thinly into ribbons)

Direction

- For the tomato jam:
- First, make your tomato jam. Dice your tomatoes and toss them in a hot pot over medium heat with your brown sugar, grated garlic and ginger, salt, cinnamon, and red pepper flakes. Turn the heat up to medium-high, stir to combine, and cook until the mixture is bubbling. Reduce the heat to medium and, stirring every so often so that the tomatoes don't burn, cook for 1 hour 30 minutes or so, until the tomatoes have thickened completely. Remove the tomatoes from the heat, taste, and adjust seasonings as needed. Allow the jam to cool. Remember that

it will thicken up as it cools, so don't overcook the jam.
- For the muffins:
- Preheat your oven to 350° F. Beat together your brown sugar and butter until well combined, at least 3 minutes, then add in your eggs, one at a time, adding the next only after the last one has been fully incorporated. Scrape down the bowl as needed throughout this process. Add in your sour cream, and once it has been fully mixed in, add in the olive oil and mix until incorporated.
- Mix together your flour, cornmeal, baking powder, baking soda, salt, and black pepper. Add 1/3 of the flour mixture to the batter, then add 1/2 cup of your milk, allowing it to fully incorporate before adding another 1/3 of your flour. Mix, add the remaining 1/2 cup of milk, and finally add in the last of your flour. Scrape down the bowl and be sure that the batter is evenly mixed. Fold in your corn kernels and your chopped basil.
- Grease and/or line about 30 muffins cups. Fill each up about 2/3 of the way full with your batter, then bake for 20 minutes or so, until lightly golden and firm. Remove from the oven and allow the muffins to cool completely.
- For assembly, cut out a small hole in the top of your muffins using a paring knife or a cupcake corer. Fill each hole with your tomato jam, then use a piping bag or plastic bag with the tip cut off to pipe a small dollop of ricotta on top of each hole. Top with a few pieces of basil chiffonade. These will keep well in an airtight container in the refrigerator for up to 24 hours, but they are best served the same day.

---

237. Seven Minutes To Heavenly Raspberry Jam

Serving: Makes 1 pint | Prep: | Cook: | Ready in:

Ingredients

- 4 pints raspberries

- 1 granny smith apple, peeled and grated
- 2 tablespoons lemon juice
- 3/4 cup turbinado sugar
- 1 sterlized pint jar with lid

Direction

- Gently rinse raspberries and let drain in a colander
- In a medium pot (this is one of the few times I like nonstick) over medium high heat, add the raspberries, lemon juice and sugar.
- Stir gently, about every minute or so. Once the raspberries start to break down and the mixture becomes quite liquid, add the grated apple.
- Crank the heat to high, stirring the mixture about every thirty seconds. You'll see the apple begin to completely dissolve. Continue for about four-five minutes.
- Take the pan off the heat and let the mixture cool for about two minutes. You should see the raspberries now have the consistency of a loose jam. Gently spoon the mixture into a pint jar, and let cool for another ten minutes. Loosely put the top on the jar and place in the refrigerator.
- Serve when cool. This keeps for a month (probably longer) in the fridge.

238.   Short Rib Jam

Serving: Serves at least 6 | Prep: | Cook: | Ready in:

Ingredients

- 1 tablespoon olive oil
- 2 pounds short ribs (not super fatty)
- 1 cup flour (for coating short ribs)
- 2 teaspoons salt (mix with flour)
- 1/2 teaspoon black pepper (mix with flour)
- 2 medium onions (1/2 lb), finely chopped
- 4 shallots, finely chopped
- 3 stalks celery, cut in half
- 2 carrots, peeled and cut in half

- 1/2 head of garlic, smashed
- 1-2 teaspoons salt
- grindings of black pepper
- 2 tablespoons honey
- 2 cups white wine (I used a Riesling for sweetness)
- 1 tablespoon white miso paste
- salt and/or pepper (if necessary), adjusting for seasoning at end

Direction

- In a heavy pot (I used my enameled cast iron) over medium-high heat, heat oil. On a plate, mix the flour, salt, and pepper together and then coat each of the short ribs in it, knocking off excess. Brown short ribs in oil until deeply caramelized on all sides (your time will vary). Remove short ribs and set aside.
- Using the short rib fat, add the onions, shallots, garlic, celery, carrots, salt and pepper to the pot and cook until softened and starting to caramelize. While it is cooking add the honey.
- De-glaze the pot with the wine and scrape up all the bits. Put the short ribs back into the pot. Bring to a boil, lower heat to low, cover, and cook for approximately 1-1/2 hours, until the meat pulls away from the bones.
- Remove the short ribs from the pot and set aside until cool enough to chop. Add the miso paste to the pot. Bring sauce to a boil again and reduce it by half. Adjust the seasoning if necessary.
- Chop the meat. I chopped it in the manner of how BBQ brisket is chopped for sandwiches, but not too fine. I also removed any large pieces of fat that had not melted into the sauce in the pot. Add the chopped meat back into the pot and let the deliciousness cool a bit before spooning it onto toasted sturdy bread. Consume.

239. Shrimp Cooked In Smoked Sausage And Roasted Red Bell Pepper Jam Sauce

Serving: Serves 4 | Prep: | Cook: |Ready in:

Ingredients

- For the Red Bell Pepper Jam (makes 1 full cup)
- • 4 meaty red bell peppers+ 1 red jalapeño pepper washed, halved, seeds and membranes removed
- • 1 large garlic clove, peeled and diced
- • 1/3 cup brown sugar
- • 1/4 cup sherry vinegar
- • 1/4 cup soy sauce
- For the Smoked Sausage and Red Bell Pepper Jam sauce
- • 1 tablespoon olive oil
- • 4 ounces any good quality smoked sausage, roughly chopped
- • 2 garlic cloves, minced
- • 1 medium shallot, diced
- • 1 teaspoon toasted cumin
- • 1 teaspoon smoked paprika
- • A pinch cayenne pepper
- • 1 cup clam juice or homemade fish stock from shrimp shells and tails
- • 1/2 cup Red Bell Pepper jam
- • 2 tablespoons butter
- • 20 Wild Jumbo Shrimp, peeled and deveined, (if making your own fish stock), shells reserved
- • 4 organic extra-large eggs for serving, fried or poached(optional)

Direction

- For the Red Bell Pepper Jam (makes 1 full cup)
- Preheat your broiler. Place only the bell pepper halves (leave the jalapeno raw), cut-side down on a baking sheet; spray with cooking spray the skins of the peppers; transfer to the upper rack of the oven and broil until the skins are charred and peppers soften, about 25 to 30 minutes.
- Cool slightly and then peel. Place the roasted peppers, jalapeño, garlic and brown sugar in the bowl of a food processor and puree until smooth.
- Transfer the mixture to a saucepan and heat over medium-high; add sherry vinegar, soy sauce and 1/4 cup water; bring to a boil. Cook, stirring often, until the liquid has evaporated and the peppers have a jam-like consistency, 25 to 30 minutes. Cool and refrigerate. Can be made 1 week in advance.
- For the Smoked Sausage and Red Bell Pepper Jam sauce
- To a sauté pan over medium heat, add the olive oil and sweat the sausage until the fat starts to render, about 2 minutes. Then add the garlic and shallots. Cook until fragrant, about 1 minute. Add the cumin, smoked paprika and cayenne pepper and cook stirring for about 1-2 minutes more.
- Deglaze with clam juice or homemade fish stock and add the red bell pepper jam. Allow to reduce by about 3/4. Finish with the butter and keep warm until ready to serve or cool and refrigerate. Can be made 1 day ahead.
- When ready to serve, add the shrimp and cook for about 2 minutes per side. Fry or poach the eggs according to your preference. Serve hot over Polenta or Grits and top with the fried egg. Garnish with some more of the Red Bell Pepper Jam.

240. Shrimp And "grits" With Kahlua Bacon Jam

Serving: Serves 4 | Prep: | Cook: |Ready in:

Ingredients

- For Kahlua Bacon Jam:
- 8 bacon strips
- 1 cup finely diced onion
- 2/3 cup diced tomatoes
- 4 garlic cloves

- 1 tablespoon balsamic vinegar
- 1 tablespoon brown sugar
- 1 teaspoon paprika
- 1 teaspoon chili powder
- 1 cup kahlua
- For shrimp and grits
- 1.5 pounds fresh shrimp (with heads and peel)
- 1 cup creme of wheat
- 2 tablespoons cooking sherry

Direction

- Cook the bacon on a frying pan until brown and crisp. Set aside on paper towel to blot out grease. Cut bacon into small pieces or tear it with your hands.
- Caramelize onion over medium heat (this takes about 8 minutes) until onion is soft and brown and sweet to taste.
- Add garlic and tomatoes. Season with vinegar, brown sugar, paprika and chili powder. Simmer for another 8 minutes for all the flavors to mix. Add kahlua and stir mixture. It will slowly thicken over 3 minutes.
- Add bacon bits and stir around. Simmer for 3 minutes until jam is thick and caramelized.
- Add cooking wine to shrimp in the pan. Pan sear shrimp with canola oil for 2-5 minutes, until shrimp turns pink throughout (that can happen very fast). Salt and pepper to taste.
- Add bacon jam to shrimp and mix thoroughly on low heat, for 1 minute. Turn heat off.
- In a separate pot, boil 3-4 cups of water. When water is boiled, add cream of wheat bit by bit and stir constantly. Keep stirring while water is boiling for 4 minutes until cream of wheat has thickened into almost a paste. Turn heat to low, simmer cream of wheat for another 4 minutes while stirring occasionally. It should thicken some more. Turn off heat when you're happy with the consistency.
- Serve bacon jammed shrimp over cream of wheat. Enjoy every bite!

241.   Sicilian Blood Orange Marmalade

Serving: Makes 9 cups | Prep: | Cook: |Ready in:

Ingredients

- 3 pounds blood oranges
- 3 pounds sugar
- 3 tablespoons lemon juice

Direction

- Using a fork or a spiky florist turtle (for quick results!) prick the oranges completely.
- Put them in a small pail or large bowl and cover with water.
- Change the water every day for 4 days.
- Drain the oranges and cut in half and remove the seeds (there will be very few).
- Slice them very thinly and turn and slice the other direction so that you mince the oranges.
- Put the minced orange pulp, lemon juice and the sugar in a large heavy pot and heat until the sugar is completely melted.
- Cool, and leave overnight to develop color and flavors.
- Next, bring to a boil, put in the thermometer, lower the heat slightly and simmer until the jell point is reached (220).
- Pour into sterilized canning jars and seal.

242.   Simple Concord Grape Jam

Serving: Makes 2 cups jam | Prep: | Cook: |Ready in:

Ingredients

- 2 pounds concord grapes cleaned and removed from stems
- 2-3 cups sugar(if jam is too loose add the full amount of sugar
- 1/2 cup water
- juice of half a lemon

- pinch of salt
- 1   apple cored and quartered

Direction

- Place grapes, water, sugar, lemon juice and salt in medium size saucepan. Bring to a rolling boil then reduce heat to med/low and simmer uncovered for 1 1/2 hours or until it reduces by about a third and becomes noticeably thicker.
- While the jam is bubbling away, sterilize 3 half pint jars and lids, lay on clean tea towel to drain and dry.
- When jam is ready place a strainer on a large (8 cup) heatproof glass measuring cup or bowl, you want to remove the skins and seeds but retain the pulp so really stir it, scraping the bottom of the strainer occasionally. Return the strained jam to saucepan and on med heat let it simmer another couple of minutes, just so it's hot. Pour into clean jars, put lid on and let come to room temperature and place in the refrigerator overnight. By morning you will have a thick jam. You can also use sure-jell if that is how you usually make jam. NOTE: be sure to test the jam before pouring into the jars by putting a saucer in the freezer and spoon a little on the ice cold saucer, if it becomes thick it's ready to put in the jar.

---

243.   Sliders With Onion Jam And Fried Bananas Foster

Serving: Makes 8 | Prep: | Cook: |Ready in:

Ingredients

- 2 pounds ground beef (use a 20% fat ratio)
- 8 pieces thick applewood-smoked bacon (any bacon works, but this bacon works the best)
- 8   slider-sized buns
- 8   slices cheddar cheese
- 3 tablespoons maple syrup
- 3   fairly ripe bananas

- 1/4 cup packed dark brown sugar
- 2 tablespoons butter
- 1/2 teaspoon cinnamon
- 1/4 cup dark rum
- 1/4 cup olive oil
- 6 cups thinly sliced red onions
- 1 cup packed dark brown sugar
- 3/4 cup apple cider vinegar
- 1/2 cup dry sherry

Direction

- As you should know about onions, the longer you cook them, the better they get. That's why we're gonna do the onion jam first; it'll let us give them all the love and attention they need, so they won't divorce us and try to take the kids.
- Heat up the olive oil on medium-high in a big pot until it starts shimmering.
- Add the onions in, cover them, and let them sweat it out for 15 minutes. Stir them once in a while too.
- Add the brown sugar, vinegar, and sherry. Stir everything together, uncover it, and stir until it gets nice and thick. Should take about 40 minutes.
- Add in a little salt and pepper, and let it cool while you do the rest of the recipe.
- For the bananas, melt a couple tablespoons of butter on low heat in a big skillet, and slice up the bananas while you do it.
- Once the butter's melted, stir in the brown sugar and cinnamon until the sugar dissolves and everything's nice and mixed together.
- Take the pan off the burner if you value your eyebrows, then slowly add the rum in. If you're clever/have any modicum of motor skills, tip the pan so it makes contact with the flame on your range. If you're like me, use a kitchen torch or a long lighter. Either way, let the rum burn until the fire naturally goes out.
- When you no longer have a fire hazard on your hands, cook the sauce for a couple more minutes until it gets syrupy.

- Add the bananas in and cook for about a minute on each side, then take them out of the pan and set aside.
- Heat up a pan to medium-high and add in the bacon. Pour the maple syrup on top, then set it aside on a plate lined with paper towels once it's crispy.
- Pour out most of the grease left behind by the bacon, leaving just enough so the bottom of the pan is lined with it. Heat it up to medium-high heat, then fry the bananas for about a minute on each side, till you get that golden-brown crispy goodness.
- Form the ground beef into small patties roughly the size of your palm (or whatever size your buns are), and season with salt and pepper.
- Heat up a grill or grill pan to medium-high heat, then throw the burgers on for about 4 minutes a side for medium-rare, or more if you want dry, overcooked garbage. Your choice, people.
- All that's left is to lightly toast the buns, melt the cheddar on top, throw the sliders together, and keep it all stable with a toothpick.

---

244.   Small Batch Strawberry Rhubarb Jam

Serving: Makes 3 half pints | Prep: | Cook: | Ready in:

Ingredients

- 1 pound strawberries
- 1 pound rhubarb stalks
- 1 1/2 cups granulated sugar

Direction

- Wash the strawberries and rhubarb well. Hull the berries and dice them into small pieces. Chop the rhubarb into segments approximately 1/2 inch in size.
- Place the chopped fruit in a glass or ceramic bowl and cover with sugar. Stir to combine

and cover. Let the fruit sit for at least an hour, until the juices are flowing.
- When you're ready to cook the jam, prepare a small boiling water bath canner and three half pint jars and bring it to a boil. Place three new canning jar lids in a small pot and bring them to a bare simmer.
- Pour the fruit and all the liquid into your jam pot and place it over high heat. For these small batches, I like to use a 12-inch, stainless steel skillet, but any low, wide, non-reactive pan will do.
- Bring the fruit to a rapid boil and stir regularly. Over high heat, this jam should take 8 to 12 minutes to cook. It is done when it is quite thick. You can tell that it's ready when you draw your spoon or spatula through the jam, and it doesn't immediately rush in to fill that space. It will also make a vigorous sizzling noise when stirred when it is finished.
- Remove the jam from the heat and funnel it into the prepared jars. Wipe rims, apply lids and rings, and process in a boiling water bath canner for 10 minutes (start your timer when the water returns to a boil, not the moment the jars go into the water bath).
- When time is up, remove jars from canner and set them to cool on a folded kitchen towel. When they are cool enough to handle, remove the rings and test the seals by grasping the edges of the lid and lifting the jar an inch or so from the countertop. If the lid holds fast, the jars are sealed. Any unsealed jars should be refrigerated and eaten promptly.

---

245.   Smoked Trout, Bacon And Tomato Sandwich With Crème Fraiche Pepper Jelly Topping

Serving: Serves 2 | Prep: | Cook: | Ready in:

Ingredients

- 4 ounces fillet of smoked trout , skin removed
- 2 whole wheat hamburger buns or 4 slices of bread, or 2 English muffins
- 1 tablespoon Butter for spreading on the bun or bread
- 2 tablespoons crème fraiche
- 2 tablespoons green pepper jelly or jam
- 1/2 cup baby spinach
- 2-4 slices ripe heirloom tomato
- 2 slices of crispy bacon that have been fried and cut in half

Direction

- Butter one side of the buns or bread and grill quickly until crisp and brown on one side. Flip and quickly toast the other side.
- Layer two pieces of bun or bread with half the baby spinach and 1-2 slices of tomato. On the other pieces, lay 2 halves of bacon, then ½ the smoked trout.
- Top with the crème fraiche mixture.
- Bite, crunch, savor!

---

246. Smoky Shitake Cranberry Cauliflower Galette With Marmalade Mustard Mascarpone

Serving: Serves 4 | Prep: | Cook: |Ready in:

Ingredients

- 1 frozen pastry sheet (about 9 ounces)
- 1/2 cup water
- 1/2 teaspoon salt
- 1 small cauliflower, cut in 1-inch florets (4-5 cups)
- 8 ounces mascarpone cheese
- 2 tablespoons orange marmalade
- 2 tablespoons honey mustard
- 1 tablespoon extra virgin olive oil
- 1/3 cup chopped shallots
- 1 cup Shitake mushrooms, cut in 1/4-inch slivers
- 2 teaspoons granulated sugar
- 1/2 teaspoon lemon pepper seasoning
- 1/3 cup dried cranberries
- 1/2 teaspoon smoked sweet paprika
- 1 tablespoon balsamic vinegar
- 1/4 cup Riesling or sweet white wine
- 4 slices fully cooked crisp bacon, cut in 1-inch pieces
- 1/2 cup grated Mandhego cheese or a smoky white cheese
- 2 tablespoons chopped fresh basil
- 1-2 tablespoons chopped chives

Direction

- Thaw pastry sheet at room temperature for 30 minutes. Preheat oven to 400 degrees F. Place a sheet of parchment paper on a large cookie sheet, set aside.
- Mix water, salt, and cauliflower florets in a microwave safe bowl; cover and microwave on high for 4 minutes. Leave covered to steam for two minutes or so and drain; set aside.
- Meanwhile, in a small bowl, mix Mascarpone cheese, marmalade, and honey mustard. Cover, and refrigerate until ready to serve.
- In a large frying pan, over medium-high, heat olive oil until warm, add shallots, mushrooms, sugar, and lemon pepper; saute and stir for 2 minutes. Reduce heat to medium, add cranberries, paprika, vinegar, stir and cook for 2 more minutes. Add Riesling and steamed cauliflower; stir and cook for 2 minutes or until wine has absorbed.
- Unfold pastry dough, in a 9" x 10" rectangle, on the center of the lined cookie sheet. Spoon the sauteed mixture on the center of dough, leaving about 1.5-inch outer edge. Sprinkle with bacon and cheese. Bake in oven 22-25 minutes or until puffed pastry is golden brown. Remove from oven; cool 5 minutes. Top with basil and serve with dollops of Marmalade-Mustard Mascarpone sprinkled with chives. This is a lovely dish served warm or at room temperature!

sections crosswise. Leave to cool in the pan for 2-3 hours or overnight. Store airtight between wax or parchment paper in a cool place for up to a week. Freeze for longer storage.

247. Sour Cherry & Marzipan Jam Bars

Serving: Makes 48 squares | Prep: | Cook: |Ready in:

Ingredients

- 1 pound unsalted butter at room temperature
- 1 1/2 cups granulated sugar
- 2   large eggs at room temperature
- 4 cups all purpose flour
- 1/2 teaspoon sea salt
- 2 cups finely chopped walnuts
- 10 ounces marzipan
- 1 1/2 cups sour cherry jam, or jam of your choice

Direction

- Heat oven to 325°F (160°C). In a large bowl, either with a mixer or by hand, cream butter and sugar until light and fluffy. Add eggs and mix well. Add flour, salt and walnuts; mix on low speed until well incorporated.
- Divide the dough in half. Flatten, wrap one half and freeze while you make the base from the other half.
- Press the remaining half of dough evenly into a 9 x 13-inch (22.5 x 32.5 cm) pan lined with parchment paper. Bake on the middle rack of the oven for 15-20 minutes until lightly golden. Let cool on a rack.
- Break the marzipan into small pieces and sprinkle over the crust. With lightly oiled fingers, press the marzipan evenly over surface. Dot with jam then spread it evenly over marzipan.
- Remove dough from freezer and shred using the large holes on a grater. Sprinkle evenly over the filling. Do not press it down. Bake for 45 minutes to 1 hour or until golden brown. Cool on a wire rack.
- While still warm, cut the pastry crosswise into 6 even sections and lengthwise into 8 even

248. Sour Cherry, Coriander & Candied Ginger Jam

Serving: Makes 4 half pints | Prep: | Cook: |Ready in:

Ingredients

- 3 pounds sour cherries with pits**
- 1 2/3 cups granulated sugar
- 1/4 cup candied ginger, minced
- 1/2 teaspoon coriander seeds
- 1/4 cup lemon juice

Direction

- Sterilize all equipment that will touch the end product (funnel, spoons, ladle, jars, lids, rings). First, I like to use Star San brewer's sanitizer. Later in the canning process, I dip utensils in boiling water right before I'm going to use them. Start a water bath canner if you intend to preserve the jam. Put a plate in the freezer.
- Look for Montmorency sour cherries. They will sometimes be sold as "tart cherries" or "pie cherries." You want cherries that are smooth, garnet red and juicy. Take a cherry between your forefinger and thumb and give it a gentle squeeze- there should be clear juice and white, not brown flesh. If you have sour cherries with pits, pit them over a bowl so that you can recapture some of the lost juice. Three pounds of sour cherries with pits will equate to about 8 cups of cherries after all the pits are removed.
- Place the coriander seeds in a tea bag or a bit of cheese cloth tied with twine. In a non-reactive pot, combine the cherries, sugar, ginger, pouch of coriander and recaptured juice.

- We want to slowly heat the cherries so we get a slow release of juice, so start off on a medium low setting. After the mixture begins to steam, about ten minutes later, add the lemon juice. Increase the heat to medium and bring the liquid to a rolling boil.
- Cook the jam for 20-25 minutes. Cooking time will depend a lot on how juicy the cherries were at the start, pot size and altitude. As the jam cooks, the juice and cherries will begin to meld together. The fruit will become very soft and flat, so it will not have the same consistency of traditional berry jam. Test a spoonful of jam on the frozen plate. Expect that there will be a little separation between the liquid and the whole cherries in the jam, but it should gently wilt away from the cherry in a small circle the size of a nickel. Spreading beyond this indicates the jam is not set.
- When the jam is set, take the pot off the stove and allow it to sit for five minutes to get out bubbles. Fish out the pouch of coriander. Skim any scum off the surface.
- Ladle the jam in to sterilized, hot jars. Wipe the rim of the jar, and place new lids on the top of the jar. Screw on rings. Process in water bath canner for ten minutes.
- Allow finished jam to sit on the counter overnight. Take off the rings and test the lids to ensure a proper seal. Label and keep in a cool, dark place for up to a year--but I don't think it will last that long!

---

249. Sour Cherry Black Pepper Jam

Serving: Makes 4¼ half-pints | Prep: | Cook: | Ready in:

Ingredients

- 8 cups washed, stemmed and pitted sour cherries and their juices
- 3¾ cups unrefined, granulated sugar
- 1½ teaspoons freshly ground black pepper
- 1 fresh orange wedge
- ½ - ¾ teaspoons best-quality, very aged Balsamic vinegar (you really want this to be like syrup because of the taste imparted)
- 1 packet liquid pectin, optional

Direction

- Set a water bath canner full of water over high heat, and bring to a boil. Get four half-pint jars and a quarter pint jar and when the water is boiling, submerge the jars in it. Throw in the lids about five minutes before your jam is ready.
- While the water comes to a boil, toss together the cherries, juices and sugar in a canning pot or large, heavy, non-reactive pot. Set over high heat and bring to a boil, stirring regularly. When you've got an active boil going, stir in the pepper and squeeze in the juice from the orange wedge.
- Keep the jam at a rapid boil, stirring regularly and mashing some of the cherries against the side of the pot with a wooden spoon or with a potato masher. I prefer to pace my jam's progress with my Thermapen so if you have one, or a good candy thermometer or the like, start checking the jam's temp at regular intervals. This should hover around 221° F when all is said and done. When you've reached about 216°, stir in the Balsamic vinegar. Its flavor will mellow some as the jam cools and sets, so unless you are totally overwhelmed at 1/2 teaspoon, add the full 3/4.
- After adding the vinegar, add the liquid pectin if you're planning to do so. Return the jam to a boil after stirring in the pectin and let boil for at least five minutes or until you've reached 221°. At that point, you can ladle the jam carefully into your sterilized jars, apply the lids and bands carefully, and then process in your water bath canner for 10 minutes. Then remove them and let cool completely.
- You can store your sealed jars in a cool, dark place for up to a year.

250.　　　Spiced Cider Jellies

Serving: Serves 100 half inch square jellies | Prep: |
Cook: | Ready in:

Ingredients

- 1 1/2 cups organic apple juice, I used Martinelli's, you just want something that is clear
- 2 tablespoons Apple Jack or Calvados
- 2 1/2 cups sugar
- 1/2 cup light corn syrup
- 1/2 cup Certo Premium Liquid Pectin
- 1/16 teaspoon cinnamon
- a heavy pinch of allspice
- a few gratings of fresh nutmeg

Direction

- Sometimes it is hard to get your thermometer to read the syrup correctly so it is important that you use a small enough pan that you get an accurate reading but also large enough the syrup doesn't boil over. I used a 1 1/2 quart reduction pan. It has sides that bevel out from the bottom.
- Take an 8 inch x 8 inch cake pan and spray the bottom with spray oil this will help the plastic wrap to stick. Take a large sheet of plastic wrap and line the pan making sure to smooth out all wrinkles. Set it aside.
- Place the 1/2 cup of pectin in a small mixing bowl. Set it aside with a small whisk and a ladle sitting next to it.
- Place the apple juice, calvados, sugar, corn syrup and the spices into a small pan. Place it over high heat and bring it to a boil stirring it a couple of time along the way to get the sugar dissolved.
- As it boils keep an eye on it so it doesn't boil over and adjust the heat as necessary. Place the candy thermometer into the syrup and leave it there. When it reaches 215 degrees using a ladle remove about a quarter cup of syrup and while whisking pour it into the

pectin to temper it. Add the pectin back to the syrup and whisk to blend.
- Bring the syrup to 219 degrees and immediately pour it into the lined cake pan. Let it sit until it is completely cool.
- Using the plastic wrap as handles gently remove the jelly from the pan. Cut into 1/2 inch squares and roll in sugar. I like to put them in pleated candy cups, and serve.
- *note* I have heard if you let these cure overnight uncovered they are easier to cut. I think I have to agree although I found a good trick to cutting them. They can be just a little sticky. I used a carving knife that I sprayed with a thin coat of neutral flavored spay oil and they cut magnificently. While they cut fine after cooling I did not try the oiled knife trick so they may be just fine then too.

251.　　　Spiced Plum And Port Jam

Serving: Serves way too many jars of jam | Prep: | Cook: | Ready in:

Ingredients

- 8 cups pitted chopped plums (about 1/2 inch chop so you have a nice chunky jam)
- 1 cup ruby port
- 1/2 cup brown sugar
- 1 teaspoon cinnamon
- 1/2 teaspoon Chinese 5 spice
- nutmeg (I ground mine in fresh - maybe 1/4 to a half tsp)
- 1 tablespoon unsalted butter
- juice from 1 lemon
- 1/2 cup white sugar
- 1.75 ounces package NO SUGAR NEEDED pectin

Direction

- If you are canning, sterilize and prepare your jars. I got 3 8 oz., 5 4 oz. plus extra for the fridge
- Mix the pectin and white sugar together and set aside. Put a tablespoon in the freezer.
- Put everything else in a pot and bring to a boil, then turn down and simmer for 10 - 15 minutes, until the plums soften. At this point I use a potato masher to mash the jam a bit, but I leave some chunks too. Do this according to how you like your jam.
- Stir in the sugar and pectin and bring your jam back to a boil for a minute or so, stirring all the while. Taste for sugar and add more if you want it sweeter. Now take a bit of the liquidy part and drizzle it onto the back of the frozen spoon. Run your finger through it - it should separate and be, well, jammy.
- If you are canning, process the jam accordingly (into sterile jars, new tops on, rings on loosely, boil for 10-15 minutes, then take them out and smile while they pop pop), if not then put it in some sort of container and refrigerate. You will have plenty for friends and neighbors.

---

252.   Spicy Sweet Potato Pommes Frites With Raspberry Preserves

Serving: Serves 2 | Prep: | Cook: |Ready in:

Ingredients

- 1 large sweet potato
- 3 tablespoons olive oil
- 1 tablespoon sugar
- 1 tablespoon salt
- 1 teaspoon chile powder
- 1 teaspoon paprika
- 1/2 teaspoon cumin
- 1/4 teaspoon cayenne
- 1 tablespoon flour

Direction

- Combine all the dry ingredients in a bowl and set aside. Peel the sweet potato and slice to desired thickness and size.
- In a bowl mix toss the sweet potatoes in olive oil. Add the dry ingredients and toss with the sweet potatoes.
- Spread potatoes in a single layer on a sheet pan. Cook at 375F for 25 minutes or until fork tender and slightly crispy.
- Serve with your favorite raspberry preserves. Enjoy!

---

253.   Steak Sandwich With Peach "jam" And Brie

Serving: Makes 4 sandwiches | Prep: | Cook: |Ready in:

Ingredients

- Peach Jam
- 3 large peaches, halved, cored, then sliced
- 1 medium-sized shallot, sliced
- 2 teaspoons balsamic vinegar
- 1 teaspoon honey
- 1 teaspoon granulated sugar
- 0.5 teaspoons salt
- Steak sandwich
- 2 1-pound NY Strip steaks
- 1 wedge of brie, half-pound max, at room temperature
- 8 slices of country bread
- salt and pepper to taste
- 1 tablespoon olive oil, plus more for drizzling

Direction

- For the peach jam: Preheat oven to 350 degrees. In a large bowl, combine all ingredients. Place in an 8x8 baking dish, and bake for 30 minutes. Once done, stir again to combine, then place in refrigerator to cool.
- Season steak liberally with salt and pepper. Heat a cast iron pan on medium-high and

pour olive oil in to coat the pan. Cook steak, turning occasionally, until desired doneness (will depend on how you want steak cooked). Let rest for 5 minutes, then thinly slice.

- Preheat oven to 350. Line baking sheet with aluminum foil. Place slices of bread on sheet and drizzle with olive oil. Bake for 5-10 minutes or until bread is lightly toasted.

- Optional: You can place brie in the oven at this time if you'd like your brie a little hotter and easier to spread. Bake this 5-6 minutes, or until gooey but not runny.

- Layer the sandwich. Spread peach jam on one side slice of bread and brie on the other. Add steak, and season with salt and pepper.

---

254.   Strawberry Balsamic Jam Infused With Star Anise And Vanilla Bean

Serving: Makes 9 pint jars | Prep: | Cook: | Ready in:

Ingredients

- 8 cups Blended strawberries
- 6 teaspoons Calcium water
- 3/4 cup Aged balsamic vinegar
- 4 pieces Star anise
- 1/2 piece Vanilla bean pod
- 3 cups Sugar
- 6 teaspoons Pectin
- 1 teaspoon Salt

Direction

- Clean and hull your strawberries and bled them, if you'd like, in a blender until smooth. Using Pomona's pectin, prepare the calcium water. Add the strawberries and calcium water to a large pot and bring to a boil.

- Meanwhile, pour the balsamic vinegar in a small saucepan. Scrape the vanilla bean seeds and add them to the pan, along with the pod and the star anise. Bring to a rolling boil and simmer for a few minutes. Add the vinegar

and its contents to the strawberries while they come to a boil, you will fish them out in a bit.

- In a separate bowl, mix together the sugar, pectin and salt. Once the strawberry pot has come to a boil, vigorously whisk the bowl of sugar/pectin/salt into the pot and continue to mix for 1-2 minutes to ensure the pectin dissolves evenly.

- Once the mixture comes back to a boil remove it from heat. Let sit for 5 minutes or so and skim the foam that has formed off the top of the jam. Fish out the vanilla bean half and the star anise pods. At this point, can in sanitized jars and process for 5 minutes, or pour into jars or a container of your choosing and keep refrigerated. If you are not canning, use within a couple weeks.

---

255.   Strawberry Cardamom 'Smoothie' Jam

Serving: Makes 1 cup | Prep: | Cook: | Ready in:

Ingredients

- 2 cups strawberries (1 punnet), washed & hulled
- Juice of 2 limes
- Seeds of 10 cardamom pods, crushed
- 1/2 - 1 cup white caster sugar
- 2 cups apple pectin (or the equivalent pectin powder)

Direction

- Combine the strawberries and lime juice in a large bowl and crush with a fork/potato masher, till liquid is released from the fruit. Add the cardamom seeds and leave to macerate, a few minutes to a couple of hours, refrigerated.

- Blitz in a blender/food processor till the strawberry mixture is smooth.

- Pour the mixture into a large pan, with the sugar and the liquid pectin. Bring to the boil and then turn down heat and let cook till reduced and edges begin to collect thickened syrup. Watch it carefully so it doesn't overheat and burn.

- If you don't have an eye for telling when the jam is ready as it may still look somewhat liquid, do the jam test, by putting a small saucer in the freezer to cool. When cold, put a small bit of jam on the cold saucer and let it rest for a couple of minutes, then touch the surface of the jam. It should wrinkle if it is ready.
- Pot/can if you like. Enjoy.

256. Strawberry Cardamom Jam

Serving: Makes 2-3 half-pints | Prep: | Cook: | Ready in:

Ingredients

- 4 cups washed and trimmed strawberries (preferably organic), cut into halves or quarters
- 1¾ cups unrefined, granulated sugar
- juice of 1/2 lemon
- 3/4 teaspoon ground cardamom; use a nice pungent one; I like Guatemalan
- 1 small apple (roughly 4 ounces), peeled, cored, grated

Direction

- Fill your canning pot with water, cover, and set over high heat. Do this first because it takes a long time to bring this much water to a rolling boil. Ready the appropriate number of jars and get out your canning funnel, ladle and such.
- In a jamming pot or other heavy-bottomed stainless pot, stir together all your ingredients. Let sit for a half hour (you can also macerate this overnight; in that instance, don't start heating your canning pot until you're ready to actually cook the jam).When a decent amount

of syrup has pooled around the strawberries, set the pot over high heat, and stir regularly (but not constantly) as the mixture comes to a boil. You want it to boil like crazy so as to evaporate as much water as possible.

- Strawberries foam a lot so if that bothers you visually, skim or carefully spoon the foam off. Keep stirring, and if your berries aren't breaking down as you'd like, crush them with a potato masher. It really depends on how much "chunk" you like in your jam. If you've not already, sterilize your jars by placing them in the boiling water bath. Sterilize your lids too either by putting them in your canning pot for 2-3 minutes as it boils or by placing them in a smaller pot of boiling water which you then remove from heat.
- If you have a Thermapen or similar instant-read thermometer, start checking the temp after about 20 minutes. You want to get to at least 217° F. When things are getting close, a rim of strawberry gunk should have adhered to the sides of your pot (at the level of the jam), the bubbles should look thick like lava, not loose like boiling water, and the jam should sheet not rain off the back of a wooden spoon.
- When the jam is ready, carefully ladle it into your prepared jars, wipe the rims, apply lids and bands, and carefully place into your canning pot. Process for 10 - 12 minutes, remove and sit on a kitchen towel for at least two hours.

257. Strawberry Chia Jam

Serving: Makes 1 cup | Prep: | Cook: | Ready in:

Ingredients

- 1 quart fresh strawberries, hulled
- 1 tablespoon raw honey
- 2 tablespoons chia seeds
- 1 orange rind or tangerine rind (a.k.a.: chen pi) (even better, if it's been dried in the sun)

Direction

- Put the strawberries and honey in a medium saucepan over medium heat. Stir often until it comes to a boil. Stir in the chia seeds. Add the optional Chen Pi (a Chinese herb that is made by drying orange peel or tangerine peel in the sun) here. Lower the heat a little and simmer for 15 minutes, stirring occasionally.
- Turn off the heat and let the mixture cool for 15 minutes. Serve it warm on toast or let it cool completely and store it in a covered jar in the fridge.

ready. You want the jam to not run very fast, but to resist the gravity a little bit.
- Take your jam off the heat when it passes your trials. But be aware that jam thickens as it cools down so be sure to take your jam off the hat before it reaches the consistency that you desire.
- Store in jars! Enjoy your jam :)

---

258.   Strawberry Jam

Serving: Serves 3-4 jars | Prep: | Cook: | Ready in:

Ingredients

- 2 pounds Strawberry
- 2 pounds Granulated white sugar
- 1/2 Lemon

Direction

- Cut the strawberries into half if you like the chunks in your jam like I do. If you want your strawberries to melt in the jam all together, cut them into smaller pieces. Put the strawberries in a pot. Add the sugar.
- Either leave the pot under the sun for a couple of hours so that the strawberries release their own juice, so you don't have to add any more water. Or, leave them in the fridge overnight.
- Boil the strawberry and sugar mix, stirring them now and then. Once it boils, turn the heat down to low to medium, add the juice of half a lemon. Continue stirring and cooking.
- Once the jam starts to look more sticky and develops a consistency that is thick, start to make trials to see if your jam is ready. To make those trials, put just a little bit of jam onto a plate that is in room temperature and tilt the plate. If the jam is very runny, it is not

---

259.   Strawberry Jam Filled Doughnut Muffins

Serving: Makes 12 muffins | Prep: | Cook: | Ready in:

Ingredients

- 2 cups flours
- 1/2 cup granulated sugar
- 1 tablespoon baking powder
- 1 teaspoon salt
- 1 egg
- 1/4 cup vegetable oil
- 1 cup milk
- 1 cup strawberry jam
- 1/2 cup melted butter
- 3/4 cup granulated sugar

Direction

- Preheat oven to 350 and butter/flour one 12-cup muffin pan (you can also use cooking spray). In a large bowl, combine flour, sugar, baking powder, and salt.
- In a separate, smaller bowl, whisk together egg, vegetable oil, and milk. Pour wet ingredients over dry ingredients and stir until just combined (a few lumps are ok!).
- Spoon 2 tbsps. of batter into each of the prepared cavities of the muffin pan, then place one tsp of strawberry jam in the center. Cover with another 2 tbsps. of muffin batter, and use a toothpick or a spatula to make sure the jam is entirely covered by muffin batter.
- Bake at 350 for 16-18 minutes or until the muffins spring back when gently pressed with

a finger or a toothpick inserted into one comes out with only a few crumbs. Let cool in pan for five minutes before carefully removing and setting on a cooling rack.

- Next, set up your dipping station. Place melted butter in a small bowl and sugar in a separate bowl. Quickly dip the outside of the muffin in melted butter, shake off excess, then roll completely in sugar. Set back on cooling rack. Repeat until all the muffins are coated.

---

260.   Strawberry Jam With Cardamom

Serving: Serves 1 320g jar | Prep: | Cook: | Ready in:

Ingredients

- 300 grams Frozen Strawberry
- 200 grams Bio-Sugar (for Jam Making)
- Juice of Half Lemon
- Pinch Salt
- 1 1/2 teaspoons Butter

Direction

- Prepare a saucer in the freezer.
- On low heat, combine Strawberry, Sugar and Lemon juice in a small pan (no non-stick pan because of the acid in lemon/strawberry), stir frequently until mixture starts to bubble.
- Continue to cook for 30 minutes, drop a bit of jam on the saucer that you've kept in the freezer, tip the plate, if it runs down very slowly, the jam is ready.
- Turn off the heat and stir in butter. This will help to get rid of the foam and clarify the jam. Add tiny pinches of Cardamom.
- Pour the hot jam into hot sterilized jars. Consume it in 2-3 weeks.

---

261.   Strawberry Lemon Jam

Serving: Serves 72 | Prep: | Cook: | Ready in:

Ingredients

- 2 quarts perfectly ripened strawberries
- 1 1.75 oz package of 100% Natural Sure Jell Premium Fruit Pectin
- 1/4 cup minus 1 Tbsp fresh squeezed lemon juice
- 6 12 oz Ball canning jelly jars with lids and rings
- A large pot of boiling water

Direction

- WASH YOUR HANDS. Fill a large pot with water and begin to heat up to a boil (this will be used for processing your jam). Place your canning jars into the dishwasher on the high heat setting to sterilize (don't use soap). If you don't have a dishwasher, sterilize them by boiling. Place your lids and rings in a small, empty pot and set aside.
- Rinse the strawberries and remove the stems and any rotten spots. Place them into a large saucepan and smash them until they have released their juices and only small pieces remain. A potato masher works well for this.
- Add 1 package of Sure Jell Pectin and the lemon juice to the saucepan and stir to evenly combine. Bring to a boil over high heat, while stirring frequently, and scraping the bottom of the pot to prevent burning. A wooden spoon works well for this.
- Once you have achieved a rolling boil, add 7 cups of sugar to the pot and stir to combine. Return the pot to a rolling boil, while continuing to stir and scrape the bottom of the pot. Boil for 1 minute and then remove the jam from the heat.
- Allow the jam to sit for a couple of minutes, until it has stopped bubbling. Scrape any foam off of the top with a large spoon and discard.
- Remove your sterilized jars from the dishwasher, taking care not to touch the inside of the jars. Add water to your small pot with

the rings and lids and clean them by heating them on the stove top until the water begins to bubble, but DO NOT BOIL, as over-heating can damage the seals on the lids. I don't boil the lids and the rings ahead of time as they tend to rust if they sit in water too long.

- Using a canning funnel, ladle the jam into your jars, leaving approximately 1/4 inch of space between the jam and the top of the jar.
- Before placing lids on the jars, wipe the rims clean with a damp paper towel to ensure a good seal. Then place the lid and the ring on the jar. Tighten the ring until you feel resistance and then loosen slightly (about 1 millimeter).
- After 10 minutes have passed remove the jam jars from the pot using your tongs. Place them on a counter top that doesn't receive direct sun, where they can sit undisturbed for 24 hours. Soon after the jars are removed from the pot, you should start hearing popping sounds as the jars seal. If after 24 hours the bubble on the top of the lid hasn't been sucked in and "pops" when you press on it, then that jar did not seal, and needs to be refrigerated and used within a month. Sealed jars are shelf stable for one year. Store in a cool, dark place with the rings removed.

---

262. Strawberry Lemon Preserves

Serving: Serves about 4 cups | Prep: | Cook: | Ready in:

Ingredients

- 7 cups   fresh strawberries
- 3 cups   granulated sugar
- zest of 2 lemons (about 2 tablespoons)
- juice from 2 lemons (about 1/3 of a cup) freshly squeezed lemon juice

Direction

- Put a couple of plates in the refrigerator to chill.
- Gently mash the strawberries in a wide-mouthed pan with the sugar, leaving some large chunks. Bring to a simmer and stir until the sugar dissolves.
- Add the lemon juice and zest. Bring the mixture to a simmer and let the preserves simmer over medium heat, stirring frequently. Cook the mixture until it thickens. The time will vary depending on your pot and the juiciness of your strawberries, but count on at least 20 minutes, and probably more like 40. Skim off the foam.
- To test the preserves to see if they have thickened, put a teaspoon of jam on one of the chilled plates and return it to the refrigerator. After a minute, remove it and tilt the plate. Most of the preserves should remain in the center of the plate, while some of it -- especially the more liquid portion -- will slowly spread out towards the edge of the plate. When the preserves have firmed up to this point, pour them into jars for storage.

---

263. Strawberry Red Currant Jam

Serving: Makes 300ml | Prep: | Cook: | Ready in:

Ingredients

- 300 grams strawberries
- 150 grams red currants
- 125 grams granulated sugar
- 1 lemon

Direction

- Put all ingredients into a pan, and heat. You want the sugar to become liquid with the juice from the fruit, once this happens give the mixture a bit to mush it up the fruit. Bring this to a boil and then boil for about 10-12 minutes. Try not to stir it, but do skim off any foam.

- After 10-12 minutes, pour into sterilized jars while hot and seal. Let cool and set, and store in the fridge. Will last about week.

264. Strawberry Rhubarb Jam

Serving: Makes 3 cups | Prep: | Cook: | Ready in:

Ingredients

- 1 pound rhubard, diced into 1/2? cubes
- 1 pound strawberries, hulled and sliced
- 3 cups granulated sugar
- 2 limes

Direction

- In a medium bowl add the rhubarb, 1.5 cups of sugar, and the juice of 1 lime. Stir until thoroughly combined. In a separate bowl combine the strawberries, the remaining 1.5 cups of sugar, and the juice of 1 lime. Stir until thoroughly combined. Cover both bowls and place in the fridge for at least 3 hours or overnight to allow the fruit to macerate and the juices to be drawn out.
- Drain the liquids from both the strawberry and the rhubarb into a large heavy bottomed pot or Dutch oven over medium heat. Bring the juices to a simmer, stirring often, for 15 minutes or until the juice has started to thicken.
- Add the fruit and continue to simmer, stirring often, for another 15 minutes or until the jam reaches 95*C or 200*F.
- Remove the jam from the heat and leave it on the stove to cool. Transfer to a bowl and refrigerate overnight. My jam was perfect consistency the next day when I took it out of the fridge, so I jarred it as it was. But if your jam isn't thick enough then simmer the mixture again the next day, remove from the heat, allow to cool, and refrigerate overnight again.

265. Strawberry Vanilla Chia Seed Jam

Serving: Makes 1 1/3 to 1 1/2 cups | Prep: | Cook: | Ready in:

Ingredients

- 3 1/2 cups frozen strawberries
- 1/4 cup pure maple syrup
- Dash fine sea salt
- 2 tablespoons chia seeds
- 2 seeded vanilla beans or 1/2 teaspoon pure vanilla bean powder
- 1 teaspoon fresh lemon juice (optional)

Direction

- In a medium pot, stir together the berries, maple syrup, and salt until combined. Bring to a simmer over medium-high heat and cook for 5 to 7 minutes, until the berries have softened (they will release a lot of liquid during this time).
- Reduce the heat to medium and carefully mash the berries with a potato masher until mostly smooth. The jam will still look very watery at this point, but this is normal!
- Add the chia seeds and stir until combined. Simmer over low-medium heat, stirring frequently (reducing heat if necessary to avoid sticking) for 8 to 15 minutes more, until a lot of the liquid has cooked off and the mixture has thickened slightly.
- Remove from the heat and stir in the vanilla beans or vanilla bean powder, and lemon juice (if using). Transfer the mixture to a bowl and refrigerate, uncovered, until cool, at least a couple of hours. For quicker cooling, pop the jam into the freezer, uncovered, for 45 minutes, stirring every 15 minutes. The chia seed jam will keep in an airtight container in the fridge for up to 2 weeks. It also freezes well for 1 to 2 months.

266. Sufganiyot (Israeli Jelly Doughnuts)

Serving: Makes 2 dozen | Prep: | Cook: | Ready in:

Ingredients

- 1 package dry yeast
- 3 tablespoons sugar, divided
- 1/4 cup water
- 1/2 cup lukewarm milk
- 3 1/2 cups unbleached all-purpose flour
- 1 large egg
- 1 additional egg yolk
- pinch salt
- Grated zest of 1 lemon
- 3 1/2 tablespoons butter, at room temperature
- 1 cup apricot jam
- Vegetable oil for deep-frying
- Neutral oil, for frying
- Confectioners or granulated sugar for rolling

Direction

- Dissolve 1 tablespoon yeast and 1 tablespoon of the sugar in water and allow yeast to bloom, then add the milk and pour into a large bowl.
- Add the egg and the yolk, salt, lemon zest, flour, the remaining 2 tablespoons sugar, and the butter. Mix together with your hands, then knead dough on a pastry board until it becomes sticky yet elastic.
- Cover the dough in a greased bowl, and let rise in a warm place for at least an hour. If you want to prepare it ahead, place the dough in the refrigerator overnight, then let it warm to room temperature before rolling and cutting.
- Dust a pastry board with flour. Roll the dough out to a 1/2-inch thickness. Using the top of a glass, cut into rounds about 2 inches in diameter, and let rise 30 minutes more.
- Pour at least 2 inches of oil into a heavy pot and heat until it is about to bubble (or do as I often do in an electric wok at 375° F).

- Drop the doughnuts into the oil, 4 or 5 at a time. Cook about 3 minutes on each side, turning when brown. Drain on paper towels. Using a pastry or cupcake injector (available at cooking stores and online), insert a teaspoon of jam into each doughnut. Roll the Sufganiyot in confectioners or granulated sugar and serve immediately.

267. Sufganiyot (Jelly Donut) Cake

Serving: Serves at least 8 | Prep: 0hours0mins | Cook: 0hours0mins | Ready in:

Ingredients

- For the brioche dough:
- 1/4 cup warm whole milk
- 1/4 cup warm water
- 1/3 cup sugar (or up to 1/2 cup if you want a sweeter cake)
- 4 teaspoons active dry yeast
- 2 3/4 cups (374 grams) all-purpose flour
- 1 1/2 teaspoons fine sea salt
- 3 large eggs, lightly beaten, at room temperature
- 2 sticks (16 tablespoons) unsalted butter, divided (12 of the tablespoons at room temperature, cut into small cubes; 4 tablespoons for melting)
- 1 pinch Sugar (plain or vanilla-scented), for coating
- For the raspberry whipped cream filling:
- 2 cups heavy cream, chilled
- 1 cup raspberry preserves (preferably seedless)

Direction

- Add the warm milk and water into the bowl of a stand mixer with a pinch of sugar. Sprinkle the yeast over top and step away for 3 minutes. The mixture may bubble (or not —

mine didn't); stir it with a wooden spoon or spatula until it looks creamy.

- Attach the dough hook to the mixer, then add the flour and salt to the bowl and pulse the mixer a few times in order to make the flour damp. Then mix at medium-low speed (scrape down the bowl as needed) until you have a shaggy mass, 2 to 3 minutes.

- Scrape down the sides of the bowl and decrease the speed to low. Pour in the beaten eggs in 3 additions, making sure that each is incorporated before you add the next part. Then, beat in the rest of the sugar and increase the speed to medium. Beat for about 3 minutes, until the dough starts to come together.

- Return the mixer to low speed and add the 12 tablespoons of butter that you've cut into small chunks. Wait until each is incorporated before adding the next one. There is a lot of butter in this recipe, which means this part is going to take some time and you might get antsy. Be patient. (I found that scraping down the sides of the bowl and aiming the butter cubes into different areas of the bowl helped ease my mind.) When all of the butter is incorporated, your dough will be very soft and silky.

- Increase the speed to medium-high and beat until the dough pulls away from the sides and begins winding its way up the dough hook, about 10 minutes. It's important to let the mixer do its thing at this stage—I set a timer and stepped away so that I wouldn't be tempted to stop the process prematurely.

- Lightly butter a large bowl and scrape the dough into it. Cover it with plastic film and let it rise at room temperature until nearly doubled in size, an hour or so. (In the winter, I recommend using the aid of a space heater.)

- Deflate the dough by lifting it up on the sides and letting it plop down into the bowl. Cover the bowl with plastic wrap and refrigerate. Deflate the dough every thirty minutes or so until it stops rising, about 2 hours (so you'll slap down your dough about 4 times). Then press plastic wrap around the surface of the dough and leave it in the refrigerator overnight.

- When you're finally ready to bake the dough, butter two 8- or 9-inch cake pans. Remove the dough from the refrigerator and divide it in half. Shape each half into a bowl, cupping it and pushing out the air. Place the balls seam side-down, one in each cake pan, and cover with parchment paper. Let them rise in a warm place for 60 to 90 minutes, until the dough balls are nearly doubled.

- Center a rack in the oven and preheat it to 400° F. Bake for 25 to 35 minutes, or until the tops are golden and you can feel that there is dry air inside of the dough balls when you tap them.

- As soon as your dough is close to being finished, melt the remaining 4 tablespoons of butter in a small saucepan and ready a bowl with sugar. Take the cakes out of the oven when they're finished and, while they're still hot, douse them with the melted butter. You should hear the butter sizzle a bit as it hits the hot pan -- that's what you're looking for. Use a spoon to generously sprinkle the sugar over the cakes. It should adhere to the melted butter.

- While the cakes cool, make the raspberry whipped cream. Chill the mixing bowl and beater for at least 15 minutes (I do this in the freezer to expedite the process). Beat the cream in the bowl until you have soft peaks (you'll be able to see beater marks in the cream, but it will still be light and cloud-like). Add the preserves and beat until they're incorporated and the peaks are a bit stiffer.

- Let your cakes cool completely before carefully slicing them through their bellies, like hamburgers. Use a spatula to apply a generous amount of jammy whipped cream to the bottom halves of the cakes, then sandwich it with the cake tops.

- This cake will be messy to eat and the filling will ooze out, so share with unfussy guests and use napkins accordingly.

268. Sungold Tomato Preserves

Serving: Makes 3 half-pints | Prep: | Cook: | Ready in:

Ingredients

- 4 pounds sungold tomatoes
- 3/4 cup lemon juice
- 2 tablespoons apple cider vinegar
- 3/4 cup brown sugar
- 2 cups granulated sugar
- 2 teaspoons ground cinnamon
- 2 teaspoons ground nutmeg

Direction

- In a food processor or blender, blend the tomatoes until mostly smooth.
- Mix the tomato puree with the rest of the ingredients in a large stockpot. Heat over medium-high heat and bring to a boil. Reduce the heat and allow to simmer for about an hour, or until the preserves will mound on the back of a spoon without sliding off. Use an immersion blender to smooth out the preserves. Savvy Tip: If you don't have an immersion blender, you can process the preserves in batches in a food processor or blender. Alternatively, don't blend the preserves any further, and enjoy the more chunky preserves.
- While the preserves cook, prepare for canning. Wash the jars and flat lids with hot, soapy water. Put the jars in the canning pot and fill the pot with hot water. Heat over medium-high heat to keep the jars hot. Place the lids in a heat-proof bowl.
- When the preserves are almost done, move some of the boiling water from the canning pot into the heat-proof bowl containing the lids. Line the hot jars up on a folded towel, then pour the water out of the heat-proof bowl and off the lids.
- Fill the jars with preserves up to ¼" below the rim. Use a clean towel to wipe any preserves off the rims, then top each jar with a lid and a tightened ring.
- Place the jars back in the canning pot and make sure they are covered by at least 1 inch of water. Bring to a boil and process for 15 minutes. Place the jars on a folded towel and allow to sit, undisturbed, for 24 hours. Check the seals of the lids after 1 hour. If a seal has not formed, refrigerate the jar immediately.

269. Sweet & Savory Tomato Jam

Serving: Makes 1 1/2 pints | Prep: 0hours0mins | Cook: 0hours0mins | Ready in:

Ingredients

- 3 1/2 pounds tomatoes, coarsely chopped
- 1 small onion, chopped
- 1/2 cup brown sugar
- 1 1/2 cups granulated sugar
- 1 teaspoon salt
- 1/2 teaspoon coriander
- 1/4 teaspoon cumin
- 1/4 cup cider vinegar
- 1 lemon, juice of

Direction

- Put all ingredients in a 2-quart pot. Bring to a gentle boil, then reduce heat to a simmer. Cook until thickened to a jam-like consistency, about 3 hours. Transfer to sterilized glass jars and store in refrigerator for up to two weeks, or use a hot-water canning bath for 15 minutes for long-term storage.

270. Sweet Cherry Pinot Grigio Jam

Serving: Makes six 8 oz jars | Prep: | Cook: | Ready in:

Ingredients

- Basic Granny Smith Apple Jelly Recipe
- 4 pounds Granny Smith Apples (whole)
- 5 cups Sugar
- 6 1/2 cups Water
- 1 Juice of a large Lemon
- Cherry Pinot Grigio Jam
- 3 pounds Cherries, pitted and split in half
- 2 1/2 pounds Sugar
- 1 Lemon, both juice and zest
- 3/4 cup Pinot Grigio

Direction

- Basic Granny Smith Apple Jelly Recipe
- Scrub the apples and cut the fruit into quarters. Leave the skin intact and place them in a large Dutch oven, cover with the 6 1/2 cups of water. Bring this up to a slow boil and simmer on low for about 35 minutes (the apples should just be starting to fall apart). Get out a container that you can place the chinois over. Pour this mixture into your chinois and use the wooden tool (or back of spatula) to press all the juice out of the mixture. You will then take this juice and strain it again. I use a smaller strainer and take a wet piece of cheesecloth and pour the mixture through again--this ensures the jelly will be clear. Now take 4 1/2 cups of this mixture and place in your preserving pan--add the sugar and lemon. Bring this mixture up to a boil and continue to hold there until your thermometer reaches 221. You can skim as you go. Once you reach 221, shut the fire and let it rest for 5 minutes. Go back now and turn the fire back up to reach 221 degrees. In my experience, this ensures a good gel. Pour this mixture into 8 oz. jars, seal and process in boiling water bath for 10 minutes. You should have 6 jars and you will be using one for the Cherry Pinot Grigio Recipe!
- Cherry Pinot Grigio Jam
- Place the 3 pounds of cherries into a non-reactive container, add sugar and lemon and cover and let this macerate overnight. The next day, pour out this mixture into your preserving pan and add 1/2 cup of the Pinot Grigio. Bring this mixture up to 219, stir all along the way to avoid sticking and burning. Once the mixture has reached 219, add the 8 oz. jar of Granny Smith Apple Jelly to the mixture. Stir and bring this up to 221. Once the mixture is holding at 221/222 add the balance of the 1/4 cup of Pinot Grigio to the mixture, this will naturally cut the foam and give it a fresh "winey" taste. Shut the fire and skim the foam off the top. Pour into your jars and process in a hot water bath canner for 11 minutes. This jam is fabulous as a dessert topping, scone topping or quick bread mix, glaze for pork--so many uses!

---

271.   Sweet Onion And Rosemary Jam With Sage Butter Crostini

Serving: Makes 3 cups | Prep: | Cook: | Ready in:

Ingredients

- For the Sweet Onion Rosemary Jam
- 3 large red onions (sliced thinly)
- 1/4 cup balsalmic vinegar
- 1/4 cup red wine vinegar
- 1/4 cup dry white wine
- 4 cloves garlic (rough chop)
- 1/4 cup honey
- 3 tablespoons sugar
- 1 bay leaf
- 3 sticks rosemary
- 1/2 teaspoon crushed red pepper flakes
- 1 tablespoon whole black peppercorns
- 1 tablespoon kosher salt
- 2 tablespoons unsalted butter
- 2 tablespoons olive oil
- For the Sage Butter
- 1 stick unsalted butter
- 5 sage leaves (rough chop)
- 1 teaspoon kosher salt

- 1 loaf of bread toasted with olive oil and salt

Direction

- In a large, thick bottomed pot, heat the butter and oil over medium heat. Add all the onion, garlic, rosemary, bay leaf, whole peppercorns and salt. Give the pot a good stir to make sure the onion is coated in oil and butter. Cover and let simmer for 20 minutes. Lower heat to medium low if anything looks like it is sticking to the bottom of the pan and burning.
- Add the balsamic and red wine vinegars, white wine, honey and sugar. Add a bit more salt. Give the pot a good stir and let cook for 20 more minutes, uncovered. Stir the mixture occasionally to ensure nothing is burning. Adjust temperature as necessary.
- Remove the rosemary sprigs and bay leaf. Some of the rosemary leaves will have fallen off, but don't worry, leave them in. The liquid should be reducing at this point. Cook for another 20 minutes (60 minutes total). Taste to see if salt should be adjusted.
- Transfer the mixture to a food processor or blender and give a few quick pulses. You want to break up any rosemary leaves, and make the jam "spreadable", but not turn it into mush.
- While the jam cooks, prepare your sage butter. Simply heat the butter, sage and salt over low heat. Let cook together for 10 minutes. Strain through cheesecloth into a small container and cool in fridge.
- Serve the sage butter and onion jam together on any kind of bread you have! I used a big loaf of freshly baked, warm multi-grain bread to make the crostini.
- The jam can also be sealed up and sent off as a wonderful holiday gift!

Serving: Makes 2 burgers | Prep: | Cook: | Ready in:

Ingredients

- 2 burger buns
- 1/2 pound ground beef
- 1/2 to 1 teaspoons crushed red pepper flakes
- 1/4 teaspoon onion powder
- 1/4 teaspoon garlic powder
- Salt and freshly ground black pepper
- 2 to 3 tablespoons fig jam (I like Trader Joe's)
- 2 ounces goat cheese
- 1 handful arugula
- 1 teaspoon olive oil

Direction

- Preheat oven to 350° F. Place buns on a baking sheet, and toast in oven for about 10 minutes.
- In a small bowl, drizzle olive oil over arugula, and season with salt and pepper. Give it a toss.
- In a mixing bowl, combine ground beef with salt, pepper, crushed red pepper, onion powder, and garlic powder. Mix with your hands. (NOTE: Any time you handle raw meat, wash your hands thoroughly with soap and water before touching anything else.) Form beef into two patties.
- Heat your cast iron skillet over medium heat. Melt butter or oil in skillet, and carefully place patties in pan. Always lay meat away from you to avoid splattering hot oil on yourself. Let patties cook for about 2 to 3 minutes before flipping (cooking time will depend on how thick your patties are). Once flipped, place goat cheese on each patty to warm and soften cheese. Cook second side for 2 to 3 minutes.
- Assemble! Spread fig jam on the bottom bun. Place patty on top of fig jam. Top patty with arugula. Top arugula with top bun.

273. Tangerine Passion Fruit Marmalade

Serving: Makes 3 cups | Prep: | Cook: | Ready in:

Ingredients

- 6 tangerines, with the thinnest skin possible
- 3 cups sugar
- 1.5 cups passion-fruit pulp

Direction

- Wash tangerines well. With a paring knife, trim the very top off each one. Cut three of the tangerines lengthwise into quarters or sixths, depending on size. Trim out the white pith in the center, then cut each piece into very thin slices--you'll have little triangular wedges. (Flick out the seeds as you go.) Put all the slices and collected juice in a 4-cup measuring cup.
- Squeeze the juice from the remaining three tangerines and add it to the measuring cup. Pull any remaining pulp out of the peel and discard. Slice the peel into thin strips and add this to the measuring cup.
- Add the passion-fruit pulp to the measuring cup. This should bring the total mix to between 3.25 and 3.75 cups, depending on the size of your tangerines. Cover the measuring cup and let sit at room temperature overnight to soften the peel.
- The next day, sterilize your jars and lids--boil for a good ten minutes. Stick a small plate in the freezer to chill--this is what you'll use to test whether the marmalade has jelled.
- Assess the amount of the mix in the measuring cup. Add a bit less sugar. For instance, if you have 3.75 cups of juice and peel, add about 3 cups of sugar. Adjust to your taste, but a 1:1 sugar: juice ratio is probably the max you'll want.
- Pour the juice, peel and sugar into a nonreactive saucepan. Set the mixture to boil over medium heat. After about 5 minutes of boiling, dab a small amount of liquid on the chilled plate. Wait a couple of seconds, then tilt the plate--If the liquid runs, the marmalade isn't ready. If it holds and looks even a bit viscous, take the pan off the heat. (For me, this takes about 8 minutes, but it depends on all kinds of factors—pan size, amount of sugar, etc. And if you increase the yield of the recipe, it will take longer.)
- Let the marmalade cool a bit, then pour into sterilized jars. Don't panic if it doesn't seem thick--it will set as it chills fully.

274. Tennessee Jam Cake

Serving: Makes one 9-inch layer cake | Prep: | Cook: | Ready in:

Ingredients

- For the cake
- 1 cup butter
- 1 1/2 cups sugar
- 10 ounces berry preserves or jam
- 4 eggs
- 2 1/2 cups flour
- 1 teaspoon baking soda
- 1 teaspoon ground nutmeg
- 1 teaspoon ground cinnamon
- 1/2 teaspoon ground cloves
- 1/2 teaspoon salt
- 1 cup buttermilk
- 1 1/2 cups chopped pecans (optional)
- For the frosting
- 1/2 cup butter
- 1 cup packed brown sugar
- 1/4 cup milk
- 3 cups confectioners' sugar
- 2 tablespoons bourbon

Direction

- Preheat the oven to 350° F. Grease and flour three 9-inch cake pans.
- Cream together the butter and sugar until light and fluffy.

- Add the jam and 4 eggs, one at a time, scraping down the bowl as you go.
- In a separate bowl, whisk together the flour, baking soda, spices, and salt.
- Add the dry ingredients and buttermilk to the wet ingredients, alternating between both.
- Fold in the nuts, if using.
- Divide the batter evenly between the three pans. Bake for 30 to 35 minutes, until the cakes begin to pull away from the sides of the pans and the tops spring back when pressed lightly.
- Let the cakes cool in the pan for 10 minutes, then turn them out onto a wire rack to finish cooling. I recommend popping the cakes in the freezer while you make the frosting—they are much easier to frost when they are fully chilled. You can also wrap them tightly in plastic wrap and freeze them for a few weeks if you want to make them in advance.
- To make the frosting, bring the butter, brown sugar, and milk to a boil in a saucepan over medium heat. Remove from the heat and let cool fully. Add the confectioners' sugar and beat for several minutes until light and fluffy. Add the bourbon and mix to incorporate.
- Frost between the layers and on the sides and top of the cake. Slice and eat!

275.   Thai Tea Jam

Serving: Makes over 1/2 a cup | Prep: 0hours5mins | Cook: 1hours15mins | Ready in:

Ingredients

- 500ml whole milk
- 180g sugar
- 2 vanilla pods, split and seeds scraped out
- 4 Thai teabags or 2 heaped tablespoons Thai tea mix

Direction

- In a heavy sided, deep pot (I used a 'small' one - about 15cm deep and 15 cm wide) - combine the milk, sugar and split vanilla pod. Bring to the boil, add the four tea bags and turn down to simmer, on low heat.
- Simmer and stir using a wooden spoon, making sure the spoon scrapes the bottom of the pan to move bits and prevent it from burning. Stir every 10 minutes. Sometimes it will foam and froth, skim - stir it in and continue
- After 45 minutes, when the mixture has taken on some colour and the flavour of tea shines through, strain, remove and discard the tea bags/ tea leaves. The mixture would have reduced in volume to about a quarter.
- Return to the pot, on simmer and keep stirring till you get a loose honey consistency. It will thicken to a paste, like Nutella or peanut butter once it cools down.
- Store in clean, sterilized jars and allow to cool. Once cool, refrigerate and allow the jam 'rest' - 2-3 days before eating. If it is too stiff when you're ready to devour it, warm it gently on the stove top, or in the microwave.

276.   The Ultimate Bacon Jam Recipe

Serving: Makes 1 regular size canning jar | Prep: | Cook: | Ready in:

Ingredients

- 2 yellow onions, diced
- 1/4 cup brown sugar, packed
- 1 tablespoon honey
- 1 tablespoon red pepper flakes
- 2 pounds cooked bacon, crumbled
- Salt & Pepper to taste
- 1 cup dark beer
- 1/4 cup red wine vinegar

Direction

- Place bacon on 2 tin foil lined baking trays and cook on 400 F for 20 to 25 minutes. You want this pretty crispy but not burnt. Place cooked bacon on paper lined dish. Reserve the bacon grease.

- In a skillet, saute onions in bacon grease until they have a nice aroma and are a nice golden color (about 10 minutes)
- Add the brown sugar, honey, red pepper flakes, and red wine vinegar. Stir until mixed. Sprinkle some salt and pepper.
- Then add the crumbled bacon and stir. Next add the beer (you can also use water)
- Cook for about 15 minutes, until the bacon is a nice dark brown color and the sauce is jam consistency. Adjust flavors to your liking (sweeter? add more honey, spicier? add more pepper flakes etc.)
- Allow the jam to cool a bit and transfer to serving dish or canning jar. You can keep refrigerated for up to 2 weeks.
- If it isn't to the consistency you want it. What I do is put the jam into the food processor and grind until you want it.

---

277.   Toasted Goat Cheese Crostini With Basil And Red Onion Jam

Serving: Serves about 30 crostini | Prep: | Cook: | Ready in:

Ingredients

- For the red onion jam
- 2 medium red onions, thinly sliced
- 2 tablespoons unsalted butter
- 1/4 cup sugar
- 1/4 teaspoon salt
- freshly ground black pepper
- 1/3 cup red wine
- 1 tablespoon sherry vinegar or red wine vinegar
- For the crostini
- 1 baguette
- 1 log fresh goat cheese

- 30-40 small basil leaves, rinsed and dried

Direction

- To make the jam, cook the onions, butter, sugar, salt and pepper in a covered saucepan over low heat, stirring occasionally, until the onions are soft and slightly caramelized, about 30 minutes. Add the wine and vinegar and simmer uncovered, stirring occasionally, until thick, about 20 minutes. Cool to room temperature before using. The jam may be prepared as much as two weeks in advance and refrigerated. (Makes about 2 cups jam.)
- Preheat the oven to 450°F. Slice the baguette thinly on the diagonal and arrange on a baking sheet. Cut the goat cheese into 1/4-inch slices (unwaxed dental floss works well for this) and top each baguette slice with a basil leaf, followed by a slice of cheese. Bake the crostini for about 5 minutes, or until the cheese starts to brown lightly. Top each toast with a small dollop of red onion jam and serve warm.

---

278.   Tomato Balsamic Jam

Serving: Serves 4-6 | Prep: | Cook: | Ready in:

Ingredients

- 2 cups Fresh red cherry tomatoes cut in half
- 1 Shallot diced
- 1 tablespoon Balsamic vinegar
- Salt and pepper
- Olive Oil to coat pan
- 1 teaspoon sugar

Direction

- Coat your fry pan with olive oil, heat should be med/high. Add shallots and saute until translucent, add tomato, salt and pepper to taste and cook until tomato starts to caramelize but there should still be some of the juices from the tomato you don't want it too dry. Add the balsamic vinegar and continue to cook stirring frequently for another 5 minutes. Remove from heat.

279. Tomato Pomegranate Jam

Serving: Makes 1 quart | Prep: | Cook: | Ready in:

Ingredients

- 4 pounds roma tomatoes, chopped (I don't bother to peel or seed, but if you prefer a smoother jam you can do so)
- 1 cup brown sugar
- 2 teaspoons kosher salt
- 1/4 cup pomegranate molasses
- 1 teaspoon freshly ground black pepper
- 1 teaspoon dried coriander

Direction

- Combine all the ingredients in a large saucepan. Bring to a boil, then lower heat to medium-low and let it simmer and bubble, stirring often, until thick and jammy (about 1 hour).
- Let cool and ladle into a 1 quart jar. The jam will keep for 2 weeks in the refrigerator.

280. Tomato Preserves

Serving: Serves 2-3 pints | Prep: | Cook: | Ready in:

Ingredients

- 2 lbs tomatoes
- 1 lb. sugar
- 1 juice of lemon
- 1 lemon peel cut into pieces 1/4" x 1/2"

Direction

- Quarter ripe tomatoes and place in big Dutch oven. Add sugar, lemon juice and lemon peel. Stir and cover. Cook over low heat for 1 hour, stirring occasionally.
- Uncover and cook for another hour and a half over very low heat, stirring frequently until volume is reduced by half. When preserves are a deep red color and thick, turn off heat and let cool.
- Strain through a food mill to remove skins. Store in glass Mason jars and freeze.

281. Tomato Basil Jam Filled Mini Phyllo Shells

Serving: Makes 15 appetizers with lots of tomato-basil jam to spare for more | Prep: | Cook: | Ready in:

Ingredients

- For the tomato-basil jam
- 5 large ripe Roma tomatoes, peeled, seeded and cut into a fine dice
- 8 large basil leaves, finely sliced
- 1/2 teaspoon granulated sugar
- 1/4 teaspoon salt
- 2 more finely sliced basil leaves
- Putting it all together
- 3 to 4 ounces fresh mozzarella cheese, cut into 1/4 inch dice
- 4 basil leaves, thinly sliced
- 1 to 2 tablespoons extra virgin olive oil
- Salt fo seasoning
- Some of the tomato-basil jam
- 1 package mini phyllo shells (15)

Direction

- For the tomato-basil jam
- In a small to medium sauce pan add the tomatoes, eight basil leaves, sugar and salt. Cook over medium heat, stirring often, until the mixture thickens up, about 15 to 20 minutes. If the tomatoes don't all break up, use a potato masher or similar utensil to finish

170

breaking them up. Remove from the heat and cool to room temperature. Stir in the two sliced basil leaves, cover and refrigerate for at least a few hours. The mixture will thicken a little more.

- Putting it all together
- Place the mini phyllo shells on a baking sheet and crisp them up a bit in a 350F oven for 3 to 4 minutes and then let them cool.
- Just before serving, mix the cheese, basil, olive oil and salt together making sure the cheese is thoroughly coated with the oil. Add a little salt to taste.
- Spoon the tomato-basil jam into the mini phyllo shells almost to their tops. Place a few cubes of the basil marinated cheese over each cup and serve.

---

282. Turkey Bacon Sliders On Homemade Parmesan Gaugeres With Bacon Moscato Marmalade

Serving: Makes 18 sliders | Prep: | Cook: | Ready in:

Ingredients

- For gaugeres and marmalade
- FOR PARMESAN GAUGERES
- 1 cup water
- 4 ounces sweet butter
- 1/2 teaspoon salt
- 11/2 teaspoon sugar
- 1 cup all purpose flour
- 3 eggs
- 1 tablespoon grated parmesan cheese
- canola oil for brushing on cookie sheet
- FOR BACON MOSCATO MARMALADE
- 4 slices jalapeño bacon (if you can't find jalapeño bacon, use regular and add ½ teaspoon hot sauce while frying it)
- 1 cup minced yellow onion
- 2 tablespoons pure maple syrup
- 2 tablespoons Moscato wine

- 1/4 teaspoon salt
- 1/8 teaspoon pepper
- For the slaw and the burgers
- FOR GREEN APPLE SLAW
- 1/2 cup shredded red cabbage
- 1/2 cup shredded green cabbage
- 1/2 cup shredded carrots
- 1/2 cup jicama, cut into matchsticks
- 1 medium green apple, cut into matchsticks
- 1 scallion
- 1 small shallot
- 1/2 cup creamy italian salad dressing
- 2 tablespoons barbeque sauce
- 2 tablespoons whole milk
- 1 teaspoon minced garlic
- FOR THE TURKEY BACON BURGERS
- 1 1/2 pounds boneless, skinless turkey thighs
- 1/2 pound jalepeno bacon
- 1 egg
- 1 small yellow onion
- 2 medium green apples
- 1/2 pound grated smoked Gouda cheese (half goes inside the burgers. half goes on top of the burgers)
- 1/2 cup Italian seasoned breadcrumbs
- 1 teaspoon minced garlic
- 2 teaspoons salt
- 1 teaspoon pepper
- Canola Oil for brushing on the grill

Direction

- For gougères and marmalade
- FOR GAUGERES: Heat the oven to 425 degrees.
- Combine the water, butter, salt, and granulated sugar in a large saucepan and bring to a rolling boil over medium-high heat. When it boils, immediately take the pan off the heat.
- Stirring with a wooden spoon, add all the flour at once and stir hard until all the flour is incorporated, 30 to 60 seconds. Return the pan to the heat and cook, stirring, about 2 minutes to evaporate some of the moisture.
- Add the eggs, one at a time, until each is fully incorporated. After each one, scrape down the

sides of the bowl with a rubber spatula. Mix until the dough is smooth and glossy and the eggs are completely incorporated. The dough should be thick, but should fall slowly and steadily from the whisk when you lift it out of the bowl.

- Fold in the Parmesan cheese.
- Grease and line 2 cookie sheets with parchment paper
- Using a pastry bag, pipe the dough into 18 half dollar size circles onto 2 cookie sheets. Dip your finger in flour and push down the points to smooth out any bumps.
- Bake 15 minutes, and then reduce the heat to 375 degrees and bake until puffed up and golden brown, about 20 minutes more. Let the gougères cool until ready to assemble the burgers.
- FOR THE MARMALADE: Chop up the bacon and fry it in a small saucepan. (5 minutes)
- When the bacon is almost crisp, add the minced onion and cook until it's browned (10 minutes).
- Add the maple syrup, salt and pepper.
- Remove from the heat and add the Moscato.
- Return to the heat and cook until the mixture becomes thick and syrupy. (5 minutes.) Set aside until ready to assemble the burgers.
- For the slaw and the burgers
- FOR SLAW: Combine all the dressing ingredients in the bottom of a large bowl. Add all the slaw ingredients on top, and toss to coat. Set aside until ready to assemble the burgers.
- FOR BURGERS: Heat grill to medium high.
- Cube turkey thighs and add to a food processor with the bacon. Pulse until it resembles ground meat.
- Peel and quarter the onion. Remove the core and seeds from the apples. Switch the food processor to the julienne attachment and add the onion and apple.
- Switch mixture from the food processor to a mixing bowl and add ½ of your grated smoked Gouda cheese. (The rest goes on top of the burgers)

- Add the remaining ingredients. Mix gently, just until it all incorporates.
- Form the mix into 18 equal size patties.
- Brush the grill with canola oil and grill the patties, 4 minutes. Flip and grill the other side for 3 minutes.
- Top evenly with the remaining shredded smoked Gouda cheese and cook another minute, letting the cheese melt.
- Remove from the grill and let rest while you slice the gougères.
- TO ASSEMBLE: Slice the gougères in half. Place 1 teaspoon of Bacon Moscato Marmalade on the bottom. Place a burger patty on top of that. Place 1 tablespoon of slaw on top of the burger. Add the top bun and serve immediately.

---

283. Valencia Orange Marmalade

Serving: Makes 9 to 10 8-ounce jars | Prep: | Cook: | Ready in:

Ingredients

- 1.75 pounds Lisbon or Eureka lemons, cut into eighths
- 2.25 pounds Valencia oranges, halved crosswise, seeds removed, and each half cut lengthwise into quarters and sliced crosswise medium-thin
- 3.5 pounds white cane sugar
- 3 ounces strained freshly squeezed juice (from 1 to 2 lemons)

Direction

- DAY 1: Place the lemon eighths in a nonreactive saucepan where they will fit snugly in a single layer. Add enough cold water for the fruit to bob freely. Cover tightly and let rest overnight at room temperature.
- DAY 1: In a separate nonreactive saucepan, place the sliced oranges with water to reach 1

inch above the tops. Cover tightly and let rest overnight at room temperature.

- DAY 2: Prepare the cooked lemon juice: Bring the pan with the lemon eighths to a boil over high heat, then reduce the heat to medium. Cook the fruit at a lively simmer, covered, for 2 to 3 hours, or until the lemons are very soft and the liquid has become slightly syrupy. As the lemons cook, press down on them gently with a spoon every 30 minutes or so, adding a little more water if necessary. The water level should stay consistently high enough for the fruit to remain well-submerged as it cooks.

- DAY 2: When the lemons are finished cooking, strain their juice by pouring the hot fruit and liquid into a medium strainer or colander suspended over a heatproof storage container or nonreactive saucepan. Cover the entire setup well with plastic wrap and let drip overnight at room temperature.

- DAY 2: Meanwhile, prepare the orange slices: Bring the pan with them to a boil over high heat, then decrease the heat to medium and cook, covered, at a lively simmer for 30 to 40 minutes, or until the fruit is very tender. If necessary, add a little more water during the cooking; the fruit should remain submerged throughout the cooking process. When the oranges have finished cooking, remove the pan from heat, cover tightly, and let rest overnight at room temperature.

- DAY 3: Place a saucer with five metal teaspoons in a flat place in your freezer for testing the marmalade later.

- DAY 3: Remove the plastic wrap from the lemon eighths and their juice and discard the lemons. Strain the juice through a very fine mesh strainer to remove any lingering solids.

- DAY 3: In a large mixing bowl, combine the sugar, cooked lemon juice, fresh lemon juice, and orange slices and their liquid, stirring well. Transfer the mixture to an 11-quart copper preserving pan or a wide nonreactive kettle.

- DAY 3: Bring the mixture to a boil over high heat. Cook at a rapid boil until the setting point is reached; this will take a minimum of 30 minutes, but may take longer, depending on your individual stove and pan. Initially, the mixture will bubble gently for several minutes; then, as more moisture cooks out of it and its sugar concentration increases, it will begin foaming. Do not stir it at all during the initial bubbling; then, once it starts to foam, stir it gently every few minutes with a heatproof rubber spatula. As it gets close to being done, stir it slowly every minute or two to prevent burning, decreasing the heat a tiny bit if necessary. The marmalade is ready for testing when its color darkens slightly and its bubbles become very small.

- DAY 3: To test the marmalade for doneness, remove it from the heat and carefully transfer a small representative half-spoonful of marmalade onto one of your frozen spoons. It should look shiny, with tiny bubbles throughout. Replace the spoon in the freezer for 3 to 4 minutes, then remove and carefully feel the underside of the spoon. It should be neither warm nor cold; if still warm, return it to the freezer for a moment. Tilt the spoon vertically to see whether the marmalade runs; if it does not run, and if its top layer has thickened to a jelly consistency, it is done. If it runs, cook it for another few minutes, stirring, and test again, repeating more times if necessary.

- DAY 3: When the marmalade has finished cooking, turn off the heat but do not stir. Using a stainless steel spoon, skim off any surface foam and discard. Pour the marmalade into sterilized jars, processing according to the manufacturer's instructions or another method of your choice.

| 284. | Vanilla Bean Semifreddo Swirled With Jam |

Serving: Serves 4-6 | Prep: | Cook: | Ready in:

Ingredients

- 3 eggs
- 2 egg yolks
- 1 vanilla bean, halved and scraped
- 1 cup sugar
- 1 1/2 cups heavy cream, whipped to medium peaks
- strawberry or other jam, to taste

Direction

- In the bowl of an electric mixer, whisk the eggs, yolks, vanilla, and sugar to combine. Place over a double boiler and heat until the sugar dissolves and the mixture reads 160 degrees on a thermometer.
- Transfer to the mixer and whip on medium high speed until pale and very thick, 4-5 minutes.
- Pour the mixture into a 13x9 casserole dish. Transfer to the freezer. It will take 2-4 hours for it to set completely. Fold gently 2-3 times while it is freezing. When it is almost frozen, generously dollop jam around the semifreddo. Use the blade of a butter knife to swirl it in. Freeze until ready to serve.

---

285. Vanilla Scented Sour Apricot Preserves

Serving: Makes 10 pints preserves | Prep: | Cook: | Ready in:

Ingredients

- 16 cups washed and pitted fresh apricots
- 4 cups sugar (I used unbleached)
- 2 vanilla beans, halved
- 1 lemon, juiced

Direction

- Place a large heavy bottomed jar on the stove and add the apricots.
- Turn heat on to medium and add the lemon juice to the pot.

- Add the halved vanilla beans.
- Add the sugar and scoop up the apricots from the bottom several times to make sure the sugar gets all over the fruit.
- Bring the apricots to a slow bubbly boil, stirring occasionally so that none sticks to the bottom and burns and then reduce heat and cook until the apricots break down completely and the preserves thicken -this can take up to 1 hour.
- Place canning jars into a dish washer and run it. Boil the lids, completely covered with water in another pot on the stove.
- Carefully remove the vanilla beans and scrape any remaining paste into the jam pot. Stir well. You should see the little black specs of the vanilla in well incorporated into the preserves.
- You are now ready to place these into the cleaned, warm jars. Once they have the lid on them I use my steam canner to preserve but some folks just immerse the whole jar into a large pot of boiling water and process for 20 minutes. Remove and turn upside down on a clean dish towel.

---

286. Vanilla Chestnut Jam

Serving: Makes 5-6 cups | Prep: | Cook: | Ready in:

Ingredients

- 2 3/4 pounds (1.25kg) unshelled chestnuts (You only need 2 ½ lbs. for the recipe. I've added an extra ¼ lb. as a margin of error for the peeling process and in case you get a few bad nuts.)
- 1 3/4 pounds (780g) sugar
- 1 vanilla bean
- 1 teaspoon lemon juice
- Sterilized jam jars (6 cups total capacity)

Direction

- To peel the chestnuts:

- Preheat the oven to 400°F. Place a rimmed sheet pan in the oven to preheat as well.
- Place a chestnut flat-side-down on a cutting board. Use a serrated knife to cut a deep "x" on the rounded side of the nut. (I find using a serrated bread knife to be the safest and easiest way to cut the chestnuts.) Repeat with remaining nuts.
- Bring a small saucepan of water to the boil. While the water is coming to the boil, place a kitchen towel inside a medium bowl.
- When the water is boiling, place a large handful of chestnuts (about 1 cup) in the pot. Boil for 2 minutes. Remove the nuts with a slotted spoon or spider and transfer them to the heated sheet pan. The boiling allows water to get beneath the inner membrane and the hot oven creates steam that helps lift the membrane from the chestnut. Roast for 7 minutes.
- Tip the nuts from the sheet pan into the towel-lined bowl and bring the corners of the towel together to keep the nuts warm. Return the sheet pan to the oven.
- Note: You might want to wear latex or rubber gloves for this step if your fingers are sensitive. Remove one of the nuts from the bowl, taking care to close the towel and keep the rest of the chestnuts warm. The corners of the "x" will have peeled back to reveal the skin beneath. Using both hands, pinch the four corners of the shell together to loosen and crack the skin beneath. Then peel the shell and skin from the chestnut. Repeat with remaining warm nuts then steam-roast another batch and peel. Continue until all the nuts have been peeled. You should have about 1 ¾ lbs. (800g) peeled nuts.
- To make the jam:
- Put a few small plates in the freezer so you can check the set of the jam later.
- Place the peeled chestnuts in a large stockpot or Dutch oven. Add a pinch of salt and enough water to cover the nuts by 2 inches. Bring to the boil, then reduce the heat and simmer until the nuts are very soft but not falling apart, 40-55 minutes. The time will vary depending on the size of your chestnuts. When done, the chestnuts should feel starchy and you should be able to easily smash them to a paste with a fork.
- Drain the nuts, reserving the cooking water. You should have roughly 2 ¼ lbs. (1kg) cooked chestnuts.
- Place the nuts in a food processor (you may need to work in batches). Measure out ⅔ cup of the cooking water, and set aside for use later. Process the nuts to a very smooth paste, adding some of the remaining cooking water as necessary to get them moving. The chestnut puree will get thick and look sandy as you process it; just keep adding cooking water until it moves again. Let your food processor run for a minute or longer to make sure the paste is quite smooth. If you use all the remaining cooking water to get your machine moving and need a bit more, just use tap water. The amount of water needed will vary depending on how powerful your food processor is and on the size of the bowl. Set the chestnut puree aside.
- Slice the vanilla bean in half lengthwise. Using a paring knife, scrape the seeds from the vanilla bean into the sugar. Rub the vanilla seeds into the sugar to distribute them evenly.
- Rinse the pot you used to cook the chestnuts. Place the vanilla sugar, the scraped vanilla bean pod, lemon juice and the reserved ⅔ cup (200mL) cooking water in the pot. Cook over medium heat, stirring frequently, until the sugar has dissolved. Increase the heat to high and bring the sugar mixture to a boil. Continue to cook over high heat until the sugar mixture starts to foam. Add the chestnut puree and whisk well to combine, taking care not to splash any of the hot sugar syrup on yourself. The jam will darken as you cook it.
- Cook at a rolling boil for 3 minutes then check for a set using the plates you placed in the freezer: place a teaspoon or so of the jam on the frozen plate and wait 10 seconds for it to cool. Rotate the plate. The jam should not run like a liquid, but have the consistency of loosely set jam. It will not wrinkle like jams

with pectin to tell you it's done, so just look for a consistency you like. If it is too loose for your taste, cook the jam for another 30-60 seconds and check for a set again. When the jam has reached your desired consistency, remove the pot from the heat and ladle the jam into the clean, sterilized jars. Process the jam or cool it and then store in the refrigerator or freezer. The jam will keep in the refrigerator for up to one month and in the freezer for up to a year.

287.   Vanilla Tomato Jam

Serving: Makes 5 half-pint jars | Prep: | Cook: |Ready in:

Ingredients

- 4 pounds tomatoes
- 2   vanilla beans
- 1   lemon, juice and zest
- 1/4 cup sugar

Direction

- Remove the stems from the tomatoes, and chop them into fairly small chunks. You don't need to remove the skins or seeds — they'll cook down into the jam and add a nice bit of texture.
- Put the tomatoes in a large non-reactive pot and simmer, uncovered, for 20-30 minutes, until they're reduced in volume to about 5 cups and the texture has thickened. Stir them occasionally so they don't burn.
- Slice the vanilla pods open lengthwise and scrape out the paste — it's where the flavor is. Add the paste to the tomatoes. (There's plenty of vanilla flavor left in the pods: use them to make vanilla-infused sugar or vodka.)
- Add the juice and zest of one lemon, and 1/4 cup sugar (or to taste).
- Simmer on low, stirring regularly, for another 10 minutes or so. Taste, and adjust lemon juice and sugar if needed.

- This is NOT a shelf-stable jam. You must store it in the freezer (about a year) or the refrigerator (about 3 weeks, once defrosted).

288.   Veal Marrowbones With Oxtails Marmalade

Serving: Serves 6 | Prep: 1hours30mins | Cook: 3hours0mins |Ready in:

Ingredients

- 3 pounds center cut veal marrowbones into 2-inch pieces
- 1 tablespoon Kosher salt
- 1 tablespoon Cracked black pepper
- 4 cups Water
- For the Oxtail marmalade 4 pounds of Oxtails, trimmed of fat
- 7 cups Port wine
- 5 cups Dry red wine
- 4 quarts Beef stock
- 1/2 bunch Fresh thymes
- 2 tablespoons Fresh black peppercorn
- 1 cup Unsalted butter
- 4 tablespoons All-Purpose flour
- 3 cups Coconut milk
- 1 1/2 pounds Fresh Carrots cut into 1/4 inch-cubes
- 2 cups Shallots diced
- 5 tablespoons Caraway seeds
- 1/2 cup Brown sugar
- 1 cup Red wine vinegar
- 1/3 cup Sea salt, black pepper to taste

Direction

- Place the bones in a large bowl. Combine salt & 4 cups of water, pour over the bones. If the water does not cover the bones, add a solution of 1 cup of water to 1 tbsp salt at a time, until the bones are covered. Soak in the fridge for 36 hours changing the water three times until the bones are bleached of color. Drain well. Combine the oxtails 3 cups of port wine, beef stock, garlic, thymes, & caraway seeds & peppercorn in a large pot. Bring the mixture to a boil, then reduce heat & simmer for 2 hours. Transfer the oxtails to a bowl, when cool enough to handle, remove the meat until ready to use. Strain the oxtail Liquid into a large skillet, discarding the solids. Bring the liquid to a boil over high heat. Reduce the heat to medium until the mixture is reduced 3 cups one 1/2 hour.

- While it reduces combine 3 tbsp of butter with flour until it forms a paste, 1 tbsp at a time, into the reduced liquid over medium heat. Cook until the mixture thickens slightly about 3 minutes. In a separate large skillet melt the remaining 5 tbsp butter. Add the carrots shallots and a pinch of salt over medium heat until slight softened, about 15 minutes. Stir in the sugar coconut milk the remaining port wine, red wine vinegar salt and pepper. Cook over medium- high heat until the liquid has completely evaporated about 30 minutes. Stir in the oxtails meat thickened oxtail cooking liquid, and remaining pepper & salt to taste. Transfer the marmalade to an airtight container and refrigerate overnight before serving reheat in a saucepan over medium heat. Add fresh mint to garnish over toasted sliced baguette bread brushed with basil pesto.

---

289.   Vegan Almond And Toasted Oat Jam Bars

Serving: Makes 8 | Prep: | Cook: | Ready in:

Ingredients

- For the base
- 1/2 cup whole wheat flour
- 1 cup almond meal
- 1 tablespoon brown sugar
- 1/3 cup coconut oil, solid
- 2 tablespoons almond milk (or other vegan milk)

- Pinch salt
- 1/2 cup jam
- For the oat topping
- 3/4 cup quick oats
- 1 1/2 teaspoons cinnamon
- 1 tablespoon brown sugar
- 1 1/2 tablespoons coconut oil, solid or melted

Direction

- Preheat the oven to 350F. Line an 8×8-inch pan with parchment paper and set aside.
- First make the base. In a food processor (or using a bowl and fork), pulse the whole wheat flour, almond meal, brown sugar, and salt until combined. Add the coconut oil and pulse until evenly distributed. Add the almond milk, one tablespoon at a time, and pulse until the mixture forms large clumps.
- Press the dough evenly into the pan, using your fingertips to pat down until smooth. Spread the jam evenly across the top of the dough.
- Now make the topping. In a small bowl, mix together the oats, cinnamon, sugar, and coconut oil. The mixture will not form clumps. Spread the oat mixture across the top of the jam until covered.
- Bake for 40 minutes until golden brown. Let cool until slicing.

---

290.   Vegetables Wrapped In Beef With Soy Marmalade Ginger Sauce

Serving: Serves 1 | Prep: | Cook: | Ready in:

Ingredients

- 7 pieces thinly sliced beef
- 1 ounce enoki mushrooms
- 4 pieces garlic stem
- 1 ounce green beans
- 1 tablespoon olive oil

- 1 pinch salt & pepper
- 1 tablespoon Japanese sake
- 1 tablespoon soy sauce
- 1 tablespoon orange marmalade
- 1 tablespoon grated ginger
- 1 piece green onion (chopped)

Direction

- Place the thinly sliced beef in a bowl. Mix with sake, salt, and pepper.
- Microwave or steam the garlic stem and green beans till they are slightly tender on the outside (we will cook them later in a frying pan, so they do not need to be throughly cooked). Cut them so that each piece is about the same width as the thinly sliced beef.
- Carefully take each piece of beef and spread it flat. Wrap each piece with enoki, green beans, or garlic stem.
- Combine all the sauce ingredients (soy sauce, orange marmalade, grated ginger, green onion) together in a small bowl and mix well. Place it in a small sauce dish.
- Put olive oil in a frying pan. Cook 3) at medium heat till the inside of the beef wrap is slightly rare. Place them on a serving plate.

291.   Whole Wheat Jelly Doughnuts (Sufganiyot)

Serving: Serves 6 | Prep: | Cook: | Ready in:

Ingredients

- 31/4 cup whole wheat flour
- 2 teaspoons baking powder
- 1/2 teaspoon cinnamon
- 1/4 teaspoon salt
- 2/3 cup sugar
- 2 pieces eggs
- 1 teaspoon vanilla
- 2/3 cup non-dairy milk
- 1/2 cup all fruit preserves
- 1/2 cup oil, divided

Direction

- Mix whole wheat flour, baking powder, cinnamon, salt, nutmeg and sugar in a large bowl. Stir eggs, vanilla, milk and ¼ cup oil in a separate bowl.
- Add wet ingredients to dry ingredients and mix to combine. Knead dough for a few minutes. Take about 2 tablespoons of the dough and roll into a small ball, flatten in your hand and spoon in a drop of jelly.
- Fold up the dough to cover the jelly and maintain the round shape. Makes about 24.
- Heat oil over high heat, once hot add doughnut and roll around in the oil until all sides are golden browned. Watch it closely, it can burn easily. Remove from heat and allow to drain on paper towels. Before serving, heat in hot oven for 5 minutes.

292.   Wild Maine Blueberry Jam

Serving: Serves 7-8 cups of jam | Prep: | Cook: | Ready in:

Ingredients

- 6 cups crushed blueberries from about 2 quarts berries (slightly underripe berries work best)
- 6 cups sugar
- 1/4 teaspoon ground cinnamon
- 1 pinch salt
- juice of half a lemon

Direction

- Combine the berries and sugar in a large, heavy pot over high heat. Cook, stirring frequently, until the berries have released a lot of juice and have just begun to simmer.
- Stir in the cinnamon, salt and lemon juice and return to a gentle, rolling boil. Boil the jam for about 40 minutes, stirring frequently, until it is quite thick and a small dollop spooned onto a

- plate and set aside to cool for a minute does not run when you tip the plate to one side.
- Fill 8 one-cup glass jars, sterilized according to the jar manufacturer's instructions, and then process according to the manufacturer's instructions.
- Once the jars have cooled, to make sure all of the lids are sealed, push down on the center of each. If the lid pops back up, the jar isn't sealed; you should refrigerate and eat any jam in unsealed jars within a couple of weeks. Properly sealed jars will keep in a cool, dry place for several months.

293.   Wine Jelly, White Chocolate And Caviar Verrine

Serving: Serves 6-8 | Prep: | Cook: | Ready in:

Ingredients

- Wine Jelly, White Chocolate and Caviar Verrine
- 750ml Champagne or sparkling wine (I used Moscato)
- 100ml creme de cassis or other berry liqueur (I used cassis/blackcurrant cordial)
- 150g caster sugar
- 6 gelatine leaves
- White chocolate shavings (recipe below)
- Black caviar (I didn't use beluga.....)
- White Chocolate Shavings
- 100-200g White chocolate

Direction

- Wine Jelly, White Chocolate and Caviar Verrines
- Place six wine glasses or 8 small glasses in the deep freezer for 15 minutes.
- Soak the gelatine leaves in a small bowl of cold water for 3 minutes. {Alternatively, follow the instructions on your pack of gelatine leaves. You can also use gelatine powder, adjust the

required amount according to the volume of liquid you're using}.
- Open the champagne/wine, pour 150 ml into a pan, and reseal the bottle with a wine cork. {This is where things could have gone really wrong for me as my cork broke. Thankfully, I had some Ikea wine corks to hand when I finally extracted the fragments of a once-whole cork!}
- Add the sugar and creme de cassis/cassis cordial to the champagne/wine and gently heat, stirring until the sugar has dissolved (without letting it boil or even get too hot). Remove from the heat.
- Squeeze the excess water from the gelatine leaves and add to the mixture, whisking continuously until dissolved. Pour into a jug. Pour around 50 ml into each glass, and slowly and gently top with champagne/wine, trying to minimize the frothing. Return the glasses to the freezer for 20 minutes, then transfer to the fridge and leave overnight before serving.
- {I used two shapes of glasses. One formed nice bubbles as soon as they came out of the freezer (Ellipse-shaped glasses). The others didn't (Tumblers). Because I'd read the trails and travails of those who had gone before me, I knew that there was still time for things to go 'right'.}
- And 'right' they did! I kept nudging them a bit 'til I went to bed, just giving the glasses a little shake and truly, the next morning, they all had bubbles in them. It was interesting to note though that the jelly in the Ellipse glasses formed differently (individual bubbles) from those in the tumblers (bubble chains).
- White Chocolate Shavings
- When Heston pairs his white chocolate with beluga, he suggests making round discs of chocolate. To quote: '… the sensation of these sweets is heightened if you place the chocolate and caviar disc on the tongue, close your mouth and leave to melt. As the chocolate melts, the caviar flavour comes through gradually. You will be amazed by the pleasure of the changing flavours and sensations'. I preferred to make shavings of mine because I

wanted melt-in-your-mouth to go with the jelly.

- Melt chocolate in a bain marie {safer than scorching and ruining it in the microwave!}
- Once melted, spread on a silicone mat (or a cold, stone surface.)
- Refrigerate it at this point…if it's on a mat.
- When cold, use a sharp knife to draw out/shave into curls. You can also cut out disks and other shapes.

294. Wintery Braised Red Cabbage, Plus Some Jelly

Serving: Serves 6 | Prep: | Cook: |Ready in:

Ingredients

- 1   medium head red cabbage (about 2 pounds)
- 4 tablespoons butter, melted
- 1/4 cup red wine vinegar
- 2   apples, relatively tart, peeled and sliced
- 1/4 cup red or black currant jelly

Direction

- Heat the oven to 325 degrees. Oil a large baking dish (9-by-13-inch, ideally) with half of the melted butter.
- Peel the outer leaves from the cabbage and cut it into 8 wedges. Nestle the wedges in the baking dish, more or less in a single layer. Salt liberally and drizzle the remaining butter and 1/4 cup water over the top. Cover tightly with foil and braise for an hour.
- After an hour, gently turn over each wedge and slide the sliced apples in among the cabbage. Drizzle the red wine vinegar over the top. Cover again with foil and braise for another hour.
- Take the cabbage out of the oven and remove the foil. It should be so tender it nearly melts. Increase the heat of the oven to 425 degrees. While the oven is warming up, drizzle the 1/4

cup currant jelly over the cabbage and gently incorporate it. Then slide the cabbage back in the oven and cook for another 15 or so minutes, until the wedges have started to brown. Serve warm or at room temperature.

295. Wintery Sunday Morning Muffins With Blood Orange Marmalade

Serving: Makes 12 muffins | Prep: | Cook: |Ready in:

Ingredients

- 7 ounces plain flour
- 2.5 ounces sugar plus 1 teaspoon for the topping
- 2 1/2 teaspoons baking powder
- 1/2 teaspoon baking soda
- 1/2 teaspoon cinnamon plus 1/2 teaspoon for the topping
- a pinch nutmeg
- a pinch salt
- 160 milliliters milk
- 2 ounces butter, melted
- 1   egg
- 1 1/2 - 2 tablespoons blood orange marmalade

Direction

- You need a muffin tray with 12 molds and paper baking cups.
- Set your oven to 390°F.
- Combine the dry ingredients in a large bowl.
- Mix the melted butter, the milk, egg and marmalade.
- Pour the liquid mixture into the dry mixture and stir with a wooden spoon until you have a lumpy dough. The more you mix it the more it will loose its light texture so don't mix it too long.

- Fill the muffin tray. Combine the sugar and cinnamon for the topping, sprinkle on top and bake for 12 minutes or until golden.

296. Yellow Plum And Apricot Jam

Serving: Makes 1 1/2 cup | Prep: | Cook: | Ready in:

Ingredients

- 1 1/2 pounds yellow plums
- 4 - 5 ripe apricots
- 1/2 cup cane sugar (or more if desired)
- 3 tablespoons Meyer lemon juice
- 1/2 pod of vanilla (seeded)
- 1/2 teaspoon almond extract

Direction

- Place the plums, apricots, sugar and lemon in a sauce pan and simmer gently until the fruit break up, about 6 to 8 minutes.
- Add the vanilla and almond extract. Bring to a soft boil, stirring constantly for at least 5 minutes.
- Reduce to a simmer, stirring occasionally until the liquid reduces by at least half and thickens to a jam consistency, about 20 minutes.
- Leave in the saucepan to cool, the jam will thicken considerably. Place in a glass jar when cool and store in the fridge.

297. Buckwheat Crepes With Homemade Fruit Jam

Serving: Makes 8 | Prep: | Cook: | Ready in:

Ingredients

- 1/3 cup buckwheat flour
- 2/3 cup soymilk

- 2 large eggs
- 1/4 teaspoon salt
- 2 cups berries, such as blueberries and raspberries
- 2 tablespoons cornstarch
- 1/4 cup agave nectar
- Splash fresh lemon juice
- plain greek yogurt

Direction

- Mix together the flour, milk and eggs with a fork. Add the salt.
- Oil a 9 inch frying pan and let it heat up. Once heated, pour a little of the crepe batter into the pan and quickly swirl it around until it covers the whole pan and goes up the edges a little.
- Meanwhile, combine the berries, cornstarch, agave nectar and lemon juice in a medium sized sauce pan. Let it simmer over medium heat for ten minutes. If the berries aren't thickening enough, add more cornstarch. After ten minutes are up, transfer the mixture to a ball jar and store in the fridge.
- When the edges pf the crepe are set and starting to curl, about 1 minute, gently run a spatula under the edges of the crepe. Flip the crepe. Cook for 30 seconds longer and then turn the crepe out onto a large plate. Repeat with the remaining crepe batter.
- Once all crepe batter is finished and the jam is done, assemble your crepes: fill with jam and a little Greek yogurt and roll up. Then, top with another dollop of yogurt and jam.

298. Kumquat Preserve

Serving: Makes 1 big jar | Prep: | Cook: | Ready in:

Ingredients

- 300 grams kumquat
- 150 grams raw sugar
- 2 pieces lemon rinds
- 50 grams roasted walnuts

Direction

- In a medium sized saucepan mix water and sugar and cook on a medium heat until sugar dissolves. Reduce heat to minimum, add lemon rinds and cook for another 5 minutes or until the liquid becomes slightly thicker or changes colour slightly. Add washed kumquats and cook for 15 minutes or until the fruit is cooked but still in one piece. The cooking time will depend on the fruit and how ripe it is, so you might have to test it a few times – remembering to leave some for the jar.
- At the end, add walnuts – previously roasted for 10 minutes on 180C.
- Leave to cool and transfer into jar. One teaspoon of this preserve and a glass of water in the morning will make a big difference to the day.

---

299. Marbled Muscadine Marmalade & Cream Cheese Brownies

Serving: Makes one 9x13 pan | Prep: | Cook: |Ready in:

Ingredients

- for the brownie batter:
- 4 ounces dark chocolate (very bitter) chocolate chips
- 1/2 cup butter, unsalted
- 1 cup sugar
- 1/2 teaspoon sea salt
- 1 teaspoon vanilla
- 2 eggs
- 2/3 cup flour
- for the marble:
- 4 ounces cream cheese, softened to room temperature
- 1/4 cup powdered sugar
- 1 egg
- 1 tablespoon flour

- 1/2 cup muscadine marmalade or jelly, room temperature

Direction

- Set the oven to 350 degrees and line a quarter sheet pan with parchment paper.
- In a large glass bowl, combine the chocolate and butter and microwave in 30-second increments or until melted. Stir to combine. Add the sugar, salt, and vanilla and stir again. Add the eggs and stir until thoroughly incorporated. Lastly, add the flour and gently fold to combine.
- Pour into the lined sheet pan and smooth into an even layer.
- In another bowl, combine the cream cheese, powdered sugar, egg, and flour and whisk together until smooth.
- Drop spoonfuls of the cream cheese mixture over the brownie batter. Repeat with the marmalade. Use a wooden skewer or the tip of a sharp knife and swirl together the cream cheese, marmalade, and batter.
- Place the sheet pan in the middle of the oven and bake until the mixture is set and the top of the brownies begins to crinkle, about 20 minutes. Cool completely before slicing and serving.

---

300. Plum Jam

Serving: Makes approx 5 x 250gr jars | Prep: | Cook: |Ready in:

Ingredients

- 1 kg plums
- 1 piece green apple
- 500 grams raw sugar
- 1 vanilla bean, scraped

Direction

- Wash your fruit even if it's organic to remove all the dirt. Pit the plums and although I know it's not an easy job, there is no way around it. Just cut them into halves and take the pip out. Place a heavy pot on the medium heat, add plums and sugar and stir a few times using wooden spoon. Add green apple, cored and sliced first. Stir again and add vanilla bean and star anise. I don't mind if any of these spices end up in my jar but you can take them out at the end of cooking.

- Cook jam for about an hour, stirring occasionally and the most important thing, take out the hull which is going to separate from the juicy part minutes after cooking starts. It's the old fashion way but it works and I don't mind doing it.
- Basically you need to cook the jam until you end up with the colour and thickness you like. When cooked, leave to cool slightly before pouring into sterilized jars (you can use dish washer for sterilizing the jars). Pour into jars and use when needed. I always leave some in a container to use straight away, because I know we will. One of my favourite desserts lately is jam poured over Greek yoghurt! You should try that. Yum!

301.   Polenta Pound Cake With Strawberry Jam Glazing

Serving: Serves 8 | Prep: | Cook: | Ready in:

Ingredients

- Cake
- 150 grams maize flour
- 30 grams polenta
- 60 grams rice flour
- 60 grams semolina
- 1 teaspoon aluminium free baking powder
- 150 milliliters milk (add half lemon juice)
- 120 milliliters olive oil
- 180 grams raw sugar
- 1 lemon zest
- Decorating & icing

- 100 grams strawberry jam
- 250 grams powdered sugar
- 1/2 lemon juice

Direction

- Heat oven to 180C.
- In a medium size bowl pulse eggs with sugar until pale. Add milk, olive oil, lemon zest and pulse again. Add flours and baking powder and mix until loosing all lumps. Pour into a greased 6" round tin and bake for 40 minutes or until cake sticker comes out dry.
- Cool onto a cooling rack until completely cool, then spread strawberry jam on the top (if jam is too thick add a drop of water to make it thinner).
- Mix powdered sugar with a few drops of lemon juice until reach desired thickness and ice the cake.

302.   Roasted Carrots With Orange Marmalade

Serving: Serves 10 | Prep: | Cook: | Ready in:

Ingredients

- 6-8 tablespoons butter
- 4 tablespoons orange marmalade
- 25 long, thin carrots with tops attached
- Dash sea salt

Direction

- Preheat oven to 450F.
- Trim off tops of carrots leaving a few inches of green. Scrub carrots clean with a vegetable brush under running water.
- Cover a rimmed baking sheet with parchment paper.
- Lay carrots on top of parchment and sprinkle with kosher salt.
- Add .5 tablespoon dollops of butter and marmalade on top.

- Roast carrots 'til cooked through (about 20 minutes).

| 303. | Tomato Jam, Mozzarella & Spinach Panini |

Serving: Serves 2 | Prep: | Cook: |Ready in:

Ingredients

- 1 teaspoon extra virgin olive oil
- 1   shallot, thinly sliced
- 1 cup packed baby spinach, well rinsed and dried
- 1 tablespoon raisins
- 4   slices, country or white pullman bread
- 3 tablespoons tomato jam
- 3 to 4 ounces fresh mozzarella, thinly sliced

Direction

- Heat olive oil in a small nonstick skillet over medium-low heat. Add the shallots and saute until fragrant, about 1 minute. Add the spinach and raisins and saute until raisins are plump and the spinach is wilted, about 1 to 2 minutes. Remove from heat and set aside.
- Heat cast iron skillet over medium flame, or alternately preheat your Panini grill.
- Meanwhile, arrange two slices of bread on a countertop or cutting board. Slather an equal amount of tomato jam on each slice. Top with equal amounts of mozzarella slices. Arrange equal amounts of spinach on top of cheese. Top with remaining slices of bread.
- Place sandwich into hot skillet and use a heavy-bottomed skillet or pot to weight it down, or alternately place it into your heated Panini press. If using the manual stovetop method, turn the sandwich once the underside is nicely browned, return heavy-bottomed pot on top of sandwich and continue to cook until golden on other side. Serve hot.

Index

A

Ale 52,53

Almond 3,7,10,12,15,25,39,102,119,177

Angostura bitters 29

Anise 3,6,12,128,156

Apple 3,5,14,32,38,107,154,165

Apricot 3,4,5,7,14,15,65,68,70,71,78,80,98,112,174,181

B

Bacon 3,4,6,7,17,18,31,32,35,36,39,57,135,147,150,168,171,172

Baguette 4,30,64

Baking 59,115

Balsamic vinegar 30,153,169

Banana 3,6,20,33,149

Basil 4,6,7,57,58,66,129,144,169,170

Beans 111

Beef 3,7,20,176,177

Berry 3,40

Biscuits 3,35

Blackberry 3,4,5,22,24,25,52,59,60,87,88,126

Blackcurrant 105

Blood orange 101

Blueberry 3,6,7,27,28,29,133,178

Bran 3,6,19,29,139

Bread 3,4,5,29,52,59,65,93,115

Brie 3,6,30,155

Brown sugar 30,74,107,115,176

Buckwheat 3,6,7,30,132,181

Burger 3,7,21,166

Butter 3,4,5,7,10,16,17,19,26,29,53,54,59,60,68,69,75,88,102,107,108,115,116,117,118,120,121,122,123,151,159,165

C

Cabbage 7,180

Cake 3,4,5,6,7,12,22,75,82,88,92,105,107,110,113,116,143,162,167,183

Calvados 32,33,154

Caramel 3,5,22,32,33,34,98,148

Caraway seeds 176

Cardamom 3,4,6,12,13,62,156,157,159

Carrot 3,7,13,34,135,176,183

Cauliflower 6,151

Caviar 7,179

Champ 3,5,35,85,179

Cheddar 3,4,35,36,76,83

Cheese 3,4,5,6,7,8,34,35,48,52,53,64,65,66,67,68,69,78,81,83,109,118,119,132,133,135,140,166,169,182

Cherry 3,5,6,7,8,30,36,37,38,59,86,137,152,153,164,165

Chestnut 7,174

Chicken 3,4,19,38,66,135

Chipotle 3,39

Chives 4,65,69

Chocolate 3,4,5,7,8,12,39,40,41,53,54,105,111,112,119,179

Ciabatta 74

Cider 6,55,154

Cinnamon 6,38,39,62,102,128,133

Clementine 4,69

Cloves 38,69

Coconut 3,4,22,23,43,44,45,79,176

Coffee 3,4,45,57

Cognac 111

Coriander 6,152

Cranberry 3,4,5,6,10,40,41,47,48,78,85,112,151

Cream
3,4,5,6,7,11,24,31,48,54,59,64,67,70,74,77,83,93,94,112,121,130,133,167,182

Croissant 5,118

Crostini 3,4,7,8,26,30,51,52,53,69,78,165,169

Crumble 52,67,112

Cumin 38

Custard 3,28

D

Date 3,4,27,55

Dijon mustard 74,89,125

Dill 3,34

Dried fruit 115

Duck 3,4,9,51,57

E

Egg 4,6,55,59,65,68,102,115,129

English muffin 151

F

Fat 66

Fennel 3,4,5,6,13,61,98,141

Feta 3,21

Fig
3,4,5,6,7,34,46,47,50,52,56,61,62,64,67,85,100,101,102,106,132,166

Fish 153,156

Flank 4,73,74

Flour 52,59,68,102,115

Focaccia 5,98

Frangipane 102

French beans 111

Fruit 7,159,167,181

G

Garlic 4,69,77

Gin
4,5,6,7,12,38,47,48,55,57,58,67,96,123,126,127,152,177

Goose 4,72

Gorgonzola 4,52

Gouda 171,172

Grapefruit 4,72

Grapes 23

H

Ham 4,46,76,80

Hazelnut 102

Heart 5,91

Honey 4,5,32,59,67,81,97,109,114,115,128,138

Horseradish 3,4,44,73,74

I

Icing 105

J

Jam
3,4,5,6,7,12,13,14,15,16,17,18,19,20,21,22,23,24,27,28,29,30,31,32,35,36,37,38,39,40,42,45,46,47,48,50,51,52,55,56,57,58,59,60,61,62,64,65,67,68,69,70,71,72,73,77,78,79,80,81,82,83,84,85,86,87,88,89,90,91,92,94,96,97,98,99,100,102,103,104,105,106,107,108,109,112,113,114,117,122,123,125,126,127,128,129,130,132,133,135,136,137,138,139,140,142,143,144,145,146,147,148,149,150,152,153,154,155,156,157,158,159,160,161,164,165,166,167,168,169,170,173,174,176,177,178,181,182,183,184

Jelly
1,3,4,5,6,7,8,10,21,22,23,24,25,30,33,35,45,46,53,54,66,75,76,78,80,81,91,99,107,112,115,116,117,118,119,120,121,125,131,133,150,162,165,178,179,180

Jus 42,57,61,64,111,171,183

K

Ketchup 73

Kumquat 4,5,7,53,54,63,85,86,181

L

Lemon
3,4,5,6,9,12,16,37,43,55,56,57,58,62,81,87,88,93,94,95,96,
102,108,110,114,136,139,158,159,160,165

Lettuce 5,89

Lime 3,5,16,31,37,95,105,143

Ling 4,74

Lychee 5,91

M

Mango 3,4,8,10,68

Marmalade
3,4,5,6,7,8,13,20,26,31,34,43,44,53,54,61,62,63,72,73,74,7
6,77,85,88,93,95,96,100,101,102,105,110,111,115,124,135,
141,148,151,167,171,172,176,177,180,182,183

Marrow 7,176

Marzipan 6,152

Mascarpone 4,5,6,52,65,111,112,126,151

Meat 3,21

Melon 5,94

Meringue 4,57,58

Milk 39,40,48,115

Mince 11

Mint 5,38,96

Morel 6,135

Mortadella 3,13

Mozzarella 5,7,66,97,184

Muffins 5,6,7,100,144,158,180

Mushroom 5,100

Mustard 4,6,30,73,74,151

N

Nut 5,106,115,168

O

Oatmeal 5,39,107

Oats 3,5,39,107,116

Oil 9,44,52,59,65,69,169,171,180,181

Olive 5,19,30,52,59,65,69,111,114,169

Onion
3,4,5,6,7,13,19,21,30,34,38,51,57,68,69,73,74,77,98,109,13
0,149,165,169

Orange
3,5,6,7,10,26,31,105,110,111,112,113,124,148,172,180,183

Oxtail 7,176

P

Pancakes 6,132

Pancetta 135

Parmesan 7,101,171,172

Pasta 5,113

Pastry 48,134

Peach 3,4,5,6,19,59,60,67,81,114,115,155

Peanut butter 115

Pear 3,4,5,6,16,73,74,78,123,124,132,139

Pecan 62,122

Pectin 108,114,115,131,142,143,154,156,159

Peel 14,16,19,33,41,71,78,109,124,143,155,172,180

Pepper
3,4,5,6,8,33,37,38,53,59,65,66,69,81,82,97,99,124,125,135,
136,147,150,153,168

Pie 4,5,50,102,120,133,134

Pine nut 68

Pineapple 5,123,126

Pistachio 4,5,55,126

Plum
3,4,5,6,7,12,70,71,89,91,125,127,128,129,132,154,181,182

Polenta 5,7,100,135,147,183

Pomegranate 7,38,109,170

Port 6,131,135,154,176

Potato 6,143,155

Preserves
3,4,5,6,7,10,30,34,40,52,59,62,70,74,78,84,95,119,124,126,
155,160,164,170,174

Prosciutto 4,52

Pulse 50,54,58,83,102,106,107,131,172

Pumpkin 5,6,112,132

Q

Quince 6,133,139

R

Raspberry 3,4,5,6,12,17,40,41,48,72,102,105,122,135,136,142,145,155

Red wine 176

Rhubarb 3,4,5,6,18,35,57,58,96,137,150,161

Rice 5,52,117

Ricotta 3,4,5,6,12,69,77,112,137,144

Rosemary 3,4,6,7,14,55,78,127,141,165

S

Sage 7,165

Salad 104

Salmon 5,93

Salt 3,4,9,13,26,30,38,39,52,54,55,59,65,68,69,102,107,110,114,115,129,135,148,156,159,166,168,169,170,180

Sausage 6,147

Savory 6,7,144,164,166

Sea salt 19,105,176

Seeds 12,39,48,156

Shallot 3,4,6,20,52,55,130,135,169,176

Shortbread 3,37,42,111,112

Soda 59

Soup 81

Spelt 6,132

Spinach 6,7,140,184

Star anise 156

Steak 4,5,6,73,74,109,110,155

Stew 133,134

Stock 38,135

Strawberry 3,4,5,6,7,9,39,40,52,63,64,80,82,103,140,150,156,157,158,159,160,161,183

Sugar 5,12,25,26,46,56,57,59,62,68,69,74,85,91,102,108,135,136,142,143,156,159,162,165

Syrup 35,37,39,55,105,108,109,118

T

Tangerine 7,167

Tapenade 111

Taro 26

Tea 3,6,7,23,41,129,168

Tequila 37

Thyme 4,57,69,135

Tomato 3,4,5,6,7,31,32,38,55,59,60,65,66,73,77,86,97,100,129,140,144,150,164,169,170,176,184

Trout 6,150

Truffle 3,8,9

Turkey 3,7,21,171

V

Veal 7,135,176

Vegan 5,7,118,177

Vegetable oil 162

Vegetables 7,177

Vinegar 55,57,69,74,135

W

Walnut 4,82,122

Watermelon 5,108

White chocolate 179

Wine 3,5,6,7,24,74,93,94,131,135,179

Worcestershire sauce 21,73

Y

Yoghurt 63

Z

Zest 18,57,58,87,88,103,122,139

Conclusion

Thank you again for downloading this book!

I hope you enjoyed reading about my book!

If you enjoyed this book, please take the time to share your thoughts and post a review on Amazon. It'd be greatly appreciated!

Write me an honest review about the book – I truly value your opinion and thoughts and I will incorporate them into my next book, which is already underway.

Thank you!

If you have any questions, **feel free to contact at:** _author@sauterecipes.com_

Mimi Lockett

sauterecipes.com

Printed in Great Britain
by Amazon

26890417R00106

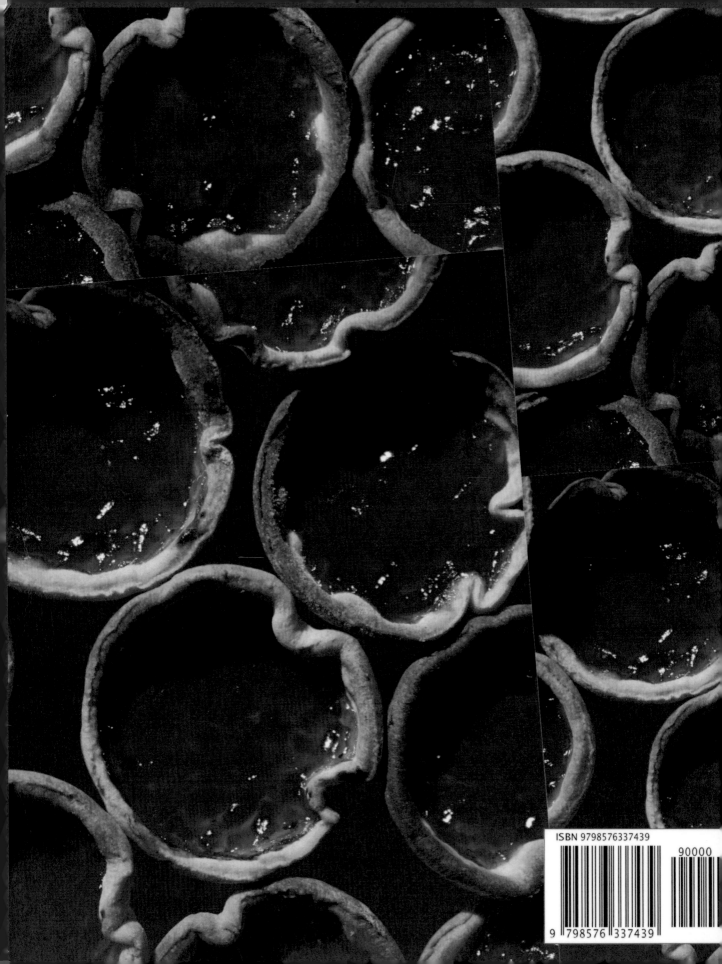

ISBN 9798576337439

Elizabeth Traill

SOUNDS AMAZING

Inspirational poems and pictures to support reading.